P.O. Box 25124
Portland, OR 97298-0124

(888) 237-2110
(877) 643-3732 FAX

Compilation, Index, Layout, Page makeup, Design and Typesetting

Copyright 1992-2010, Pocket Press, Inc.

No claim of copyright is made for statutes from the Oregon Revised Statutes or other rules or codes.

PRINTED IN THE UNITED STATES OF AMERICA

ISBN 978-1-884493-28-7

All rights reserved. No part of this book may be reproduced or transmitted in any form or by any means, electronic or mechanical, including photocopying, recording, or any information or storage and retrieval system, without permission in writing from the Publisher.

Published by:

Pocket Press, Inc.

CCOR10-2010 Oregon Criminal Laws

Foreword

This book is intended as a convenient guide to the laws of this state. It is not a replacement for a full text version of the statutes. Although our intent is to provide a more compact form, the full text version is the ultimate authority.

Every attempt has been made to ensure the accuracy of the sections contained herein. However, no express or implied warranties or guarantees are made.

Not all laws are contained in this book.

Conventions Used in this Book

Notes such as "Note: See..." mean to refer to that section in this book if provided, or otherwise to refer to the full text version of the statutes for complete information.

Sections in this book which were amended or added by act of the latest session of the legislature denote that following the title of the section.

Amendments–Text amended in the current year is denoted by ***bold italics***. Deleted text or numbering changes are not shown.

Added sections–Sections added by the latest legislative session have ADDED on the title line, AND are shown in ***bold italics***.

Deletions–Material deleted by legislative change is not indicated to avoid confusion. If deletions are the only change in the sections, a note will indicate that.

Information included within brackets [ ] is added for clarification and is not an inherent part of the section itself.

Some subsections are omitted as their content is not directly related to the intent of this guide. Where this occurs, the omission is represented by (...). The original numbering of the statutes is maintained where omissions occur.

Time Dependent Material

Contents of this book are applicable until the effective date of the next legislative enactments. In addition, material may be affected by existing or future appellate court decisions.

Sections affected in 2009

163.115	Murder	Amended
163.160	Assault in the fourth degree	Amended
163.165	Assault in the third degree	Amended
163.185	Assault in the first degree	Amended
163.196	Aggravated driving while suspended or revoked	Added
163.197	Hazing	Amended
163.206	Exceptions–Criminal mistreatment	Amended
163.235	Kidnapping in the first degree	Amended
163.305	Definitions–Sexual offenses	Amended
163.415	Sexual abuse in the third degree	Amended
163.425	Sexual abuse in the second degree	Amended
163.426	Definitions–Sexual abuse in the second degree by a coach	Added
163.431	Definitions–Online sexual corruption of a child	Amended
163.700	Invasion of personal privacy	Amended
163.702	Exceptions–Invasion of personal privacy	Amended
163.730	Definitions–Stalking	Amended
164.043	Theft in the third degree	Amended
164.045	Theft in the second degree	Amended
164.055	Theft in the first degree	Amended
164.095	Theft by receiving	Amended
164.125	Theft of services	Amended
164.162	Mail theft or receipt of stolen mail	Amended
164.354	Criminal mischief in the second degree	Amended
164.365	Criminal mischief in the first degree	Amended
164.857	Unlawfully transporting metal property	Added
164.885	Endangering aircraft in the first degree	Amended
165.055	Fraudulent use of credit card	Amended
165.107	Failing to maintain metal purchase record	Amended
165.116	Metal property offenses–Definitions	Added
165.118	Metal property offenses	Added
165.124	Metal property offenses–Exceptions	Added
165.540	Obtaining contents of communications	Amended
166.065	Harassment	Amended
166.070	Aggravated harassment	Added
166.210	Definitions–Weapons	Amended
166.220	Unlawful use of weapon	Amended

166.250	Unlawful possession of firearms	*Amended*
166.260	Exemptions–Unlawful possession of firearms	*Amended*
166.270	Possession of weapon by felon	*Amended*
166.370	Possession of firearm or dangerous weapon in public building or court–Discharging firearm at school	*Amended*
166.460	Exceptions–Antique firearms	*Amended*
166.470	Sale/transfer of firearm	*Amended*
166.630	Discharging weapon on or across highway, ocean shore recreation area or public utility facility	*Amended*
167.310	Definitions–Animal offenses	*Amended*
167.332	Pet possession restrictions	*Amended*
167.337	Interfering with law enforcement animal	*Amended*
167.339	Assaulting law enforcement animal	*Amended*
167.340	Animal abandonment	*Amended*
167.355	Involvement in animal fighting	*Amended*
167.360	Definitions–Dogfighting	*Amended**
167.370	Participation in dogfighting	*Amended**
167.372	Possessing dogfighting paraphernalia	*Amended**
167.431	Participation in cockfighting	*Amended*
181.594	Definitions–Sex offender registration	*Amended*
181.599	Failure to report as sex offender	*Amended*
471.410	Providing liquor to minor or intoxicated person–Allowing consumption by minor	*Amended*
471.430	Purchase or possession of liquor or entry of licensed premises by minor	*Amended*
475.005	Definitions–Controlled substance offenses	*Amended*
475.302	Definitions–Medical marijuana	*Amended*
475.316	Limitations on medical marijuana immunity	*Amended*
475.320	Medical marijuana limits	*Amended*
475.840	Controlled substance offenses	*Amended*
475.860	Unlawful delivery of marijuana	*Amended*

* Amended in the 2008 Special Session.

127.995 Altering, forging, concealing or destroying an advance directive

(1) It shall be a Class A felony for a person without authorization of the principal to willfully alter, forge, conceal or destroy an instrument, the reinstatement or revocation of an instrument or any other evidence or document reflecting the principal's desires and interests, with the intent and effect of causing a withholding or withdrawal of life-sustaining procedures or of artificially administered nutrition and hydration which hastens the death of the principal.

(2) Except as provided in subsection (1) of this section, it shall be a Class A misdemeanor for a person without authorization of the principal to willfully alter, forge, conceal or destroy an instrument, the reinstatement or revocation of an instrument, or any other evidence or document reflecting the principal's desires and interests with the intent or effect of affecting a health care decision.

131.605 Definitions–Stopping of persons

As used in ORS 131.605 to 131.625, unless the context requires otherwise:
(1) "Crime" has the meaning provided for that term in ORS 161.515.
(2) "Dangerous weapon," "deadly weapon" and "person" have the meaning provided for those terms in ORS 161.015.
(3) "Frisk" is an external patting of a person's outer clothing.
(4) "Is about to commit" means unusual conduct that leads a peace officer reasonably to conclude in light of the officer's training and experience that criminal activity may be afoot.
(5) "Reasonably suspects" means that a peace officer holds a belief that is reasonable under the totality of the circumstances existing at the time and place the peace officer acts as authorized in ORS 131.605 to 131.625.
(6) A "stop" is a temporary restraint of a person's liberty by a peace officer lawfully present in any place.

131.615 Stopping of persons

(1) A peace officer who reasonably suspects that a person has committed or is about to commit a crime may stop the person and, after informing the person that the peace officer is a peace officer, make a reasonable inquiry.
(2) The detention and inquiry shall be conducted in the vicinity of the stop and for no longer than a reasonable time.
(3) The inquiry shall be considered reasonable if it is limited to:
  (a) The immediate circumstances that aroused the officer's suspicion;
  (b) Other circumstances arising during the course of the detention and inquiry that give rise to a reasonable suspicion of criminal activity; and
  (c) Ensuring the safety of the officer, the person stopped or other persons present, including an inquiry regarding the presence of weapons.

(4) The inquiry may include a request for consent to search in relation to the circumstances specified in subsection (3) of this section or to search for items of evidence otherwise subject to search or seizure under ORS 133.535.

(5) A peace officer making a stop may use the degree of force reasonably necessary to make the stop and ensure the safety of the peace officer, the person stopped or other persons who are present.

131.625 Frisk of stopped persons

(1) A peace officer may frisk a stopped person for dangerous or deadly weapons if the officer reasonably suspects that the person is armed and dangerous to the officer or other persons present.

(2) If, in the course of the frisk, the peace officer feels an object which the peace officer reasonably suspects is a dangerous or deadly weapon, the peace officer may take such action as is reasonably necessary to take possession of the weapon.

133.033 Community caretaking

(1) Except as otherwise expressly prohibited by law, any peace officer of this state, as defined in ORS 133.005, is authorized to perform community caretaking functions.

(2) As used in this section, "community caretaking functions" means any lawful acts that are inherent in the duty of the peace officer to serve and protect the public. "Community caretaking functions" includes, but is not limited to:

(a) The right to enter or remain upon the premises of another if it reasonably appears to be necessary to:
  (A) Prevent serious harm to any person or property;
  (B) Render aid to injured or ill persons; or
  (C) Locate missing persons.
(b) The right to stop or redirect traffic or aid motorists or other persons when such action reasonably appears to be necessary to:
  (A) Prevent serious harm to any person or property;
  (B) Render aid to injured or ill persons; or
  (C) Locate missing persons.

(3) Nothing contained in this section shall be construed to limit the authority of a peace officer that is inherent in the office or that is granted by any other provision of law.

133.076 Failure to appear on criminal citation

(1) A person commits the offense of failure to appear on a criminal citation if the person has been served with a criminal citation issued under ORS 133.055 to 133.076 and the person knowingly fails to do any of the following:
  (a) Make an appearance in the manner required by ORS 133.060.
  (b) Make appearance at the time set for trial in the criminal proceeding.
  (c) Appear at any other time required by the court or by law.

(2) Failure to appear on a criminal citation is a Class A misdemeanor.

133.318 False foreign restraining order
(1) Any person who provides to a peace officer a copy of a writing purporting to be a foreign restraining order as defined by ORS 24.190 knowing that no valid foreign restraining order is in effect shall be guilty of a Class A misdemeanor.

(2) Any person who represents to a police officer that a foreign restraining order is the most recent order in effect between the parties or that the person restrained by the order has been personally served with a copy of the order or has actual notice of the order knowing that the representation is false commits a Class A misdemeanor.

161.015 Definitions–General
As used in chapter 743, Oregon Laws 1971, and ORS 166.635, unless the context requires otherwise:

(1) "Dangerous weapon" means any weapon, device, instrument, material, or substance which under the circumstances in which it is used, attempted to be used or threatened to be used, is readily capable of causing death or serious physical injury.

(2) "Deadly weapon" means any instrument, article or substance specifically designed for and presently capable of causing death or serious physical injury.

(3) "Deadly physical force" means physical force that under the circumstances in which it is used is readily capable of causing death or serious physical injury.

(4) "Peace officer" means a sheriff, constable, marshal, municipal police officer, member of the Oregon State Police, investigator of the Criminal Justice Division of the Department of Justice or investigator of a district attorney's office and such other persons as may be designated by law.

(5) "Person" means a human being and, where appropriate, a public or private corporation, an unincorporated association, a partnership, a government or a governmental instrumentality.

(6) "Physical force" includes, but is not limited to, the use of an electrical stun gun, tear gas or mace.

(7) "Physical injury" means impairment of physical condition or substantial pain.

(8) "Serious physical injury" means physical injury which creates a substantial risk of death or which causes serious and protracted disfigurement, protracted impairment of health or protracted loss or impairment of the function of any bodily organ.

(9) "Possess" means to have physical possession or otherwise to exercise dominion or control over property.

(10) "Public place" means a place to which the general public has access and includes, but is not limited to, hallways, lobbies and other parts of apartment houses and hotels not constituting rooms or apartments designed

for actual residence, and highways, streets, schools, places of amusement, parks, playgrounds and premises used in connection with public passenger transportation.

161.085 Definitions–Culpability

As used in chapter 743, Oregon Laws 1971, and ORS 166.635, unless the context requires otherwise:

(1) "Act" means a bodily movement.

(2) "Voluntary act" means a bodily movement performed consciously and includes the conscious possession or control of property.

(3) "Omission" means a failure to perform an act the performance of which is required by law.

(4) "Conduct" means an act or omission and its accompanying mental state.

(5) "To act" means either to perform an act or to omit to perform an act.

(6) "Culpable mental state" means intentionally, knowingly, recklessly or with criminal negligence as these terms are defined in subsections (7), (8), (9) and (10) of this section.

(7) "Intentionally" or "with intent," when used with respect to a result or to conduct described by a statute defining an offense, means that a person acts with a conscious objective to cause the result or to engage in the conduct so described.

(8) "Knowingly" or "with knowledge," when used with respect to conduct or to a circumstance described by a statute defining an offense, means that a person acts with an awareness that the conduct of the person is of a nature so described or that a circumstance so described exists.

(9) "Recklessly," when used with respect to a result or to a circumstance described by a statute defining an offense, means that a person is aware of and consciously disregards a substantial and unjustifiable risk that the result will occur or that the circumstance exists. The risk must be of such nature and degree that disregard thereof constitutes a gross deviation from the standard of care that a reasonable person would observe in the situation.

(10) "Criminal negligence" or "criminally negligent," when used with respect to a result or to a circumstance described by a statute defining an offense, means that a person fails to be aware of a substantial and unjustifiable risk that the result will occur or that the circumstance exists. The risk must be of such nature and degree that the failure to be aware of it constitutes a gross deviation from the standard of care that a reasonable person would observe in the situation.

161.125 Defenses–Intoxication or drug use

(1) The use of drugs or controlled substances, dependence on drugs or controlled substances or voluntary intoxication shall not, as such, constitute a defense to a criminal charge, but in any prosecution for an offense, evidence that the defendant used drugs or controlled substances, or was dependent on drugs or controlled substances, or was intoxicated may be offered by the defendant whenever it is relevant to negative an element of the crime charged.

(2) When recklessness establishes an element of the offense, if the defendant, due to the use of drugs or controlled substances, dependence on drugs or controlled substances or voluntary intoxication, is unaware of a risk of which the defendant would have been aware had the defendant been not intoxicated, not using drugs or controlled substances, or not dependent on drugs or controlled substances, such unawareness is immaterial.

161.150 Criminal liability–Defined

A person is guilty of a crime if it is committed by the person's own conduct or by the conduct of another for which the person is criminally liable, or both.

161.155 Criminal liability for conduct of another

A person is criminally liable for the conduct of another person constituting a crime if:
(1) The person is made criminally liable by the statute defining the crime; or
(2) With the intent to promote or facilitate the commission of the crime the person:
  (a) Solicits or commands such other person to commit the crime; or
  (b) Aids or abets or agrees or attempts to aid or abet such other person in planning or committing the crime; or
  (c) Having a legal duty to prevent the commission of the crime, fails to make an effort the person is legally required to make.

161.165 Exemptions to criminal liability for conduct of another

Except as otherwise provided by the statute defining the crime, a person is not criminally liable for conduct of another constituting a crime if:
(1) The person is a victim of that crime; or
(2) The crime is so defined that the conduct of the person is necessarily incidental thereto.

161.190 Justification as defense

In any prosecution for an offense, justification, as defined in ORS 161.195 to 161.275, is a defense.

161.195 Justification–Defined

(1) Unless inconsistent with other provisions of chapter 743, Oregon Laws 1971, defining justifiable use of physical force, or with some other provision of law, conduct which would otherwise constitute an offense is justifiable and not criminal when it is required or authorized by law or by a judicial decree or is performed by a public servant in the reasonable exercise of official powers, duties or functions.
(2) As used in subsection (1) of this section, "laws and judicial decrees" include but are not limited to:
  (a) Laws defining duties and functions of public servants;
  (b) Laws defining duties of private citizens to assist public servants in the performance of certain of their functions;
  (c) Laws governing the execution of legal process;

(d) Laws governing the military services and conduct of war; and
(e) Judgments and orders of courts.

161.200 Choice of evils

(1) Unless inconsistent with other provisions of chapter 743, Oregon Laws 1971, defining justifiable use of physical force, or with some other provision of law, conduct which would otherwise constitute an offense is justifiable and not criminal when:
(a) That conduct is necessary as an emergency measure to avoid an imminent public or private injury; and
(b) The threatened injury is of such gravity that, according to ordinary standards of intelligence and morality, the desirability and urgency of avoiding the injury clearly outweigh the desirability of avoiding the injury sought to be prevented by the statute defining the offense in issue.
(2) The necessity and justifiability of conduct under subsection (1) of this section shall not rest upon considerations pertaining only to the morality and advisability of the statute, either in its general application or with respect to its application to a particular class of cases arising thereunder.

161.205 Use of physical force

The use of physical force upon another person that would otherwise constitute an offense is justifiable and not criminal under any of the following circumstances:
(1) A parent, guardian or other person entrusted with the care and supervision of a minor or an incompetent person may use reasonable physical force upon such minor or incompetent person when and to the extent the person reasonably believes it necessary to maintain discipline or to promote the welfare of the minor or incompetent person. A teacher may use reasonable physical force upon a student when and to the extent the teacher reasonably believes it necessary to maintain order in the school or classroom or at a school activity or event, whether or not it is held on school property.
(2) An authorized official of a jail, prison or correctional facility may use physical force when and to the extent that the official reasonably believes it necessary to maintain order and discipline or as is authorized by law.
(3) A person responsible for the maintenance of order in a common carrier of passengers, or a person acting under the direction of the person, may use physical force when and to the extent that the person reasonably believes it necessary to maintain order, but the person may use deadly physical force only when the person reasonably believes it necessary to prevent death or serious physical injury.
(4) A person acting under a reasonable belief that another person is about to commit suicide or to inflict serious physical self-injury may use physical force upon that person to the extent that the person reasonably believes it necessary to thwart the result.
(5) A person may use physical force upon another person in self-defense or in defending a third person, in defending property, in making an arrest

or in preventing an escape, as hereafter prescribed in chapter 743 Oregon Laws 1971.

161.209 Use of physical force in defense of a person

Except as provided in ORS 161.215 and 161.219, a person is justified in using physical force upon another person for self-defense or to defend a third person from what the person reasonably believes to be the use or imminent use of unlawful physical force, and the person may use a degree of force which the person reasonably believes to be necessary for the purpose.

161.215 Limitations on use of physical force in defense of a person

Notwithstanding ORS 161.209, a person is not justified in using physical force upon another person if:
(1) With intent to cause physical injury or death to another person, the person provokes the use of unlawful physical force by that person; or
(2) The person is the initial aggressor, except that the use of physical force upon another person under such circumstances is justifiable if the person withdraws from the encounter and effectively communicates to the other person the intent to do so, but the latter nevertheless continues or threatens to continue the use of unlawful physical force; or
(3) The physical force involved is the product of a combat by agreement not specifically authorized by law.

161.219 Limitations on use of deadly physical force in defense of a person

Notwithstanding the provisions of ORS 161.209, a person is not justified in using deadly physical force upon another person unless the person reasonably believes that the other person is:
(1) Committing or attempting to commit a felony involving the use or threatened imminent use of physical force against a person; or
(2) Committing or attempting to commit a burglary in a dwelling; or
(3) Using or about to use unlawful deadly physical force against a person.

161.225 Use of physical force in defense of premises

(1) A person in lawful possession or control of premises is justified in using physical force upon another person when and to the extent that the person reasonably believes it necessary to prevent or terminate what the person reasonably believes to be the commission or attempted commission of a criminal trespass by the other person in or upon the premises.
(2) A person may use deadly physical force under the circumstances set forth in subsection (1) of this section only:
(a) In defense of a person as provided in ORS 161.219; or

(b) When the person reasonably believes it necessary to prevent the commission of arson or a felony by force and violence by the trespasser.

(3) As used in subsection (1) and subsection (2)(a) of this section, "premises" includes any building as defined in ORS 164.205 and any real property. As used in subsection (2)(b) of this section, "premises" includes any building.

161.229 Use of physical force in defense of property

A person is justified in using physical force, other than deadly physical force, upon another person when and to the extent that the person reasonably believes it to be necessary to prevent or terminate the commission or attempted commission by the other person of theft or criminal mischief of property.

161.235 Use of physical force in making arrest or in preventing escape

Except as provided in ORS 161.239, a peace officer is justified in using physical force upon another person only when and to the extent that the peace officer reasonably believes it necessary:

(1) To make an arrest or to prevent the escape from custody of an arrested person unless the peace officer knows that the arrest is unlawful; or
(2) For self-defense or to defend a third person from what the peace officer reasonably believes to be the use or imminent use of physical force while making or attempting to make an arrest or while preventing or attempting to prevent an escape.

161.239 Use of deadly physical force in making arrest or in preventing escape

(1) Notwithstanding the provisions of ORS 161.235, a peace officer may use deadly physical force only when the peace officer reasonably believes that:
(a) The crime committed by the person was a felony or an attempt to commit a felony involving the use or threatened imminent use of physical force against a person; or
(b) The crime committed by the person was kidnapping, arson, escape in the first degree, burglary in the first degree or any attempt to commit such a crime; or
(c) Regardless of the particular offense which is the subject of the arrest or attempted escape, the use of deadly physical force is necessary to defend the peace officer or another person from the use or threatened imminent use of deadly physical force; or
(d) The crime committed by the person was a felony or an attempt to commit a felony and under the totality of the circumstances existing at the time and place, the use of such force is necessary; or
(e) The officer's life or personal safety is endangered in the particular circumstances involved.

(2) Nothing in subsection (1) of this section constitutes justification for reckless or criminally negligent conduct by a peace officer amounting to an offense against or with respect to innocent persons whom the peace officer is not seeking to arrest or retain in custody.

161.245 Reasonable belief–Defined

(1) For the purposes of ORS 161.235 and 161.239, a reasonable belief that a person has committed an offense means a reasonable belief in facts or circumstances which if true would in law constitute an offense. If the believed facts or circumstances would not in law constitute an offense, an erroneous though not unreasonable belief that the law is otherwise does not render justifiable the use of force to make an arrest or to prevent an escape from custody.

(2) A peace officer who is making an arrest is justified in using the physical force prescribed in ORS 161.235 and 161.239 unless the arrest is unlawful and is known by the officer to be unlawful.

161.249 Use of physical force by private person assisting arrest

(1) Except as provided in subsection (2) of this section, a person who has been directed by a peace officer to assist the peace officer to make an arrest or to prevent an escape from custody is justified in using physical force when and to the extent that the person reasonably believes that force to be necessary to carry out the peace officer's direction.

(2) A person who has been directed to assist a peace officer under circumstances specified in subsection (1) of this section may use deadly physical force to make an arrest or to prevent an escape only when:
  (a) The person reasonably believes that force to be necessary for self-defense or to defend a third person from what the person reasonably believes to be the use or imminent use of deadly physical force; or
  (b) The person is directed or authorized by the peace officer to use deadly physical force unless the person knows that the peace officer is not authorized to use deadly physical force under the circumstances.

161.255 Use of physical force by private person making citizen's arrest

(1) Except as provided in subsection (2) of this section, a private person acting on the person's own account is justified in using physical force upon another person when and to the extent that the person reasonably believes it necessary to make an arrest or to prevent the escape from custody of an arrested person whom the person has arrested under ORS 133.225.

(2) A private person acting under the circumstances prescribed in subsection (1) of this section is justified in using deadly physical force only when the person reasonably believes it necessary for self-defense or to defend a third person from what the person reasonably believes to be the use or imminent use of deadly physical force.

161.260 Use of physical force in resisting arrest prohibited

A person may not use physical force to resist an arrest by a peace officer who is known or reasonably appears to be a peace officer, whether the arrest is lawful or unlawful.

161.265 Use of physical force to prevent escape

(1) A guard or other peace officer employed in a correctional facility, as that term is defined in ORS 162.135, is justified in using physical force, including deadly physical force, when and to the extent that the guard or peace officer reasonably believes it necessary to prevent the escape of a prisoner from a correctional facility.

(2) Notwithstanding subsection (1) of this section, a guard or other peace officer employed by the Department of Corrections may not use deadly physical force in the circumstances described in ORS 161.267 (3).

161.267 Use of physical force by corrections officer

(1) As used in this section:
  (a) "Colocated minimum security facility" means a Department of Corrections institution that has been designated by the Department of Corrections as a minimum security facility and has been located by the department on the grounds of a medium or higher security Department of Corrections institution.
  (b) "Department of Corrections institution" has the meaning given that term in ORS 421.005.
  (c) "Stand-alone minimum security facility" means a Department of Corrections institution that has been designated by the department as a minimum security facility and has been located by the department separate and apart from other Department of Corrections institutions.

(2) A corrections officer or other official employed by the Department of Corrections is justified in using physical force, including deadly physical force, when and to the extent that the officer or official reasonably believes it necessary to:
  (a) Prevent the escape of an inmate from a Department of Corrections institution, including the grounds of the institution, or from custody;
  (b) Maintain or restore order and discipline in a Department of Corrections institution, or any part of the institution, in the event of a riot, disturbance or other occurrence that threatens the safety of inmates, department employees or other persons; or
  (c) Prevent serious physical injury to or the death of the officer, official or another person.

(3) Notwithstanding subsection (2)(a) of this section, a corrections officer or other official employed by the department may not use deadly physical force to prevent the escape of an inmate from:
  (a) A stand-alone minimum security facility;

(b) A colocated minimum security facility, if the corrections officer or other official knows that the inmate has been classified by the department as minimum custody; or
(c) Custody outside of a Department of Corrections institution:
  (A) While the inmate is assigned to an inmate work crew; or
  (B) During transport or other supervised activity, if the inmate is classified by the department as minimum custody and the inmate is not being transported or supervised with an inmate who has been classified by the department as medium or higher custody.
(4) Nothing in this section limits the authority of a person to use physical force under ORS 161.205 (2) or 161.265.

161.270 Duress

(1) The commission of acts which would otherwise constitute an offense, other than murder, is not criminal if the actor engaged in the proscribed conduct because the actor was coerced to do so by the use or threatened use of unlawful physical force upon the actor or a third person, which force or threatened force was of such nature or degree to overcome earnest resistance.
(2) Duress is not a defense for one who intentionally or recklessly places oneself in a situation in which it is probable that one will be subjected to duress.
(3) It is not a defense that a spouse acted on the command of the other spouse, unless the spouse acted under such coercion as would establish a defense under subsection (1) of this section.

161.275 Entrapment

(1) The commission of acts which would otherwise constitute an offense is not criminal if the actor engaged in the proscribed conduct because the actor was induced to do so by a law enforcement official, or by a person acting in cooperation with a law enforcement official, for the purpose of obtaining evidence to be used against the actor in a criminal prosecution.
(2) As used in this section, "induced" means that the actor did not contemplate and would not otherwise have engaged in the proscribed conduct. Merely affording the actor an opportunity to commit an offense does not constitute entrapment.

161.405 Attempt

(1) A person is guilty of an attempt to commit a crime when the person intentionally engages in conduct which constitutes a substantial step toward commission of the crime.
(2) An attempt is a:
  (a) Class A felony if the offense attempted is murder or treason.
  (b) Class B felony if the offense attempted is a Class A felony.
  (c) Class C felony if the offense attempted is a Class B felony.
  (d) Class A misdemeanor if the offense attempted is a Class C felony or an unclassified felony.
  (e) Class B misdemeanor if the offense attempted is a Class A misdemeanor.
  (f) Class C misdemeanor if the offense attempted is a Class B misdemeanor.

(g) Violation if the offense attempted is a Class C misdemeanor or an unclassified misdemeanor.

161.425 Impossibility not a defense

In a prosecution for an attempt, it is no defense that it was impossible to commit the crime which was the object of the attempt where the conduct engaged in by the actor would be a crime if the circumstances were as the actor believed them to be.

161.430 Renunciation as defense to attempt

(1) A person is not liable under ORS 161.405 if, under circumstances manifesting a voluntary and complete renunciation of the criminal intent of the person, the person avoids the commission of the crime attempted by abandoning the criminal effort and, if mere abandonment is insufficient to accomplish this avoidance, doing everything necessary to prevent the commission of the attempted crime.

(2) The defense of renunciation is an affirmative defense.

161.435 Solicitation

(1) A person commits the crime of solicitation if with the intent of causing another to engage in specific conduct constituting a crime punishable as a felony or as a Class A misdemeanor or an attempt to commit such felony or Class A misdemeanor the person commands or solicits such other person to engage in that conduct.

(2) Solicitation is a:

(a) Class A felony if the offense solicited is murder or treason.
(b) Class B felony if the offense solicited is a Class A felony.
(c) Class C felony if the offense solicited is a Class B felony.
(d) Class A misdemeanor if the offense solicited is a Class C felony.
(e) Class B misdemeanor if the offense solicited is a Class A misdemeanor.

161.440 Defenses–Renunciation as defense to solicitation

(1) It is a defense to the crime of solicitation that the person soliciting the crime, after soliciting another person to commit a crime, persuaded the person solicited not to commit the crime or otherwise prevented the commission of the crime, under circumstances manifesting a complete and voluntary renunciation of the criminal intent.

(2) The defense of renunciation is an affirmative defense.

161.450 Conspiracy

(1) A person is guilty of criminal conspiracy if with the intent that conduct constituting a crime punishable as a felony or a Class A misdemeanor be performed, the person agrees with one or more persons to engage in or cause the performance of such conduct.

(2) Criminal conspiracy is a:

(a) Class A felony if an object of the conspiracy is commission of murder, treason or a Class A felony.

(b) Class B felony if an object of the conspiracy is commission of a Class B felony.
(c) Class C felony if an object of the conspiracy is commission of a Class C felony.
(d) Class A misdemeanor if an object of the conspiracy is commission of a Class A misdemeanor.

161.455 Conspiratorial relationship

If a person is guilty of conspiracy, as defined in ORS 161.450, and knows that a person with whom the person conspires to commit a crime has conspired or will conspire with another person or persons to commit the same crime, the person is guilty of conspiring with such other person or persons, whether or not the person knows their identity, to commit such crime.

161.460 Defenses–Renunciation as defense to conspiracy

(1) It is a defense to a charge of conspiracy that the actor, after conspiring to commit a crime, thwarted commission of the crime which was the object of the conspiracy, under circumstances manifesting a complete and voluntary renunciation of the criminal purpose of the actor. Renunciation by one conspirator does not, however, affect the liability of another conspirator who does not join in the renunciation of the conspiratorial objective.

(2) The defense of renunciation is an affirmative defense.

161.465 Duration of conspiracy

For the purpose of application of ORS 131.125:

(1) Conspiracy is a continuing course of conduct which terminates when the crime or crimes which are its object are completed or the agreement that they be committed is abandoned by the defendant and by those with whom the defendant conspired.

(2) Abandonment is presumed if neither the defendant nor anyone with whom the defendant conspired does any overt act in pursuance of the conspiracy during the applicable period of limitation.

(3) If an individual abandons the agreement, the conspiracy is terminated as to the individual only if and when the individual advises those with whom the individual conspired of the abandonment or the individual informs the law enforcement authorities of the existence of the conspiracy and of the participation of the individual therein.

161.475 Defenses–Solicitation and conspiracy

(1) Except as provided in subsection (2) of this section, it is immaterial to the liability of a person who solicits or conspires with another to commit a crime that:

(a) The person or the person whom the person solicits or with whom the person conspires does not occupy a particular position or have a particular characteristic which is an element of such crime, if the person believes that one of them does; or

(b) The person whom the person solicits or with whom the person conspires is irresponsible or has an immunity to prosecution or conviction for the commission of the crime, or, in the case of conspiracy, has feigned the agreement; or

(c) The person with whom the person conspires has not been prosecuted for or convicted of the conspiracy or a crime based upon the conduct in question, or has previously been acquitted.

(2) It is a defense to a charge of solicitation or conspiracy to commit a crime that if the criminal object were achieved, the actor would not be guilty of a crime under the law defining the offense or as an accomplice under ORS 161.150 to 161.165.

162.015 Bribe giving

(1) A person commits the crime of bribe giving if the person offers, confers or agrees to confer any pecuniary benefit upon a public servant with the intent to influence the public servant's vote, opinion, judgment, action, decision or exercise of discretion in an official capacity.

(2) Bribe giving is a Class B felony.

162.025 Bribe receiving

(1) A public servant commits the crime of bribe receiving if the public servant:

(a) Solicits any pecuniary benefit with the intent that the vote, opinion, judgment, action, decision or exercise of discretion as a public servant will thereby be influenced; or

(b) Accepts or agrees to accept any pecuniary benefit upon an agreement or understanding that the vote, opinion, judgment, action, decision or exercise of discretion as a public servant will thereby be influenced.

(2) Bribe receiving is a Class B felony.

162.035 Bribery defenses

(1) In any prosecution under ORS 162.015, it is a defense that the defendant offered, conferred or agreed to confer the pecuniary benefit as a result of the public servant's conduct constituting extortion or coercion.

(2) It is no defense to a prosecution under ORS 162.015 and 162.025 that the person sought to be influenced was not qualified to act in the desired way, whether because the person had not assumed office, lacked jurisdiction or for any other reason.

162.055 Definitions–Public justice offenses

As used in ORS 162.055 to 162.425 and 162.465, unless the context requires otherwise:

(1) "Benefit" means gain or advantage to the beneficiary or to a third person pursuant to the desire or consent of the beneficiary.
(2) "Material" means that which could have affected the course or outcome of any proceeding or transaction. Whether a false statement is "material" in a given factual situation is a question of law.
(3) "Statement" means any representation of fact and includes a representation of opinion, belief or other state of mind where the representation clearly relates to state of mind apart from or in addition to any facts which are the subject of the representation.
(4) "Sworn statement" means any statement that attests to the truth of what is stated and that is knowingly given under any form of oath or affirmation or by declaration under penalty of perjury as described in ORCP 1 E [Oregon Rules of Civil Procedure].

162.065 Perjury
(1) A person commits the crime of perjury if the person makes a false sworn statement in regard to a material issue, knowing it to be false.
(2) Perjury is a Class C felony.

162.075 False swearing
(1) A person commits the crime of false swearing if the person makes a false sworn statement, knowing it to be false.
(2) False swearing is a Class A misdemeanor.

162.085 Unsworn falsification
(1) A person commits the crime of unsworn falsification if the person knowingly makes any false written statement to a public servant in connection with an application for any benefit.
(2) Unsworn falsification is a Class B misdemeanor.

162.095 Defenses–Perjury & false swearing
It is no defense to a prosecution for perjury or false swearing that:
(1) The statement was inadmissible under the rules of evidence; or
(2) The oath or affirmation was taken or administered in an irregular manner; or
(3) The defendant mistakenly believed the false statement to be immaterial.

162.105 Defenses–Retraction
(1) It is a defense to a prosecution for perjury or false swearing committed in an official proceeding that the defendant retracted the false statement:
  (a) In a manner showing a complete and voluntary retraction of the prior false statement; and
  (b) During the course of the same official proceeding in which it was made; and
  (c) Before the subject matter of the official proceeding is submitted to the ultimate trier of fact.

(2) "Official proceeding," as used in this section, means a proceeding before any judicial, legislative or administrative body or officer, wherein sworn statements are received, and includes any referee, hearing examiner, commissioner, notary or other person taking sworn statements in connection with such proceedings. Statements made in separate stages of the same trial or administrative proceeding shall be considered to have been made in the course of the same proceeding.

162.135 Definitions–Escape & contraband

As used in ORS 162.135 to 162.205, unless the context requires otherwise:

(1)(a) "Contraband" means:
   (A) Controlled substances as defined in ORS 475.005;
   (B) Drug paraphernalia as defined in ORS 475.525;
   (C) Except as otherwise provided in paragraph (b) of this subsection, currency possessed by or in the control of an inmate confined in a correctional facility; or
   (D) Any article or thing which a person confined in a correctional facility, youth correction facility or state hospital is prohibited by statute, rule or order from obtaining or possessing, and whose use would endanger the safety or security of such institution or any person therein.
  (b) "Contraband" does not include authorized currency possessed by an inmate in a work release facility.

(2) "Correctional facility" means any place used for the confinement of persons charged with or convicted of a crime or otherwise confined under a court order and includes but is not limited to a youth correction facility. "Correctional facility" applies to a state hospital or a secure intensive community inpatient facility only as to persons detained therein charged with or convicted of a crime, or detained therein after having been found guilty except for insanity of a crime under ORS 161.290 to 161.370.

(3) "Currency" means paper money and coins that are within the correctional institution.

(4) "Custody" means the imposition of actual or constructive restraint by a peace officer pursuant to an arrest or court order, but does not include detention in a correctional facility, youth correction facility or a state hospital.

(5) "Escape" means the unlawful departure of a person from custody or a correctional facility. "Escape" includes the unauthorized departure or absence from this state or failure to return to this state by a person who is under the jurisdiction of the Psychiatric Security Review Board. "Escape" does not include failure to comply with provisions of a conditional release in ORS 135.245.

(6) "Youth correction facility" means:
  (a) A youth correction facility as defined in ORS 420.005; and
  (b) A detention facility as defined in ORS 419A.004.

(7) "State hospital" means the Oregon State Hospital, Blue Mountain Recovery Center, Eastern Oregon Training Center and any other hospital established by law for similar purposes.

(8) "Unauthorized departure" means the unauthorized departure of a person confined by court order in a youth correction facility or a state hospital that, because of the nature of the court order, is not a correctional facility as defined in this section, or the failure to return to custody after any form of temporary release or transitional leave from a correctional facility.

162.145 Escape in the third degree

(1) A person commits the crime of escape in the third degree if the person escapes from custody.
(2) It is a defense to a prosecution under this section that the person escaping or attempting to escape was in custody pursuant to an illegal arrest.
(3) Escape in the third degree is a Class A misdemeanor.

162.155 Escape in the second degree

(1) A person commits the crime of escape in the second degree if:
  (a) The person uses or threatens to use physical force escaping from custody; or
  (b) Having been convicted or found guilty of a felony, the person escapes from custody imposed as a result thereof; or
  (c) The person escapes from a correctional facility; or
  (d) While under the jurisdiction of the Psychiatric Security Review Board, the person departs, is absent from or fails to return to this state without authorization of the board.
(2) Escape in the second degree is a Class C felony.

162.165 Escape in the first degree

(1) A person commits the crime of escape in the first degree if:
  (a) Aided by another person actually present, the person uses or threatens to use physical force in escaping from custody or a correctional facility; or
  (b) The person uses or threatens to use a dangerous or deadly weapon escaping from custody or a correctional facility.
(2) Escape in the first degree is a Class B felony.

162.175 Unauthorized departure

(1) A person commits the crime of unauthorized departure if:
  (a) The person makes an unauthorized departure; or
  (b) Not being an inmate therein, the person aids another in making or attempting to make an unauthorized departure.
(2) Unauthorized departure is a Class A misdemeanor.

162.185 Supplying contraband

(1) A person commits the crime of supplying contraband if:

(a) The person knowingly introduces any contraband into a correctional facility, youth correction facility or state hospital; or
(b) Being confined in a correctional facility, youth correction facility or state hospital, the person knowingly makes, obtains, or possesses any contraband.

(2) Supplying contraband is a Class C felony.

162.195 Failure to appear in the second degree

(1) A person commits the crime of failure to appear in the second degree if the person knowingly fails to appear as required after:
(a) Having by court order been released from custody or a correctional facility under a release agreement or security release upon the condition that the person will subsequently appear personally in connection with a charge against the person of having committed a misdemeanor; or
(b) Having been released from a correctional facility subject to a forced release agreement under ORS 169.046 in connection with a charge against the person of having committed a misdemeanor.

(2) Failure to appear in the second degree is a Class A misdemeanor.

162.205 Failure to appear in the first degree

(1) A person commits the crime of failure to appear in the first degree if the person knowingly fails to appear as required after:
(a) Having by court order been released from custody or a correctional facility under a release agreement or security release upon the condition that the person will subsequently appear personally in connection with a charge against the person of having committed a felony; or
(b) Having been released from a correctional facility subject to a forced release agreement under ORS 169.046 in connection with a charge against the person of having committed a felony.

(2) Failure to appear in the first degree is a Class C felony.

162.225 Definitions–Obstructing government

As used in ORS 162.225 to 162.375 and 162.465, unless the context requires otherwise:

(1) "Firefighter" means any fire or forestry department employee, or authorized fire department volunteer, vested with the duty of preventing or combating fire or preventing the loss of life or property by fire.

(2) "Official proceeding" means a proceeding before any judicial, legislative or administrative body or officer, wherein sworn statements are received, and includes any referee, hearing examiner, commissioner, notary or other person taking sworn statements in connection with such proceedings.

(3) "Physical evidence" means any article, object, record, document or other evidence of physical substance.
(4) "Public record" means any book, document, paper, file, photograph, sound recording, computerized recording in machine storage, records or other materials, regardless of physical form or characteristic, made, received, filed or recorded in any government office or agency pursuant to law or in connection with the transaction of public business, whether or not confidential or restricted in use.
(5) "Testimony" means oral or written statements that may be offered by a witness in an official proceeding.

162.235 Obstructing governmental or judicial administration

(1) A person commits the crime of obstructing governmental or judicial administration if the person intentionally obstructs, impairs or hinders the administration of law or other governmental or judicial function by means of intimidation, force, physical or economic interference or obstacle.
(2) This section shall not apply to the obstruction of unlawful governmental or judicial action or interference with the making of an arrest.
(3) Obstructing governmental or judicial administration is a Class A misdemeanor.

162.245 Refusing to assist a peace officer

(1) A person commits the offense of refusing to assist a peace officer if upon command by a person known by the person to be a peace officer the person unreasonably refuses or fails to assist in effecting an authorized arrest or preventing another from committing a crime.
(2) Refusing to assist a peace officer is a Class B violation.

162.247 Interfering with a peace officer

(1) A person commits the crime of interfering with a peace officer or parole and probation officer if the person, knowing that another person is a peace officer or a parole and probation officer as defined in ORS 181.610:
  (a) Intentionally acts in a manner that prevents, or attempts to prevent, a peace officer or parole and probation officer from performing the lawful duties of the officer with regards to another person; or
  (b) Refuses to obey a lawful order by the peace officer or parole and probation officer.
(2) Interfering with a peace officer or parole and probation officer is a Class A misdemeanor.

(3) This section does not apply in situations in which the person is engaging in:
  (a) Activity that would constitute resisting arrest under ORS 162.315; or
  (b) Passive resistance.

162.255 Refusing to assist in fire-fighting operations

(1) A person commits the offense of refusing to assist in fire-fighting operations if:
  (a) Upon command by a person known by the person to be a firefighter the person unreasonably refuses or fails to assist in extinguishing a fire or protecting property threatened thereby; or
  (b) Upon command by a person known by the person to be a firefighter or peace officer the person intentionally and unreasonably disobeys a lawful order relating to the conduct of the person in the vicinity of a fire.
(2) Subsection (1) of this section does not apply to a person working for a news organization if the person is reporting on the fire and the person does not unreasonably interfere with fire-fighting operations.
(3) Refusing to assist in fire-fighting operations is a Class B violation.

162.257 Interfering with a firefighter or EMT

(1) A person commits the crime of interfering with a firefighter or emergency medical technician if the person, knowing that another person is a firefighter or emergency medical technician, intentionally acts in a manner that prevents, or attempts to prevent, a firefighter or emergency medical technician from performing the lawful duties of the firefighter or emergency medical technician.
(2) Interfering with a firefighter or emergency medical technician is a Class A misdemeanor.
(3) As used in this section, "emergency medical technician" has the meaning given that term in ORS 682.025.

162.285 Tampering with a witness

(1) A person commits the crime of tampering with a witness if:
  (a) The person knowingly induces or attempts to induce a witness or a person the person believes may be called as a witness in any official proceeding to offer false testimony or unlawfully withhold any testimony; or
  (b) The person knowingly induces or attempts to induce a witness to be absent from any official proceeding to which the person has been legally summoned.
(2) Tampering with a witness is a Class C felony.

162.295 Tampering with physical evidence
(1) A person commits the crime of tampering with physical evidence if, with intent that it be used, introduced, rejected or unavailable in an official proceeding which is then pending or to the knowledge of such person is about to be instituted, the person:
  (a) Destroys, mutilates, alters, conceals or removes physical evidence impairing its verity or availability; or
  (b) Knowingly makes, produces or offers any false physical evidence; or
  (c) Prevents the production of physical evidence by an act of force, intimidation or deception against any person.
(2) Tampering with physical evidence is a Class A misdemeanor.

162.305 Tampering with public records
(1) A person commits the crime of tampering with public records if, without lawful authority, the person knowingly destroys, mutilates, conceals, removes, makes a false entry in or falsely alters any public record, including records relating to the Oregon State Lottery.
(2)(a) Except as provided in paragraph (b) of this subsection, tampering with public records is a Class A misdemeanor.
  (b) Tampering with records relating to the Oregon State Lottery is a Class C felony.

162.315 Resisting arrest
(1) A person commits the crime of resisting arrest if the person intentionally resists a person known by the person to be a peace officer or parole and probation officer in making an arrest.
(2) As used in this section:
  (a) "Arrest" has the meaning given that term in ORS 133.005 and includes, but is not limited to, the booking process.
  (b) "Parole and probation officer" has the meaning given that term in ORS 181.610.
  (c) "Resists" means the use or threatened use of violence, physical force or any other means that creates a substantial risk of physical injury to any person and includes, but is not limited to, behavior clearly intended to prevent being taken into custody by overcoming the actions of the arresting officer. The behavior does not have to result in actual physical injury to an officer. Passive resistance does not constitute behavior intended to prevent being taken into custody.
(3) It is no defense to a prosecution under this section that the peace officer or parole and probation officer lacked legal authority to make the arrest or book the person, provided the officer was acting under color of official authority.
(4) Resisting arrest is a Class A misdemeanor.

162.325 Hindering prosecution
(1) A person commits the crime of hindering prosecution if, with intent to hinder the apprehension, prosecution, conviction or punishment of a person who has committed a crime punishable as a felony, or with the intent to assist a person who has committed a crime punishable as a felony in profiting or benefiting from the commission of the crime, the person:
(a) Harbors or conceals such person; or
(b) Warns such person of impending discovery or apprehension; or
(c) Provides or aids in providing such person with money, transportation, weapon, disguise or other means of avoiding discovery or apprehension; or
(d) Prevents or obstructs, by means of force, intimidation or deception, anyone from performing an act which might aid in the discovery or apprehension of such person; or
(e) Suppresses by any act of concealment, alteration or destruction physical evidence which might aid in the discovery or apprehension of such person; or
(f) Aids such person in securing or protecting the proceeds of the crime.
(2) Hindering prosecution is a Class C felony.

162.335 Compounding
(1) A person commits the crime of compounding if the person accepts or agrees to accept any pecuniary benefit as consideration for refraining from reporting to law enforcement authorities the commission or suspected commission of any felony or information relating to a felony.
(2) Compounding is a Class A misdemeanor.

162.345 Defenses–Hindering or compounding
It is no defense to a prosecution for hindering prosecution or compounding that the principal offender is not apprehended, prosecuted, convicted or punished.

162.355 Simulating legal process
(1) A person commits the crime of simulating legal process if, with the intent to harass, injure or defraud another person, the person knowingly issues or delivers to another person any document that in form and substance falsely simulates civil or criminal process.
(2) As used in this section:
(a) "Civil or criminal process" means a document or order, including, but not limited to, a summons, lien, complaint, warrant, injunction, writ,

notice, pleading or subpoena, that is issued by a court or that is filed or recorded for the purpose of:
(A) Exercising jurisdiction;
(B) Representing a claim against a person or property;
(C) Directing a person to appear before a court or tribunal; or
(D) Directing a person to perform or refrain from performing a specified act.
(b) "Person" has the meaning given that term in ORS 161.015, except that in relation to a defendant, "person" means a human being, a public or private corporation, an unincorporated association or a partnership.
(3) Simulating legal process is a Class C felony.

162.365 Criminal impersonation

(1) A person commits the crime of criminal impersonation if with intent to obtain a benefit, to injure or defraud another or to facilitate an unlawful activity, the person does an act in the assumed character of:
(a) A public servant; or
(b) An active member or veteran of the Armed Forces of the United States.
(2) It is no defense to a prosecution for criminal impersonation that:
(a) The office, position or title that the person pretended to hold did not in fact exist; or
(b) The unit of government that the person pretended to represent did not in fact exist.
(3)(a) Criminal impersonation is a Class A misdemeanor.
(b) Notwithstanding paragraph (a) of this subsection, criminal impersonation is a Class C felony if the public servant impersonated is a peace officer, judge or justice of the peace.

162.367 Criminal impersonation of peace officer

(1) A person commits the crime of criminal impersonation of a peace officer if the person, with the intent to obtain a benefit or to injure or defraud another person, uses false law enforcement identification or wears a law enforcement uniform to give the impression that the person is a peace officer and does an act in that assumed character.
(2) Criminal impersonation of a peace officer is a Class C felony.
(3) As used in this section:
(a) "False law enforcement identification" means a badge or an identification card that:
(A) Identifies the possessor of the badge or card as a member of a law enforcement unit; and
(B) Was not lawfully issued to the possessor by the law enforcement unit.

(b) "Law enforcement uniform" means clothing bearing words such as "police," "sheriff," "state trooper" or "law enforcement," or clothing that is an official uniform or substantially similar to an official uniform of a law enforcement unit that would make it reasonably likely that a person would believe that the wearer is a peace officer.

162.369 Possession of false law enforcement identification card

(1) A person commits the crime of possession of a false law enforcement identification card if the person possesses a false law enforcement identification card.

(2) Possession of a false law enforcement identification card is a Class A misdemeanor.

(3) As used in this section, "false law enforcement identification card" means an identification card that:
  (a) Identifies the possessor of the card as a member of a law enforcement unit; and
  (b) Was not lawfully issued to the possessor by the law enforcement unit.

162.375 Initiating false report

(1) A person commits the crime of initiating a false report if the person knowingly initiates a false alarm or report which is transmitted to a fire department, law enforcement agency or other organization that deals with emergencies involving danger to life or property.

(2) Initiating a false report is a Class C misdemeanor.

162.385 False information to a police officer

(1) A person commits the crime of giving false information to a peace officer for issuance or service of a citation or for an arrest on a warrant if the person knowingly uses or gives a false or fictitious name, address or date of birth to any peace officer for the purpose of:
  (a) The officer's issuing or serving the person a citation under authority of ORS 133.055 to 133.076 or ORS chapter 153; or
  (b) The officer's arresting the person on a warrant.

(2) A person who violates this section commits a Class A misdemeanor.

Note: See 807.620 for "false information to an officer enforcing motor vehicle laws."

162.405 Official misconduct in the second degree

(1) A public servant commits the crime of official misconduct in the second degree if the person knowingly violates any statute relating to the office of the person.

(2) Official misconduct in the second degree is a Class C misdemeanor.

162.415 Official misconduct in the first degree

(1) A public servant commits the crime of official misconduct in the first degree if with intent to obtain a benefit or to harm another:
  (a) The public servant knowingly fails to perform a duty imposed upon the public servant by law or one clearly inherent in the nature of office; or
  (b) The public servant knowingly performs an act constituting an unauthorized exercise in official duties.

(2) Official misconduct in the first degree is a Class A misdemeanor.

163.005 Criminal homicide

(1) A person commits criminal homicide if, without justification or excuse, the person intentionally, knowingly, recklessly or with criminal negligence causes the death of another human being.

(2) "Criminal homicide" is murder, manslaughter, criminally negligent homicide or aggravated vehicular homicide.

(3) "Human being" means a person who has been born and was alive at the time of the criminal act.

163.095 Aggravated murder

As used in ORS 163.105 and this section, "aggravated murder" means murder as defined in ORS 163.115 which is committed under, or accompanied by, any of the following circumstances:

(1)(a) The defendant committed the murder pursuant to an agreement that the defendant receive money or other thing of value for committing the murder.
  (b) The defendant solicited another to commit the murder and paid or agreed to pay the person money or other thing of value for committing the murder.
  (c) The defendant committed murder after having been convicted previously in any jurisdiction of any homicide, the elements of which constitute the crime of murder as defined in ORS 163.115 or manslaughter in the first degree as defined in ORS 163.118.
  (d) There was more than one murder victim in the same criminal episode as defined in ORS 131.505.
  (e) The homicide occurred in the course of or as a result of intentional maiming or torture of the victim.
  (f) The victim of the intentional homicide was a person under the age of 14 years.

(2)(a) The victim was one of the following and the murder was related to the performance of the victim's official duties in the justice system:
  (A) A police officer as defined in ORS 181.610;
  (B) A correctional, parole and probation officer or other person charged with the duty of custody, control or supervision of convicted persons;
  (C) A member of the Oregon State Police;
  (D) A judicial officer as defined in ORS 1.210;
  (E) A juror or witness in a criminal proceeding;
  (F) An employee or officer of a court of justice; or
  (G) A member of the State Board of Parole and Post-Prison Supervision.
(b) The defendant was confined in a state, county or municipal penal or correctional facility or was otherwise in custody when the murder occurred.
(c) The defendant committed murder by means of an explosive as defined in ORS 164.055.
(d) Notwithstanding ORS 163.115 (1)(b), the defendant personally and intentionally committed the homicide under the circumstances set forth in ORS 163.115 (1)(b).
(e) The murder was committed in an effort to conceal the commission of a crime, or to conceal the identity of the perpetrator of a crime.
(f) The murder was committed after the defendant had escaped from a state, county or municipal penal or correctional facility and before the defendant had been returned to the custody of the facility.

163.115 Murder *Amended 2009*

(1) Except as provided in ORS 163.118 and 163.125, criminal homicide constitutes murder:
  (a) When it is committed intentionally, except that it is an affirmative defense that, at the time of the homicide, the defendant was under the influence of an extreme emotional disturbance;
  (b) When it is committed by a person, acting either alone or with one or more persons, who commits or attempts to commit any of the following crimes and in the course of and in furtherance of the crime the person is committing or attempting to commit, or during the immediate flight therefrom, the person, or another participant if there be any, causes the death of a person other than one of the participants:
    (A) Arson in the first degree as defined in ORS 164.325;
    (B) Criminal mischief in the first degree by means of an explosive as defined in ORS 164.365;
    (C) Burglary in the first degree as defined in ORS 164.225;
    (D) Escape in the first degree as defined in ORS 162.165;
    (E) Kidnapping in the second degree as defined in ORS 163.225;
    (F) Kidnapping in the first degree as defined in ORS 163.235;
    (G) Robbery in the first degree as defined in ORS 164.415;

(H) Any felony sexual offense in the first degree defined in this chapter;
(I) Compelling prostitution as defined in ORS 167.017; or
(J) Assault in the first degree, as defined in ORS 163.185, and the victim is under 14 years of age, or assault in the second degree, as defined in ORS 163.175 (1)(a) or (b), and the victim is under 14 years of age; or

(c) By abuse when a person, recklessly under circumstances manifesting extreme indifference to the value of human life, causes the death of a child under 14 years of age or a dependent person, as defined in ORS 163.205, and:
(A) The person has previously engaged in a pattern or practice of assault or torture of the victim or another child under 14 years of age or a dependent person; or
(B) The person causes the death by neglect or maltreatment.

(2) An accusatory instrument alleging murder by abuse under subsection (1)(c) of this section need not allege specific incidents of assault or torture.
(3) It is an affirmative defense to a charge of violating subsection (1)(b) of this section that the defendant:
(a) Was not the only participant in the underlying crime;
(b) Did not commit the homicidal act or in any way solicit, request, command, importune, cause or aid in the commission thereof;
(c) Was not armed with a dangerous or deadly weapon;
(d) Had no reasonable ground to believe that any other participant was armed with a dangerous or deadly weapon; and
(e) Had no reasonable ground to believe that any other participant intended to engage in conduct likely to result in death.
(4) It is an affirmative defense to a charge of violating subsection (1)(c)(B) of this section that the child or dependent person was under care or treatment solely by spiritual means pursuant to the religious beliefs or practices of the child or person or the parent or guardian of the child or person.

• • •

(6) As used in this section:
(a) "Assault" means to intentionally, knowingly or recklessly cause physical injury to another person. "Assault" does not include the causing of physical injury in a motor vehicle accident that occurs by reason of the reckless conduct of a defendant.
(b) "Neglect or maltreatment" means a violation of ORS 163.535, 163.545 or 163.547 or a failure to provide adequate food, clothing, shelter or medical care that is likely to endanger the health or welfare of a child under 14 years of age or a dependent person. This paragraph is not intended to replace or affect the duty or standard of care required under ORS chapter 677.
(c) "Pattern or practice" means one or more previous episodes.
(d) "Torture" means to intentionally inflict intense physical pain upon an unwilling victim as a separate objective apart from any other purpose.

Note: *The 2009 amendments to this section occurred in omitted subsection(s).*

163.117 Causing or aiding commission of suicide is not murder

It is a defense to a charge of murder that the defendant's conduct consisted of causing or aiding, without the use of duress or deception, another person to commit suicide. Nothing contained in this section shall constitute a defense to a prosecution for, or preclude a conviction of, manslaughter or any other crime.

163.118 Manslaughter in the first degree

(1) Criminal homicide constitutes manslaughter in the first degree when:
 (a) It is committed recklessly under circumstances manifesting extreme indifference to the value of human life;
 (b) It is committed intentionally by a defendant under the influence of extreme emotional disturbance as provided in ORS 163.135, which constitutes a mitigating circumstance reducing the homicide that would otherwise be murder to manslaughter in the first degree and need not be proved in any prosecution;
 (c) A person recklessly causes the death of a child under 14 years of age or a dependent person, as defined in ORS 163.205, and:
  (A) The person has previously engaged in a pattern or practice of assault or torture of the victim or another child under 14 years of age or a dependent person; or
  (B) The person causes the death by neglect or maltreatment, as defined in ORS 163.115; or
 (d) It is committed recklessly or with criminal negligence by a person operating a motor vehicle while under the influence of intoxicants in violation of ORS 813.010 and:
  (A) The person has at least three previous convictions for driving while under the influence of intoxicants under ORS 813.010, or its statutory counterpart in any jurisdiction, in the 10 years prior to the date of the current offense; or
  (B)(i) The person has a previous conviction for any of the crimes described in subsection (2) of this section, or their statutory counterparts in any jurisdiction; and
   (ii) The victim's serious physical injury in the previous conviction was caused by the person driving a motor vehicle.
(2) The previous convictions to which subsection (1)(d)(B) of this section applies are:
 (a) Assault in the first degree under ORS 163.185;
 (b) Assault in the second degree under ORS 163.175; or

(c) Assault in the third degree under ORS 163.165.
(3) Manslaughter in the first degree is a Class A felony.
(4) It is an affirmative defense to a charge of violating:
  (a) Subsection (1)(c)(B) of this section that the child or dependent person was under care or treatment solely by spiritual means pursuant to the religious beliefs or practices of the child or person or the parent or guardian of the child or person.
  (b) Subsection (1)(d)(B) of this section that the defendant was not under the influence of intoxicants at the time of the conduct that resulted in the previous conviction.

163.125 Manslaughter in the second degree

(1) Criminal homicide constitutes manslaughter in the second degree when:
  (a) It is committed recklessly;
  (b) A person intentionally causes or aids another person to commit suicide; or
  (c) A person, with criminal negligence, causes the death of a child under 14 years of age or a dependent person, as defined in ORS 163.205, and:
    (A) The person has previously engaged in a pattern or practice of assault or torture of the victim or another child under 14 years of age or a dependent person; or
    (B) The person causes the death by neglect or maltreatment, as defined in ORS 163.115.
(2) Manslaughter in the second degree is a Class B felony.

163.135 Extreme emotional disturbance as affirmative defense to murder

(1) It is an affirmative defense to murder for purposes of ORS 163.115 (1)(a) that the homicide was committed under the influence of extreme emotional disturbance if the disturbance is not the result of the person's own intentional, knowing, reckless or criminally negligent act and if there is a reasonable explanation for the disturbance. The reasonableness of the explanation for the disturbance must be determined from the standpoint of an ordinary person in the actor's situation under the circumstances that the actor reasonably believed them to be. Extreme emotional disturbance does not constitute a defense to a prosecution for, or preclude a conviction of, manslaughter in the first degree or any other crime.
(2) The defendant may not introduce in the defendant's case in chief expert testimony regarding extreme emotional disturbance under this section unless the defendant gives notice of the defendant's intent to do so.
(3) The notice required must be in writing and must be filed at the time the defendant pleads not guilty. The defendant may file the notice at any time

after the defendant pleads but before trial if the court determines that there was just cause for failure to file the notice at the time of the defendant's plea.

(4) If the defendant fails to file notice, the defendant may not introduce evidence for the purpose of proving extreme emotional disturbance under ORS 163.115 unless the court, in its discretion, determines that there was just cause for failure to file notice.

(5) After the defendant files notice as provided in this section, the state may have at least one psychiatrist or licensed psychologist of its selection examine the defendant in the same manner and subject to the same provisions as provided in ORS 161.315.

163.145 Criminally negligent homicide

(1) A person commits the crime of criminally negligent homicide when, with criminal negligence, the person causes the death of another person.

(2) Criminally negligent homicide is a Class B felony.

163.149 Aggravated vehicular homicide

(1) Criminal homicide constitutes aggravated vehicular homicide when it is committed with criminal negligence, recklessly or recklessly under circumstances manifesting extreme indifference to the value of human life by a person operating a motor vehicle while under the influence of intoxicants in violation of ORS 813.010 and:
  (a) The person has a previous conviction for any of the crimes described in subsection (2) of this section, or their statutory counterparts in any jurisdiction; and
  (b) The victim's death in the previous conviction was caused by the person driving a motor vehicle.

(2) The previous convictions to which subsection (1) of this section applies are:
  (a) Manslaughter in the first degree under ORS 163.118;
  (b) Manslaughter in the second degree under ORS 163.125; or
  (c) Criminally negligent homicide under ORS 163.145.

(3) It is an affirmative defense to a prosecution under this section that the defendant was not under the influence of intoxicants at the time of the conduct that resulted in the previous conviction.

(4) Aggravated vehicular homicide is a Class A felony.

163.160 Assault in the fourth degree
Amended 2009

(1) A person commits the crime of assault in the fourth degree if the person:
  (a) Intentionally, knowingly or recklessly causes physical injury to another; or

Amended 2009

  (b) With criminal negligence causes physical injury to another by means of a deadly weapon.

(2) Assault in the fourth degree is a Class A misdemeanor.

(3) Notwithstanding subsection (2) of this section, assault in the fourth degree is a Class C felony if the person commits the crime of assault in the fourth degree and:

  (a) The person has previously been convicted of assaulting the same victim;

  (b) The person has previously been convicted at least three times under this section or under equivalent laws of another jurisdiction and all of the assaults involved domestic violence, as defined in ORS 135.230;

  (c) The assault is committed in the immediate presence of, or is witnessed by, the person's or the victim's minor child or stepchild or a minor child residing within the household of the person or victim; *or*

  (d) The person commits the assault knowing that the victim is pregnant.

(4) For the purposes of subsection (3) of this section, an assault is witnessed if the assault is seen or directly perceived in any other manner by the child.

163.165 Assault in the third degree
Amended 2009

(1) A person commits the crime of assault in the third degree if the person:

  (a) Recklessly causes serious physical injury to another by means of a deadly or dangerous weapon;

  (b) Recklessly causes serious physical injury to another under circumstances manifesting extreme indifference to the value of human life;

  (c) Recklessly causes physical injury to another by means of a deadly or dangerous weapon under circumstances manifesting extreme indifference to the value of human life;

  (d) Intentionally, knowingly or recklessly causes, by means other than a motor vehicle, physical injury to the operator of a public transit vehicle while the operator is in control of or operating the vehicle. As used in this paragraph, "public transit vehicle" has the meaning given that term in ORS 166.116;

  (e) While being aided by another person actually present, intentionally or knowingly causes physical injury to another;

  (f) While committed to a youth correction facility, intentionally or knowingly causes physical injury to another knowing the other person is a staff member of a youth correction facility while the other person is acting in the course of official duty;

  (g) Intentionally, knowingly or recklessly causes physical injury to an emergency medical technician, *as* defined in ORS 682.025, *or a paramedic* while the ***emergency medical*** technician or paramedic is performing official duties;

(h) Being at least 18 years of age, intentionally or knowingly causes physical injury to a child 10 years of age or younger; or

(i) Intentionally, knowingly or recklessly causes, by means other than a motor vehicle, physical injury to the operator of a taxi while the operator is in control of the taxi.

(2)***(a)*** Assault in the third degree is a Class C felony.

(b) Notwithstanding paragraph (a) of this subsection, assault in the third degree under subsection (1)(a) or (b) of this section is a Class B felony if:

(A) The assault resulted from the operation of a motor vehicle; and

(B) The defendant was the driver of the motor vehicle and was driving while under the influence of intoxicants.

(3) As used in this section:

(a) "Staff member" means:

(A) A corrections officer as defined in ORS 181.610, a youth correction officer, a Department of Corrections or Oregon Youth Authority staff member or a person employed pursuant to a contract with the department or youth authority to work with, or in the vicinity of, inmates or youth offenders; and

(B) A volunteer authorized by the department, youth authority or other entity in charge of a corrections facility to work with, or in the vicinity of, inmates or youth offenders.

(b) "Youth correction facility" has the meaning given that term in ORS 162.135.

Note: *The 2009 amendments to this section also deleted the definition of Dangerous substance formerly found at (3)(a).*

163.175 Assault in the second degree

(1) A person commits the crime of assault in the second degree if the person:

(a) Intentionally or knowingly causes serious physical injury to another;

(b) Intentionally or knowingly causes physical injury to another by means of a deadly or dangerous weapon; or

(c) Recklessly causes serious physical injury to another by means of a deadly or dangerous weapon under circumstances manifesting extreme indifference to the value of human life.

(2) Assault in the second degree is a Class B felony.

163.185 Assault in the first degree
Amended 2009

(1) A person commits the crime of assault in the first degree if the person:
 (a) Intentionally causes serious physical injury to another by means of a deadly or dangerous weapon;
 (b) Intentionally or knowingly causes serious physical injury to a child under six years of age;
 (c) Violates ORS 163.175 knowing that the victim is pregnant; or
 (d) Intentionally, knowingly or recklessly causes serious physical injury to another while operating a motor vehicle under the influence of intoxicants in violation of ORS 813.010 and:
  (A) The person has at least three previous convictions for driving while under the influence of intoxicants under ORS 813.010, or its statutory counterpart in any jurisdiction, in the 10 years prior to the date of the current offense; or
  (B)(i) The person has a previous conviction for any of the crimes described in subsection (2) of this section, or their statutory counterparts in any jurisdiction; and
   (ii) The victim's death or serious physical injury in the previous conviction was caused by the person driving a motor vehicle.
(2) The previous convictions to which *subsection (1)(d)(B)* of this section apply are:
 (a) Manslaughter in the first degree under ORS 163.118;
 (b) Manslaughter in the second degree under ORS 163.125;
 (c) Criminally negligent homicide under ORS 163.145;
 (d) Assault in the first degree under this section;
 (e) Assault in the second degree under ORS 163.175; or
 (f) Assault in the third degree under ORS 163.165.
(3) Assault in the first degree is a Class A felony.
(4) It is an affirmative defense to a prosecution under *subsection (1)(d)(B)* of this section that the defendant was not under the influence of intoxicants at the time of the conduct that resulted in the previous conviction.

163.187 Strangulation

(1) A person commits the crime of strangulation if the person knowingly impedes the normal breathing or circulation of the blood of another person by:
 (a) Applying pressure on the throat or neck of the other person; or
 (b) Blocking the nose or mouth of the other person.
(2) Subsection (1) of this section does not apply to legitimate medical or dental procedures or good faith practices of a religious belief.
(3) Strangulation is a Class A misdemeanor.

163.190 Menacing
(1) A person commits the crime of menacing if by word or conduct the person intentionally attempts to place another person in fear of imminent serious physical injury.
(2) Menacing is a Class A misdemeanor.

163.195 Recklessly endangering another person
(1) A person commits the crime of recklessly endangering another person if the person recklessly engages in conduct which creates a substantial risk of serious physical injury to another person.
(2) Recklessly endangering another person is a Class A misdemeanor.

163.196 Aggravated driving while suspended or revoked *Added 2009*
(1) A person commits the crime of aggravated driving while suspended or revoked if the person operates a motor vehicle that causes serious physical injury to, or the death of, another person while knowingly violating ORS 811.175 or 811.182, if the suspension or revocation resulted from, or if the hardship or probationary permit violated is based upon a suspension or revocation that resulted from, a conviction for a criminal offense involving the use of a motor vehicle.
(2) Aggravated driving while suspended or revoked is a Class C felony.
(3) The Oregon Criminal Justice Commission shall classify aggravated driving while suspended or revoked as crime category 7 of the sentencing guidelines grid of the commission.

163.197 Hazing *Amended 2009*
(1) A student organization or a member of a student organization commits the offense of hazing if, as a condition or precondition of attaining membership in the organization or of attaining any office or status in the organization, the organization or member intentionally hazes any member, potential member or person pledged to be a member of the organization.
(2)(a) A student organization that violates subsection (1) of this section commits a Class A violation.
(b) A member of a student organization who personally violates subsection (1) of this section commits a Class B violation.
(3) Consent of the person who is hazed is not a defense in a prosecution under this section.
(4) As used in this section:
(a) "Haze" means:

(A) To subject an individual to whipping, beating, striking, branding or electronic shocking, to place a harmful substance on an individual's body or to subject an individual to other similar forms of physical brutality;
(B) To subject an individual to sleep deprivation, exposure to the elements, confinement in a small space or other similar activity that subjects the individual to an unreasonable risk of harm or adversely affects the physical health or safety of the individual;
(C) To compel an individual to consume food, liquid, alcohol, controlled substances or other substances that subject the individual to an unreasonable risk of harm or adversely affect the physical health or safety of the individual; or
(D) To induce, cause or require an individual to perform a duty or task that involves the commission of a crime or an act of hazing.
(b) "Member" includes volunteers, coaches and faculty advisers of a student organization.
(c) "Student organization" means a fraternity, sorority, athletic team or other organization that is organized or operating on a college, university or elementary or secondary school campus for the purpose of providing members an opportunity to participate in student activities of the college, university or elementary or secondary school.

163.200 Criminal mistreatment in the second degree

(1) A person commits the crime of criminal mistreatment in the second degree if, with criminal negligence and:
 (a) In violation of a legal duty to provide care for another person, the person withholds necessary and adequate food, physical care or medical attention from that person; or
 (b) Having assumed the permanent or temporary care, custody or responsibility for the supervision of another person, the person withholds necessary and adequate food, physical care or medical attention from that person.
(2) Criminal mistreatment in the second degree is a Class A misdemeanor.
(3) As used in this section, "legal duty" includes but is not limited to a duty created by familial relationship, court order, contractual agreement or statutory or case law.

163.205 Criminal mistreatment in the first degree

(1) A person commits the crime of criminal mistreatment in the first degree if:
 (a) The person, in violation of a legal duty to provide care for another person, or having assumed the permanent or temporary care, custody or responsibility for the supervision of another person, intentionally or knowingly withholds necessary and

adequate food, physical care or medical attention from that other person; or
(b) The person, in violation of a legal duty to provide care for a dependent person or elderly person, or having assumed the permanent or temporary care, custody or responsibility for the supervision of a dependent person or elderly person, intentionally or knowingly:
(A) Causes physical injury or injuries to the dependent person or elderly person;
(B) Deserts the dependent person or elderly person in a place with the intent to abandon that person;
(C) Leaves the dependent person or elderly person unattended at a place for such a period of time as may be likely to endanger the health or welfare of that person;
(D) Hides the dependent person's or elderly person's money or property or takes the money or property for, or appropriates the money or property to, any use or purpose not in the due and lawful execution of the person's responsibility;
(E) Takes charge of a dependent or elderly person for the purpose of fraud; or
(F) Leaves the dependent person or elderly person, or causes the dependent person or elderly person to enter or remain, in or upon premises where a chemical reaction involving one or more precursor substances:
(i) Is occurring as part of unlawfully manufacturing a controlled substance or grinding, soaking or otherwise breaking down a precursor substance for the unlawful manufacture of a controlled substance; or
(ii) Has occurred as part of unlawfully manufacturing a controlled substance or grinding, soaking or otherwise breaking down a precursor substance for the unlawful manufacture of a controlled substance and the premises have not been certified as fit for use under ORS 453.885.
(2) As used in this section:
(a) "Controlled substance" has the meaning given that term in ORS 475.005.
(b) "Dependent person" means a person who because of either age or a physical or mental disability is dependent upon another to provide for the person's physical needs.
(c) "Elderly person" means a person 65 years of age or older.

(d) "Legal duty" includes but is not limited to a duty created by familial relationship, court order, contractual agreement or statutory or case law.
(e) "Precursor substance" has the meaning given that term in ORS 475.940.
(3) Criminal mistreatment in the first degree is a Class C felony.

163.206 Exceptions–Criminal mistreatment Amended 2009

ORS 163.200 and 163.205 do not apply:
(1) To a person acting pursuant to a court order, an advance directive or a power of attorney for health care pursuant to ORS 127.505 to 127.660 *or a POLST, as defined in ORS 127.663*;
(2) To a person withholding or withdrawing life-sustaining procedures or artificially administered nutrition and hydration pursuant to ORS 127.505 to 127.660;
(3) When a competent person refuses food, physical care or medical care;
(4) To a person who provides an elderly person or a dependent person who is at least 15 years of age with spiritual treatment through prayer from a duly accredited practitioner of spiritual treatment as provided in ORS 124.095, in lieu of medical treatment, in accordance with the tenets and practices of a recognized church or religious denomination of which the elderly or dependent person is a member or an adherent; or
(5) To a duly accredited practitioner of spiritual treatment as provided in ORS 124.095.

163.208 Assaulting a public safety officer

(1) A person commits the crime of assaulting a public safety officer if the person intentionally or knowingly causes physical injury to the other person, knowing the other person to be a peace officer, corrections officer, youth correction officer, parole and probation officer, animal control officer, firefighter or staff member, and while the other person is acting in the course of official duty.
(2) Assaulting a public safety officer is a Class C felony.
(3)(a) Except as otherwise provided in paragraph (b) of this subsection, a person convicted under this section shall be sentenced to not less than seven days of imprisonment and shall not be granted bench parole or suspension of sentence nor released on a sentence of probation before serving at least seven days of the sentence of confinement.
(b) A person convicted under this section shall be sentenced to not less than 14 days of imprisonment and shall not be granted bench parole or suspension of sentence nor released on a sentence of probation before serving at least 14 days of the sentence of confinement if the victim is a peace officer.
(4) As used in this section:
(a) "Animal control officer" has the meaning given that term in ORS 609.500; and
(b) "Staff member" means:

(A) A corrections officer as defined in ORS 181.610, a youth correction officer, a Department of Corrections or Oregon Youth Authority staff member or a person employed pursuant to a contract with the department or youth authority to work with, or in the vicinity of, inmates or youth offenders; and
(B) A volunteer authorized by the department, youth authority or other entity in charge of a corrections facility to work with, or in the vicinity of, inmates or youth offenders.

163.211 Definitions–Mace and tear gas

As used in ORS 163.211 to 163.213:
(1) "Corrections officer" and "parole and probation officer" have the meanings given those terms in ORS 181.610.
(2) "Mace, tear gas, pepper mace or any similar deleterious agent" means a sternutator, lacrimator or any substance composed of a mixture of a sternutator or lacrimator including, but not limited to, chloroacetophenone, alpha-chloroacetophenone, phenylchloromethylketone, orthochlorobenzalmalononitrile, oleoresin capsicum or a chemically similar sternutator or lacrimator by whatever name known, or phosgene or other gas or substance capable of generating offensive, noxious or suffocating fumes, gases or vapor or capable of immobilizing a person.
(3) "Tear gas weapon" includes:
(a) Any shell, cartridge or bomb capable of being discharged or exploded, when the discharge or explosion will cause or permit the release or emission of tear gas or oleoresin capsicum.
(b) Any revolver, pistol, fountain pen gun, billy or other form of device, portable or fixed, intended for the projection or release of tear gas or oleoresin capsicum.

163.212 Unlawful use of an electrical stun gun, tear gas or mace in the second degree

(1) A person commits the crime of unlawful use of an electrical stun gun, tear gas or mace in the second degree if the person recklessly discharges an electrical stun gun, tear gas weapon, mace, tear gas, pepper mace or any similar deleterious agent against another person.
(2) Unlawful use of an electrical stun gun, tear gas or mace in the second degree is a Class A misdemeanor.

163.213 Unlawful use of an electrical stun gun, tear gas or mace in the first degree

(1) A person commits the crime of unlawful use of an electrical stun gun, tear gas or mace in the first degree if the person knowingly discharges or causes to be discharged any electrical stun gun, tear gas weapon, mace, tear gas, pepper mace or any similar deleterious

Amended 2009

agent against another person, knowing the other person to be a peace officer, corrections officer, parole and probation officer, firefighter or emergency medical technician or paramedic and while the other person is acting in the course of official duty.

(2) Unlawful use of an electrical stun gun, tear gas or mace in the first degree is a Class C felony.

163.215 Definitions–Kidnapping & related offenses

As used in ORS 163.215 to 163.257, unless the context requires otherwise:

(1) "Without consent" means that the taking or confinement is accomplished by force, threat or deception, or, in the case of a person under 16 years of age or who is otherwise incapable of giving consent, that the taking or confinement is accomplished without the consent of the lawful custodian of the person.

(2) "Lawful custodian" means a parent, guardian or other person responsible by authority of law for the care, custody or control of another.

(3) "Relative" means a parent, ancestor, brother, sister, uncle or aunt.

163.225 Kidnapping in the second degree

(1) A person commits the crime of kidnapping in the second degree if, with intent to interfere substantially with another's personal liberty, and without consent or legal authority, the person:
  (a) Takes the person from one place to another; or
  (b) Secretly confines the person in a place where the person is not likely to be found.

(2) It is a defense to a prosecution under subsection (1) of this section if:
  (a) The person taken or confined is under 16 years of age;
  (b) The defendant is a relative of that person; and
  (c) The sole purpose of the person is to assume control of that person.

(3) Kidnapping in the second degree is a Class B felony.

163.235 Kidnapping in the first degree
Amended 2009

(1) A person commits the crime of kidnapping in the first degree if the person violates ORS 163.225 with any of the following purposes:
  (a) To compel any person to pay or deliver money or property as ransom;
  (b) To hold the victim as a shield or hostage;
  (c) To cause physical injury to the victim;
  (d) To terrorize the victim or another person; *or*
  (e) To further the commission or attempted commission of any of the following crimes against the victim:
    (A) Rape in the first degree, as defined in ORS 163.375 (1)(b);

(B) *Sodomy in the first degree, as defined in ORS 163.405 (1)(b); or*

(C) *Unlawful sexual penetration in the first degree, as defined in ORS 163.411 (1)(b).*

(2) Kidnapping in the first degree is a Class A felony.

163.245 Custodial interference in the second degree

(1) A person commits the crime of custodial interference in the second degree if, knowing or having reason to know that the person has no legal right to do so, the person takes, entices or keeps another person from the other person's lawful custodian or in violation of a valid joint custody order with intent to hold the other person permanently or for a protracted period.

(2) Expenses incurred by a lawful custodial parent or a parent enforcing a valid joint custody order in locating and regaining physical custody of the person taken, enticed or kept in violation of this section are "economic damages" for purposes of restitution under ORS 137.103 to 137.109.

(3) Custodial interference in the second degree is a Class C felony.

163.257 Custodial interference in the first degree

(1) A person commits the crime of custodial interference in the first degree if the person violates ORS 163.245 and:

(a) Causes the person taken, enticed or kept from the lawful custodian or in violation of a valid joint custody order to be removed from the state; or

(b) Exposes that person to a substantial risk of illness or physical injury.

(2) Expenses incurred by a lawful custodial parent or a parent enforcing a valid joint custody order in locating and regaining physical custody of the person taken, enticed or kept in violation of this section are "economic damages" for purposes of restitution under ORS 137.103 to 137.109.

(3) Custodial interference in the first degree is a Class B felony.

163.261 Definitions–Involuntary servitude and human trafficking

As used in ORS 163.263 and 163.264, "services" means activities performed by one person under the supervision or for the benefit of another person.

163.263 Subjecting another person to involuntary servitude in the second degree

(1) A person commits the crime of subjecting another person to involuntary servitude in the second degree if the person know-

ingly and without lawful authority forces or attempts to force the other person to engage in services by:
(a) Abusing or threatening to abuse the law or legal process;
(b) Destroying, concealing, removing, confiscating or possessing an actual or purported passport or immigration document or another actual or purported government identification document of a person;
(c) Threatening to report a person to a government agency for the purpose of arrest or deportation;
(d) Threatening to collect an unlawful debt; or
(e) Instilling in the other person a fear that the actor will withhold from the other person the necessities of life, including but not limited to lodging, food and clothing.
(2) Subjecting another person to involuntary servitude in the second degree is a Class C felony.

163.264 Subjecting another person to involuntary servitude in the first degree

(1) A person commits the crime of subjecting another person to involuntary servitude in the first degree if the person knowingly and without lawful authority forces or attempts to force the other person to engage in services by:
(a) Causing or threatening to cause the death of or serious physical injury to a person; or
(b) Physically restraining or threatening to physically restrain a person.
(2) Subjecting another person to involuntary servitude in the first degree is a Class B felony.

163.266 Trafficking in persons

(1) A person commits the crime of trafficking in persons if the person knowingly:
(a) Recruits, entices, harbors, transports, provides or obtains by any means, or attempts to recruit, entice, harbor, transport, provide or obtain by any means, another person knowing that the other person will be subjected to involuntary servitude as described in ORS 163.263 or 163.264; or
(b) Benefits financially or receives something of value from participation in a venture that involves an act prohibited by this section or ORS 163.263 or 163.264.
(2) Trafficking in persons is a Class B felony.

163.275 Coercion

(1) A person commits the crime of coercion when the person compels or induces another person to engage in conduct from which the other person has a legal right to abstain, or to abstain from engaging in conduct in which the other person has a legal right to engage, by means of instilling in the other person a fear that, if the other person refrains from the conduct compelled or induced or engages in conduct contrary to the compulsion or inducement, the actor or another will:

(a) Unlawfully cause physical injury to some person;

(b) Unlawfully cause damage to property;

(c) Engage in conduct constituting a crime;

(d) Falsely accuse some person of a crime or cause criminal charges to be instituted against the person;

(e) Cause or continue a strike, boycott or other collective action injurious to some person's business, except that such a threat is not deemed coercive when the act or omission compelled is for the benefit of the group in whose interest the actor purports to act;

(f) Testify falsely or provide false information or withhold testimony or information with respect to another's legal claim or defense; or

(g) Unlawfully use or abuse the person's position as a public servant by performing some act within or related to official duties, or by failing or refusing to perform an official duty, in such manner as to affect some person adversely.

(2) Coercion is a Class C felony.

163.285 Defenses–Coercion

In any prosecution for coercion committed by instilling in the victim a fear that the victim or another person would be charged with a crime, it is a defense that the defendant reasonably believed the threatened charge to be true and that the sole purpose of the defendant was to compel or induce the victim to take reasonable action to make good the wrong which was the subject of the threatened charge.

163.305 Definitions–Sexual offenses
Amended 2009

As used in chapter 743, Oregon Laws 1971, unless the context requires otherwise:

(1) "Deviate sexual intercourse" means sexual conduct between persons consisting of contact between the sex organs of one person and the mouth or anus of another.

(2) "Forcible compulsion" means to compel by:
  (a) Physical force; or
  (b) A threat, express or implied, that places a person in fear of immediate or future death or physical injury to self or another person, or in fear that the person or another person will immediately or in the future be kidnapped.
(3) "Mentally defective" means that a person suffers from a mental disease or defect that renders the person incapable of appraising the nature of the conduct of the person.
(4) "Mentally incapacitated" means that a person is rendered incapable of appraising or controlling the conduct of the person at the time of the alleged offense.
(5) "Physically helpless" means that a person is unconscious or for any other reason is physically unable to communicate unwillingness to an act.
(6) "Sexual contact" means any touching of the sexual or other intimate parts of a person or causing such person to touch the sexual or other intimate parts of the actor for the purpose of arousing or gratifying the sexual desire of either party.
(7) "Sexual intercourse" has its ordinary meaning and occurs upon any penetration, however slight; emission is not required.

Note: *The 2009 amendments to this section consist solely of deletions in subsection (4).*

163.315 Incapacity to consent

(1) A person is considered incapable of consenting to a sexual act if the person is:
  (a) Under 18 years of age;
  (b) Mentally defective;
  (c) Mentally incapacitated; or
  (d) Physically helpless.
(2) A lack of verbal or physical resistance does not, by itself, constitute consent but may be considered by the trier of fact along with all other relevant evidence.

163.325 Defenses–Ignorance or mistake

(1) In any prosecution under ORS 163.355 to 163.445 in which the criminality of conduct depends on a child's being under the age of 16, it is no defense that the defendant did not know the child's age or that the defendant reasonably believed the child to be older than the age of 16.
(2) When criminality depends on the child's being under a specified age other than 16, it is an affirmative defense for the defendant to prove that the defendant reasonably believed the child to be above the specified age at the time of the alleged offense.
(3) In any prosecution under ORS 163.355 to 163.445 in which the victim's lack of consent is based solely upon the incapacity of the victim to consent because the victim is mentally defective, mentally incapacitated or physically helpless, it is an affirmative defense for the defendant to prove that at

the time of the alleged offense the defendant did not know of the facts or conditions responsible for the victim's incapacity to consent.

163.345 Defenses–Age as defense
(1) In any prosecution under ORS 163.355, 163.365, 163.385, 163.395, 163.415, 163.425, 163.427 or 163.435 in which the victim's lack of consent was due solely to incapacity to consent by reason of being less than a specified age, it is a defense that the actor was less than three years older than the victim at the time of the alleged offense.
(2) In any prosecution under ORS 163.408, when the object used to commit the unlawful sexual penetration was the hand or any part thereof of the actor and in which the victim's lack of consent was due solely to incapacity to consent by reason of being less than a specified age, it is a defense that the actor was less than three years older than the victim at the time of the alleged offense.
(3) In any prosecution under ORS 163.445 in which the victim's lack of consent was due solely to incapacity to consent by reason of being less than a specified age, it is a defense that the actor was less than three years older than the victim at the time of the alleged offense if the victim was at least 15 years of age at the time of the alleged offense.

163.355 Rape in the third degree
(1) A person commits the crime of rape in the third degree if the person has sexual intercourse with another person under 16 years of age.
(2) Rape in the third degree is a Class C felony.

163.365 Rape in the second degree
(1) A person who has sexual intercourse with another person commits the crime of rape in the second degree if the other person is under 14 years of age.
(2) Rape in the second degree is a Class B felony.

163.375 Rape in the first degree
(1) A person who has sexual intercourse with another person commits the crime of rape in the first degree if:
  (a) The victim is subjected to forcible compulsion by the person;
  (b) The victim is under 12 years of age;
  (c) The victim is under 16 years of age and is the person's sibling, of the whole or half blood, the person's child or the person's spouse's child; or
  (d) The victim is incapable of consent by reason of mental defect, mental incapacitation or physical helplessness.
(2) Rape in the first degree is a Class A felony.

163.385 Sodomy in the third degree
(1) A person commits the crime of sodomy in the third degree if the person engages in deviate sexual intercourse with another person under 16 years of age or causes that person to engage in deviate sexual intercourse.
(2) Sodomy in the third degree is a Class C felony.

163.395 Sodomy in the second degree
(1) A person who engages in deviate sexual intercourse with another person or causes another to engage in deviate sexual intercourse commits the crime of sodomy in the second degree if the victim is under 14 years of age.
(2) Sodomy in the second degree is a Class B felony.

163.405 Sodomy in the first degree
(1) A person who engages in deviate sexual intercourse with another person or causes another to engage in deviate sexual intercourse commits the crime of sodomy in the first degree if:
  (a) The victim is subjected to forcible compulsion by the actor;
  (b) The victim is under 12 years of age;
  (c) The victim is under 16 years of age and is the actor's brother or sister, of the whole or half blood, the son or daughter of the actor or the son or daughter of the actor's spouse; or
  (d) The victim is incapable of consent by reason of mental defect, mental incapacitation or physical helplessness.
(2) Sodomy in the first degree is a Class A felony.

163.408 Unlawful sexual penetration in the second degree
(1) Except as permitted under ORS 163.412, a person commits the crime of unlawful sexual penetration in the second degree if the person penetrates the vagina, anus or penis of another with any object other than the penis or mouth of the actor and the victim is under 14 years of age.
(2) Unlawful sexual penetration in the second degree is a Class B felony.

163.411 Unlawful sexual penetration in the first degree
(1) Except as permitted under ORS 163.412, a person commits the crime of unlawful sexual penetration in the first degree if the person penetrates the vagina, anus or penis of another with any object other than the penis or mouth of the actor and:

(a) The victim is subjected to forcible compulsion;
(b) The victim is under 12 years of age; or
(c) The victim is incapable of consent by reason of mental defect, mental incapacitation or physical helplessness.

(2) Unlawful sexual penetration in the first degree is a Class A felony.

163.412 Exceptions to unlawful sexual penetration

Nothing in ORS 163.408, 163.411 or 163.452 prohibits a penetration described in those sections when:

(1) The penetration is part of a medically recognized treatment or diagnostic procedure; or

(2) The penetration is accomplished by a peace officer or a corrections officer acting in official capacity, or by medical personnel at the request of such an officer, in order to search for weapons, contraband or evidence of crime.

163.415 Sexual abuse in the third degree
Amended 2009

(1) A person commits the crime of sexual abuse in the third degree if:
  (a) The person subjects another person to sexual contact and:
    (A) The victim does not consent to the sexual contact; or
    (B) The victim is incapable of consent by reason of being under 18 years of age; *or*
  (b) For the purpose of arousing or gratifying the sexual desire of the person or another person, the person intentionally propels any dangerous substance at a victim without the consent of the victim.

(2) Sexual abuse in the third degree is a Class A misdemeanor.

(3) As used in this section, "dangerous substance" means blood, urine, semen or feces.

163.425 Sexual abuse in the second degree
Amended 2009

(1) A person commits the crime of sexual abuse in the second degree when:
  (a) The person subjects another person to sexual intercourse, deviate sexual intercourse or, except as provided in ORS 163.412, penetration of the vagina, anus or penis with any object other than the penis or mouth of the actor and the victim does not consent thereto; *or*
  (b)(A) The person violates ORS 163.415 (1)(a)(B);
    (B) The person is 21 years of age or older; and

(C) At any time before the commission of the offense, the person was the victim's coach as defined in ORS 163.426.

(2) Sexual abuse in the second degree is a Class C felony.

163.426 Definitions–Sexual abuse in the second degree by a coach Added 2009

(1) As used in this section, "coach" means a person who instructs or trains an individual or members of a team in a sport.

(2) The Oregon Criminal Justice Commission shall classify sexual abuse in the second degree as described in ORS 163.425 (1)(a) as a crime category 8 of the sentencing guidelines grid of the commission if:

(a) The victim is incapable of consent by reason of being under 18 years of age;

(b) The offender is 21 years of age or older; and

(c) At any time before the commission of the offense, the offender was the victim's coach.

163.427 Sexual abuse in the first degree

(1) A person commits the crime of sexual abuse in the first degree when that person:

(a) Subjects another person to sexual contact and:

(A) The victim is less than 14 years of age;

(B) The victim is subjected to forcible compulsion by the actor; or

(C) The victim is incapable of consent by reason of being mentally defective, mentally incapacitated or physically helpless; or

(b) Intentionally causes a person under 18 years of age to touch or contact the mouth, anus or sex organs of an animal for the purpose of arousing or gratifying the sexual desire of a person.

(2) Sexual abuse in the first degree is a Class B felony.

163.431 Definitions–Online sexual corruption of a child Amended 2009

As used in **ORS 163.431** to 163.434:

(1) "Child" means a person who the defendant reasonably believes to be under 16 years of age.

(2) "Online communication" means communication that occurs via *telephone text messaging,* electronic mail, personal or instant messaging, chat rooms, bulletin boards or any other *transmission of information by wire, radio, optical cable, cellular system, electromagnetic system or other similar means.*

(3) "Sexual contact" has the meaning given that term in ORS 163.305.

(4) "Sexually explicit conduct" has the meaning given that term in ORS 163.665.

(5) "Solicit" means to invite, request, seduce, lure, entice, persuade, prevail upon, coax, coerce or attempt to do so.

163.432 Online sexual corruption of a child in the second degree

(1) A person commits the crime of online sexual corruption of a child in the second degree if the person is 18 years of age or older and:
  (a) For the purpose of arousing or gratifying the sexual desire of the person or another person, knowingly uses an online communication to solicit a child to engage in sexual contact or sexually explicit conduct; and
  (b) Offers or agrees to physically meet with the child.
(2) Online sexual corruption of a child in the second degree is a Class C felony.

163.433 Online sexual corruption of a child in the first degree

(1) A person commits the crime of online sexual corruption of a child in the first degree if the person violates ORS 163.432 and intentionally takes a substantial step toward physically meeting with or encountering the child.
(2) Online sexual corruption of a child in the first degree is a Class B felony.

163.434 Defenses—Online sexual corruption of a child

(1) It is an affirmative defense to a prosecution for online sexual corruption of a child in the first or second degree that the person was not more than three years older than the person reasonably believed the child to be.
(2) It is not a defense to a prosecution for online sexual corruption of a child in the first or second degree that the person was in fact communicating with a law enforcement officer, as defined in ORS 163.730, or a person working under the direction of a law enforcement officer, who is 16 years of age or older.
(3) Online sexual corruption of a child in the first or second degree is committed in either the county in which the communication originated or the county in which the communication was received.

163.435 Contributing to the sexual delinquency of a minor

(1) A person 18 years of age or older commits the crime of contributing to the sexual delinquency of a minor if:
  (a) Being a male, he engages in sexual intercourse with a female under 18 years of age; or
  (b) Being a female, she engages in sexual intercourse with a male under 18 years of age; or

(c) The person engages in deviate sexual intercourse with another person under 18 years of age or causes that person to engage in deviate sexual intercourse.

(2) Contributing to the sexual delinquency of a minor is a Class A misdemeanor.

163.445 Sexual misconduct

(1) A person commits the crime of sexual misconduct if the person engages in sexual intercourse or deviate sexual intercourse with an unmarried person under 18 years of age.

(2) Sexual misconduct is a Class C misdemeanor.

163.448 Correctional facility–Defined

As used in ORS 163.452 and 163.454, "correctional facility" has the meaning given that term in ORS 162.135.

163.452 Custodial sexual misconduct in the first degree

(1) A person commits the crime of custodial sexual misconduct in the first degree if the person:

(a) Engages in sexual intercourse or deviate sexual intercourse with another person or penetrates the vagina, anus or penis of another person with any object other than the penis or mouth of the actor knowing that the other person is:

(A) In the custody of a law enforcement agency following arrest;

(B) Confined or detained in a correctional facility;

(C) Participating in an inmate or offender work crew or work release program;

(D) On probation, parole, post-prison supervision or other form of conditional or supervised release; and

(b) Is employed by or under contract with the state or local agency that:

(A) Employs the officer who arrested the other person;

(B) Operates the correctional facility in which the other person is confined or detained;

(C) Is responsible for supervising the other person in a work crew or work release program or on probation, parole, post-prison supervision or other form of conditional or supervised release; or

(D) Engages the other person in work or on-the-job training pursuant to ORS 421.354 (1).

(2) Consent of the other person to sexual intercourse, deviate sexual intercourse or the sexual penetration is not a defense to a prosecution under this section.

(3) Lack of supervisory authority over the other person is an affirmative defense to a prosecution under this section when the other person is on probation, parole, post-prison supervision or other form of conditional or supervised release.

(4) Custodial sexual misconduct in the first degree is a Class C felony.

163.454 Custodial sexual misconduct in the second degree

(1) A person commits the crime of custodial sexual misconduct in the second degree if the person:

(a) Engages in sexual contact with another person knowing that the other person is:

(A) In the custody of a law enforcement agency following arrest;

(B) Confined or detained in a correctional facility;

(C) Participating in an inmate or offender work crew or work release program; or

(D) On probation, parole, post-prison supervision or other form of conditional or supervised release; and

(b) Is employed by or under contract with the state or local agency that:

(A) Employs the officer who arrested the other person;

(B) Operates the correctional facility in which the other person is confined or detained;

(C) Is responsible for supervising the other person in a work crew or work release program or on probation, parole, post-prison supervision or other form of conditional or supervised release; or

(D) Engages the other person in work or on-the-job training pursuant to ORS 421.354 (1).

(2) Consent of the other person to sexual contact is not a defense to a prosecution under this section.

(3) Lack of supervisory authority over the other person is an affirmative defense to a prosecution under this section when the other person is on probation, parole, post-prison supervision or other form of conditional or supervised release.

(4) Custodial sexual misconduct in the second degree is a Class A misdemeanor.

163.465 Public indecency

(1) A person commits the crime of public indecency if while in, or in view of, a public place the person performs:

(a) An act of sexual intercourse;

(b) An act of deviate sexual intercourse; or

(c) An act of exposing the genitals of the person with the intent of arousing the sexual desire of the person or another person.
(2)(a) Public indecency is a Class A misdemeanor.
  (b) Notwithstanding paragraph (a) of this subsection, public indecency is a Class C felony if the person has a prior conviction for public indecency or a crime described in ORS 163.355 to 163.445 or for a crime in another jurisdiction that, if committed in this state, would constitute public indecency or a crime described in ORS 163.355 to 163.445.

163.467 Private indecency

(1) A person commits the crime of private indecency if the person exposes the genitals of the person with the intent of arousing the sexual desire of the person or another person and:
  (a) The person is in a place where another person has a reasonable expectation of privacy;
  (b) The person is in view of the other person;
  (c) The exposure reasonably would be expected to alarm or annoy the other person; and
  (d) The person knows that the other person did not consent to the exposure.
(2) Private indecency is a Class A misdemeanor.
(3) Subsection (1) of this section does not apply to a person who commits the act described in subsection (1) of this section if the person cohabits with and is involved in a sexually intimate relationship with the other person.
(4) For purposes of this section, "place where another person has a reasonable expectation of privacy" includes, but is not limited to, residences, yards of residences, working areas and offices.

163.476 Unlawfully being in location where children regularly congregate

(1) A person commits the crime of unlawfully being in a location where children regularly congregate if the person:
  (a)(A) Has been designated a sexually violent dangerous offender under ORS 137.765;
    (B) Has been designated a predatory sex offender under ORS 181.585 and does not have written approval from the State Board of Parole and Post-Prison Supervision or the person's supervisory authority or supervising officer to be in or upon the specific premises;
    (C) Has been sentenced as a dangerous offender under ORS 161.725 upon conviction of a sex crime; or

(D) Has been given a similar designation or been sentenced under a similar law of another jurisdiction; and

(b) Knowingly enters or remains in or upon premises where persons under 18 years of age regularly congregate.

(2) As used in this section:

(a) "Premises where persons under 18 years of age regularly congregate" means schools, child care centers, playgrounds, other places intended for use primarily by persons under 18 years of age and places where persons under 18 years of age gather for regularly scheduled educational and recreational programs.

(b) "Sex crime" has the meaning given that term in ORS 181.594.

(3) Unlawfully being in a location where children regularly congregate is a Class A misdemeanor.

163.479 Unlawful contact with a child

(1) A person commits the crime of unlawful contact with a child if the person:

(a)(A) Has been designated a sexually violent dangerous offender under ORS 137.765;

(B) Has been designated a predatory sex offender under ORS 181.585;

(C) Has been sentenced as a dangerous offender under ORS 161.725 upon conviction of a sex crime; or

(D) Has been given a similar designation or been sentenced under a similar law of another jurisdiction; and

(b) Knowingly contacts a child with the intent to commit a crime or for the purpose of arousing or satisfying the sexual desires of the person or another person.

(2) As used in this section:

(a) "Child" means a person under 18 years of age.

(b) "Contact" means to communicate in any manner.

(c) "Sex crime" has the meaning given that term in ORS 181.594.

(3) Unlawful contact with a child is a Class C felony.

163.505 Definitions–Family offenses

As used in ORS 163.505 to 163.575, unless the context requires otherwise:

(1) "Controlled substance" has the meaning given that term in ORS 475.005.

(2) "Descendant" includes persons related by descending lineal consanguinity, stepchildren and lawfully adopted children.

(3) "Precursor substance" has the meaning given that term in ORS 475.940.

(4) "Support" includes, but is not limited to, necessary and proper shelter, food, clothing, medical attention and education.

163.515 Bigamy
(1) A person commits the crime of bigamy if the person knowingly marries or purports to marry another person at a time when either is lawfully married.
(2) Bigamy is a Class C felony.

163.525 Incest
(1) A person commits the crime of incest if the person marries or engages in sexual intercourse or deviate sexual intercourse with a person whom the person knows to be related to the person, either legitimately or illegitimately, as an ancestor, descendant or brother or sister of either the whole or half blood.
(2) Incest is a Class C felony.

163.535 Abandonment of a child
(1) A person commits the crime of abandonment of a child if, being a parent, lawful guardian or other person lawfully charged with the care or custody of a child under 15 years of age, the person deserts the child in any place with intent to abandon it.
(2) Abandonment of a child is a Class C felony.
(3) It is an affirmative defense to a charge of violating subsection (1) of this section that the child was left in accordance with ORS 418.017.

163.537 Buying or selling a person under 18 years of age
(1) A person commits the crime of buying or selling a person under 18 years of age if the person buys, sells, barters, trades or offers to buy or sell the legal or physical custody of a person under 18 years of age.
(2) Subsection (1) of this section does not:
  (a) Prohibit a person in the process of adopting a child from paying the fees, costs and expenses related to the adoption as allowed in ORS 109.311.
  (b) Prohibit a negotiated satisfaction of child support arrearages or other settlement in favor of a parent of a child in exchange for consent of the parent to the adoption of the child by the current spouse of the child's other parent.
  (c) Apply to fees for services charged by the Department of Human Services or adoption agencies licensed under ORS 412.001 to 412.161 and 412.991 and ORS chapter 418.
  (d) Apply to fees for services in an adoption pursuant to a surrogacy agreement.
  (e) Prohibit discussion or settlement of disputed issues between parties in a domestic relations proceeding.
(3) Buying or selling a person under 18 years of age is a Class B felony.

163.545 Child neglect in the second degree

(1) A person having custody or control of a child under 10 years of age commits the crime of child neglect in the second degree if, with criminal negligence, the person leaves the child unattended in or at any place for such period of time as may be likely to endanger the health or welfare of such child.

(2) Child neglect in the second degree is a Class A misdemeanor.

163.547 Child neglect in the first degree

(1)(a) A person having custody or control of a child under 16 years of age commits the crime of child neglect in the first degree if the person knowingly leaves the child, or allows the child to stay:
  (A) In a vehicle where controlled substances are being criminally delivered or manufactured;
  (B) In or upon premises and in the immediate proximity where controlled substances are criminally delivered or manufactured for consideration or profit or where a chemical reaction involving one or more precursor substances:
    (i) Is occurring as part of unlawfully manufacturing a controlled substance or grinding, soaking or otherwise breaking down a precursor substance for the unlawful manufacture of a controlled substance; or
    (ii) Has occurred as part of unlawfully manufacturing a controlled substance or grinding, soaking or otherwise breaking down a precursor substance for the unlawful manufacture of a controlled substance and the premises have not been certified as fit for use under ORS 453.885; or
  (C) In or upon premises that have been determined to be not fit for use under ORS 453.855 to 453.912.
(b) As used in this subsection, "vehicle" and "premises" do not include public places, as defined in ORS 161.015.
(2) Child neglect in the first degree is a Class B felony.
(3) Subsection (1) of this section does not apply if the controlled substance is marijuana and is delivered for no consideration.
(4) The Oregon Criminal Justice Commission shall classify child neglect in the first degree as crime category 6 of the sentencing guidelines grid of the commission if the controlled substance being delivered or manufactured is methamphetamine.

163.555 Criminal nonsupport

(1) A person commits the crime of criminal nonsupport if, being the parent, lawful guardian or other person lawfully charged with the

support of a child under 18 years of age, born in or out of wedlock, the person knowingly fails to provide support for such child.

(2) It is no defense to a prosecution under this section that either parent has contracted a subsequent marriage, that issue has been born of a subsequent marriage, that the defendant is the parent of issue born of a prior marriage or that the child is being supported by another person or agency.

(3) It is an affirmative defense to a prosecution under this section that the defendant has a lawful excuse for failing to provide child support.

(4) If the defendant intends to rely on the affirmative defense created in subsection (3) of this section, the defendant must give the district attorney written notice of the intent to do so at least 30 days prior to trial. The notice must describe the nature of the lawful excuse upon which the defendant proposes to rely. If the defendant fails to file notice as required by this subsection, the defendant may not introduce evidence of a lawful excuse unless the court finds there was just cause for the defendant's failure to file the notice within the required time.

(5) Criminal nonsupport is a Class C felony.

163.565 Evidence of paternity

(1) Proof that a child was born to a woman during the time a man lived and cohabited with her, or held her out as his wife, is prima facie evidence that he is the father of the child. This subsection does not exclude any other legal evidence tending to establish the parental relationship.

(2) No provision of law prohibiting the disclosure of confidential communications between husband and wife apply to prosecutions for criminal nonsupport. A husband or wife is a competent and compellable witness for or against either party.

163.575 Endangering the welfare of a minor

(1) A person commits the crime of endangering the welfare of a minor if the person knowingly:

  (a) Induces, causes or permits an unmarried person under 18 years of age to witness an act of sexual conduct or sadomasochistic abuse as defined by ORS 167.060; or

  (b) Permits a person under 18 years of age to enter or remain in a place where unlawful activity involving controlled substances is maintained or conducted; or

  (c) Induces, causes or permits a person under 18 years of age to participate in gambling as defined by ORS 167.117; or

  (d) Distributes, sells, or causes to be sold, tobacco in any form to a person under 18 years of age; or

  (e) Sells to a person under 18 years of age any device in which tobacco, marijuana, cocaine or any controlled substance, as defined in ORS 475.005, is burned and the principal design and

use of which is directly or indirectly to deliver tobacco smoke, marijuana smoke, cocaine smoke or smoke from any controlled substance into the human body including but not limited to:
(A) Pipes, water pipes, hookahs, wooden pipes, carburetor pipes, electric pipes, air driven pipes, corncob pipes, meerschaum pipes and ceramic pipes, with or without screens, permanent screens, hashish heads or punctured metal bowls;
(B) Carburetion tubes and devices, including carburetion masks;
(C) Bongs;
(D) Chillums;
(E) Ice pipes or chillers;
(F) Cigarette rolling papers and rolling machines; and
(G) Cocaine free basing kits.
(2) Endangering the welfare of a minor by violation of subsection (1)(a), (b), (c) or (e) of this section, involving other than a device for smoking tobacco, is a Class A misdemeanor.
(3) Endangering the welfare of a minor by violation of subsection (1)(d) of this section or by violation of subsection (1)(e) of this section, involving a device for smoking tobacco, is a Class A violation and the court shall impose a fine of not less than $100.

163.577 Failing to supervise a child

(1) A person commits the offense of failing to supervise a child if the person is the parent, lawful guardian or other person lawfully charged with the care or custody of a child under 15 years of age and the child:
(a) Commits an act that brings the child within the jurisdiction of the juvenile court under ORS 419C.005;
(b) Violates a curfew law of a county or any other political subdivision; or
(c) Fails to attend school as required under ORS 339.010.
(2) Nothing in this section applies to a child-caring agency as defined in ORS 418.205 or to foster parents.
(3) In a prosecution of a person for failing to supervise a child under subsection (1)(a) of this section, it is an affirmative defense that the person:
(a) Is the victim of the act that brings the child within the jurisdiction of the juvenile court; or
(b) Reported the act to the appropriate authorities.
(4) In a prosecution of a person for failing to supervise a child under subsection (1) of this section, it is an affirmative defense that the person took reasonable steps to control the conduct of the child at the time the person is alleged to have failed to supervise the child.
(5)(a) Except as provided in subsection (6) or (7) of this section, in a prosecution of a person for failing to supervise a child under subsection (1)(a) of

this section, the court shall order the person to pay restitution under ORS 137.103 to 137.109 to a victim for economic damages arising from the act of the child that brings the child within the jurisdiction of the juvenile court.

(b) The amount of restitution ordered under this subsection may not exceed $2,500.

(6) If a person pleads guilty or is found guilty of failing to supervise a child under this section and if the person has not previously been convicted of failing to supervise a child, the court:

(a) Shall warn the person of the penalty for future convictions of failing to supervise a child and shall suspend imposition of sentence.

(b) May not order the person to pay restitution under this section.

(7)(a) If a person pleads guilty or is found guilty of failing to supervise a child under this section and if the person has only one prior conviction for failing to supervise a child, the court, with the consent of the person, may suspend imposition of sentence and order the person to complete a parent effectiveness program approved by the court. Upon the person's completion of the parent effectiveness program to the satisfaction of the court, the court may discharge the person. If the person fails to complete the parent effectiveness program to the satisfaction of the court, the court may impose a sentence authorized by this section.

(b) There may be only one suspension of sentence under this subsection with respect to a person.

(8) The juvenile court has jurisdiction over a first offense of failing to supervise a child under this section.

(9) Failing to supervise a child is a Class A violation.

163.580 Smoking devices–Posting sign of sales prohibition

(1) Any person who sells any of the smoking devices listed in ORS 163.575 (1)(e) shall display a sign clearly stating that the sale of such devices to persons under 18 years of age is prohibited by law.

(2) Any person who violates this section commits a Class B violation.

163.665 Definitions–Child pornography

As used in ORS 163.670 to 163.693:

(1) "Child" means a person who is less than 18 years of age, and any reference to a child in relation to a photograph, motion picture, videotape or other visual recording of the child is a reference to a person who was less than 18 years of age at the time the original image in the photograph, motion picture, videotape or other visual recording was created and not the age of the person at the time of an alleged offense relating to the subsequent reproduction, use or possession of the visual recording.

(2) "Child abuse" means conduct that constitutes, or would constitute if committed in this state, a crime in which the victim is a child.

(3) "Sexually explicit conduct" means actual or simulated:

(a) Sexual intercourse or deviant sexual intercourse;

(b) Genital-genital, oral-genital, anal-genital or oral-anal contact, whether between persons of the same or opposite sex or between humans and animals;
(c) Penetration of the vagina or rectum by any object other than as part of a medical diagnosis or treatment or as part of a personal hygiene practice;
(d) Masturbation;
(e) Sadistic or masochistic abuse; or
(f) Lewd exhibition of sexual or other intimate parts.
(4) "Visual depiction" includes, but is not limited to, photographs, films, videotapes, pictures or computer or computer-generated images or pictures, whether made or produced by electronic, mechanical or other means.

163.670 Using child in display of sexually explicit conduct

(1) A person commits the crime of using a child in a display of sexually explicit conduct if the person employs, authorizes, permits, compels or induces a child to participate or engage in sexually explicit conduct for any person to observe or to record in a photograph, motion picture, videotape or other visual recording.
(2) Using a child in a display of sexually explicit conduct is a Class A felony.

163.676 Exemption–Encouraging child sexual abuse in the first degree

(1) No employee shall be liable to prosecution under ORS 163.684 or under any city or home rule county ordinance for exhibiting or possessing with intent to exhibit any obscene matter or performance provided the employee is acting within the scope of regular employment at a showing open to the public.
(2) As used in this section, "employee" means any person regularly employed by the owner or operator of a motion picture theater if the person has no financial interest other than salary or wages in the ownership or operation of the motion picture theater, no financial interest in or control over the selection of the motion pictures shown in the theater, and is working within the motion picture theater where the person is regularly employed, but does not include a manager of the motion picture theater.

163.682 Exceptions–Child sexual abuse

The provisions of ORS 163.665 to 163.693 do not apply to:
(1) Any legitimate medical procedure performed by or under the direction of a person licensed to provide medical services for the purpose of medical diagnosis or treatment, including the recording of medical procedures;
(2) Any activity undertaken in the course of bona fide law enforcement activity or necessary to the proper functioning of the criminal justice system, except that this exception shall not apply to any activity prohibited by ORS 163.670;
(3) Any bona fide educational activity, including studies and lectures, in the fields of medicine, psychotherapy, sociology or criminology, except that this exception shall not apply to any activity prohibited by ORS 163.670;

(4) Obtaining, viewing or possessing a photograph, motion picture, videotape or other visual recording as part of a bona fide treatment program for sexual offenders; or

(5) A public library, as defined in ORS 357.400, or a library exempt from taxation under ORS 307.090 or 307.130, except that these exceptions do not apply to any activity prohibited by ORS 163.670.

163.684 Encouraging child sexual abuse in the first degree

(1) A person commits the crime of encouraging child sexual abuse in the first degree if the person:

(a)(A) Knowingly develops, duplicates, publishes, prints, disseminates, exchanges, displays, finances, attempts to finance or sells any photograph, motion picture, videotape or other visual recording of sexually explicit conduct involving a child or possesses such matter with the intent to develop, duplicate, publish, print, disseminate, exchange, display or sell it; or

(B) Knowingly brings into this state, or causes to be brought or sent into this state, for sale or distribution, any photograph, motion picture, videotape or other visual recording of sexually explicit conduct involving a child; and

(b) Knows or is aware of and consciously disregards the fact that creation of the visual recording of sexually explicit conduct involved child abuse.

(2) Encouraging child sexual abuse in the first degree is a Class B felony.

163.686 Encouraging child sexual abuse in the second degree

(1) A person commits the crime of encouraging child sexual abuse in the second degree if the person:

(a)(A)(i) Knowingly possesses or controls any photograph, motion picture, videotape or other visual recording of sexually explicit conduct involving a child for the purpose of arousing or satisfying the sexual desires of the person or another person; or

(ii) Knowingly pays, exchanges or gives anything of value to obtain or view a photograph, motion picture, videotape or other visual recording of sexually explicit conduct involving a child for the purpose of arousing or satisfying the sexual desires of the person or another person; and

(B) Knows or is aware of and consciously disregards the fact that creation of the visual recording of sexually explicit conduct involved child abuse; or

(b)(A) Knowingly pays, exchanges or gives anything of value to observe sexually explicit conduct by a child or knowingly observes, for the purpose of arousing or gratifying the sexual desire of the person, sexually explicit conduct by a child; and

(B) Knows or is aware of and consciously disregards the fact that the conduct constitutes child abuse.

(2) Encouraging child sexual abuse in the second degree is a Class C felony.

163.687 Encouraging child sexual abuse in the third degree

(1) A person commits the crime of encouraging child sexual abuse in the third degree if the person:

(a)(A)(i) Knowingly possesses or controls any photograph, motion picture, videotape or other visual recording of sexually explicit conduct involving a child for the purpose of arousing or satisfying the sexual desires of the person or another person; or

(ii) Knowingly pays, exchanges or gives anything of value to obtain or view a photograph, motion picture, videotape or other visual recording of sexually explicit conduct involving a child for the purpose of arousing or satisfying the sexual desires of the person or another person; and

(B) Knows or fails to be aware of a substantial and unjustifiable risk that the creation of the visual recording of sexually explicit conduct involved child abuse; or

(b)(A) Knowingly pays, exchanges or gives anything of value to observe sexually explicit conduct by a child or knowingly observes, for the purpose of arousing or gratifying the sexual desire of the person, sexually explicit conduct by a child; and

(B) Knows or fails to be aware of a substantial and unjustifiable risk that the conduct constitutes child abuse.

(2) Encouraging child sexual abuse in the third degree is a Class A misdemeanor.

163.688 Possession of materials depicting sexually explicit conduct of a child in the first degree

(1) A person commits the crime of possession of materials depicting sexually explicit conduct of a child in the first degree if the person:

Amended 2009

(a) Knowingly possesses any visual depiction of sexually explicit conduct involving a child or any visual depiction of sexually explicit conduct that appears to involve a child; and

(b) Uses the visual depiction to induce a child to participate or engage in sexually explicit conduct.

(2) Possession of materials depicting sexually explicit conduct of a child in the first degree is a Class B felony.

163.689 Possession of materials depicting sexually explicit conduct of a child in the second degree

(1) A person commits the crime of possession of materials depicting sexually explicit conduct of a child in the second degree if the person:

(a) Knowingly possesses any visual depiction of sexually explicit conduct involving a child or any visual depiction of sexually explicit conduct that appears to involve a child; and

(b) Intends to use the visual depiction to induce a child to participate or engage in sexually explicit conduct.

(2) Possession of materials depicting sexually explicit conduct of a child in the second degree is a Class C felony.

163.690 Defenses–Lack of knowledge of age of child

It is an affirmative defense to any prosecution under ORS 163.684, 163.686, 163.687 or 163.693 that the defendant, at the time of engaging in the conduct prohibited therein, did not know and did not have reason to know that the relevant sexually explicit conduct involved a child.

163.700 Invasion of personal privacy
Amended 2009

(1) Except as provided in ORS 163.702, a person commits the crime of invasion of personal privacy if:

(a)(A) The person knowingly makes or records a photograph, motion picture, videotape or other visual recording of another person in a state of nudity without the consent of the person being recorded; and

 (B) At the time the visual recording is made or recorded the person being recorded is in a place and circumstances where the person has a reasonable expectation of personal privacy; or

(b)(A) For the purpose of arousing or gratifying the sexual desire of the person, the person is in a location to observe another

person in a state of nudity without the consent of the other person; and
  (B) The other person is in a place and circumstances where the person has a reasonable expectation of personal privacy.
(2) As used in this section:
  (a) "Makes or records a photograph, motion picture, videotape or other visual recording" includes, but is not limited to, making or recording or employing, authorizing, permitting, compelling or inducing another person to make or record a photograph, motion picture, videotape or other visual recording.
  (b) "Nudity" means *any part of the* uncovered, or less than opaquely covered,:
    (A) Genitals;
    (B) Pubic area; or
    (C) Female breast below a point immediately above the top of the areola.
  (c) "Places and circumstances where the person has a reasonable expectation of personal privacy" includes, but is not limited to, a bathroom, dressing room, locker room that includes an enclosed area for dressing or showering, tanning booth and any area where a person undresses in an enclosed space that is not open to public view.
  (d) "Public view" means that an area can be readily seen and that a person within the area can be distinguished by normal unaided vision when viewed from a public place as defined in ORS 161.015.
(3) Invasion of personal privacy is a Class A misdemeanor.

163.702 Exceptions–Invasion of personal privacy
Amended 2009

(1) The provisions of ORS 163.700 do not apply to:
  (a) Any legitimate medical procedure performed by or under the direction of a person licensed to provide medical service for the purpose of medical diagnosis, treatment, education or research, including, but not limited to, the recording of medical procedures; and
  (b) Any activity undertaken in the course of bona fide law enforcement or corrections activity or necessary to the proper functioning of the criminal justice system, including but not limited to the operation and management of jails, prisons and other youth and adult corrections facilities.
(2) The provisions of ORS 163.700 (1)(a) do not apply to a visual recording of a person under 12 years of age if:
  (a) The person who makes or records the visual recording is the father, mother, sibling, grandparent, aunt, uncle or first cousin, by blood, adoption or marriage, of the person under 12 years of age; and
  (b) The visual recording is made or recorded for a purpose other than arousing or gratifying the sexual desire of the person or another person.

163.709 Unlawful directing of light from a laser pointer

(1) A person commits the offense of unlawful directing of light from a laser pointer if the person knowingly directs light from a laser pointer at another person without the consent of the other person and the other person is:
  (a) A peace officer as defined in ORS 161.015 who is acting in the course of official duty; or
  (b) A uniformed private security professional as defined in ORS 181.870 who is on duty.
(2) The offense described in this section, unlawful directing of light from a laser pointer, is a Class A misdemeanor.
(3) As used in this section, "laser pointer" means a device that emits light amplified by the stimulated emission of radiation that is visible to the human eye.

163.730 Definitions–Stalking   *Amended 2009*

As used in ORS 30.866 and 163.730 to 163.750, unless the context requires otherwise:
(1) "Alarm" means to cause apprehension or fear resulting from the perception of danger.
(2) "Coerce" means to restrain, compel or dominate by force or threat.
(3) "Contact" includes but is not limited to:
  (a) Coming into the visual or physical presence of the other person;
  (b) Following the other person;
  (c) Waiting outside the home, property, place of work or school of the other person or of a member of the other person's family or household;
  (d) Sending or making written or electronic communications in any form to the other person;
  (e) Speaking with the other person by any means;
  (f) Communicating with the other person through a third person;
  (g) Committing a crime against the other person;
  (h) Communicating with a third person who has some relationship to the other person with the intent of affecting the third person's relationship with the other person;
  (i) Communicating with business entities with the intent of affecting some right or interest of the other person;
  (j) Damaging the other person's home, property, place of work or school;
  (k) Delivering directly or through a third person any object to the home, property, place of work or school of the other person; ***or***
  (L) Service of process or other legal documents unless the other person is served as provided in ORCP 7 or 9.
(4) "Household member" means any person residing in the same residence as the victim.

(5) "Immediate family" means father, mother, child, sibling, spouse, grandparent, stepparent and stepchild.
(6) "Law enforcement officer" means any person employed in this state as a police officer by a county sheriff, constable, marshal or municipal or state police agency.
(7) "Repeated" means two or more times.
(8) "School" means a public or private institution of learning or a child care facility.

163.732 Stalking

(1) A person commits the crime of stalking if:
  (a) The person knowingly alarms or coerces another person or a member of that person's immediate family or household by engaging in repeated and unwanted contact with the other person;
  (b) It is objectively reasonable for a person in the victim's situation to have been alarmed or coerced by the contact; and
  (c) The repeated and unwanted contact causes the victim reasonable apprehension regarding the personal safety of the victim or a member of the victim's immediate family or household.
(2)(a) Stalking is a Class A misdemeanor.
  (b) Notwithstanding paragraph (a) of this subsection, stalking is a Class C felony if the person has a prior conviction for:
    (A) Stalking; or
    (B) Violating a court's stalking protective order.
  (c) When stalking is a Class C felony pursuant to paragraph (b) of this subsection, stalking shall be classified as a person felony and as crime category 8 of the sentencing guidelines grid of the Oregon Criminal Justice Commission.

163.735 Stalking citation

(1) Upon a complaint initiated as provided in ORS 163.744, a law enforcement officer shall issue a citation ordering the person to appear in court within three judicial days and show cause why the court should not enter a court's stalking protective order when the officer has probable cause to believe that:
  (a) The person intentionally, knowingly or recklessly engages in repeated and unwanted contact with the other person or a member of that person's immediate family or household thereby alarming or coercing the other person;
  (b) It is objectively reasonable for a person in the victim's situation to have been alarmed or coerced by the contact; and
  (c) The repeated and unwanted contact causes the victim reasonable apprehension regarding the personal safety of the victim or a member of the victim's immediate family or household.
(2) The Department of State Police shall develop and distribute a form for the citation. The form shall be uniform throughout the state and shall

contain substantially the following in addition to any other material added by the department:

• • •

Note: Pursuant to ORS 163.738 (1)(b), the officer shall notify the petitioner in writing of the place and time set for the hearing.

163.750 Violating court's stalking protective order

(1) A person commits the crime of violating a court's stalking protective order when:

(a) The person has been served with a court's stalking protective order as provided in ORS 30.866 or 163.738 or if further service was waived under ORS 163.741 because the person appeared before the court;

(b) The person, subsequent to the service of the order, has engaged intentionally, knowingly or recklessly in conduct prohibited by the order; and

(c) If the conduct is prohibited contact as defined in ORS 163.730 (3)(d), (e), (f), (h) or (i), the subsequent conduct has created reasonable apprehension regarding the personal safety of a person protected by the order.

(2)(a) Violating a court's stalking protective order is a Class A misdemeanor.

(b) Notwithstanding paragraph (a) of this subsection, violating a court's stalking protective order is a Class C felony if the person has a prior conviction for:

(A) Stalking; or

(B) Violating a court's stalking protective order.

(c) When violating a court's stalking protective order is a Class C felony pursuant to paragraph (b) of this subsection, violating a court's stalking protective order shall be classified as a person felony and as crime category 8 of the sentencing guidelines grid of the Oregon Criminal Justice Commission.

163.755 Exemptions–Stalking protective order

(1) Nothing in ORS 30.866 or 163.730 to 163.750 shall be construed to permit the issuance of a court's stalking protective order under ORS 30.866 or 163.738, the issuance of a citation under ORS 163.735, a criminal prosecution under ORS 163.732 or a civil action under ORS 30.866:

(a) For conduct that is authorized or protected by the labor laws of this state or of the United States.

(b) By or on behalf of a person who is in the legal or physical custody of a law enforcement unit or is in custody under ORS chapter 419C.

(c) By or on behalf of a person not described in paragraph (b) of this subsection to or against another person who:

(A) Is a parole and probation officer or an officer, employee or agent of a law enforcement unit, a county juvenile department or the Oregon Youth Authority; and
(B) Is acting within the scope of the other person's official duties.
(2) As used in this section, "law enforcement unit" and "parole and probation officer" have the meanings given those terms in ORS 181.610.

164.005 Definitions–Theft

As used in chapter 743, Oregon Laws 1971, unless the context requires otherwise:
(1) "Appropriate property of another to oneself or a third person" or "appropriate" means to:
(a) Exercise control over property of another, or to aid a third person to exercise control over property of another, permanently or for so extended a period or under such circumstances as to acquire the major portion of the economic value or benefit of such property; or
(b) Dispose of the property of another for the benefit of oneself or a third person.
(2) "Deprive another of property" or "deprive" means to:
(a) Withhold property of another or cause property of another to be withheld from that person permanently or for so extended a period or under such circumstances that the major portion of its economic value or benefit is lost to that person; or
(b) Dispose of the property in such manner or under such circumstances as to render it unlikely that an owner will recover such property.
(3) "Obtain" includes, but is not limited to, the bringing about of a transfer or purported transfer of property or of a legal interest therein, whether to the obtainer or another.
(4) "Owner of property taken, obtained or withheld" or "owner" means any person who has a right to possession thereof superior to that of the taker, obtainer or withholder.
(5) "Property" means any article, substance or thing of value, including, but not limited to, money, tangible and intangible personal property, real property, choses-in-action, evidence of debt or of contract.

164.015 Theft

A person commits theft when, with intent to deprive another of property or to appropriate property to the person or to a third person, the person:
(1) Takes, appropriates, obtains or withholds such property from an owner thereof;
(2) Commits theft of property lost, mislaid or delivered by mistake as provided in ORS 164.065;
(3) Commits theft by extortion as provided in ORS 164.075;
(4) Commits theft by deception as provided in ORS 164.085; or
(5) Commits theft by receiving as provided in ORS 164.095.

164.035 Defenses–Theft
(1) In a prosecution for theft it is a defense that the defendant acted under an honest claim of right, in that:
   (a) The defendant was unaware that the property was that of another; or
   (b) The defendant reasonably believed that the defendant was entitled to the property involved or had a right to acquire or dispose of it as the defendant did.
(2) In a prosecution for theft by extortion committed by instilling in the victim a fear that the victim or another person would be charged with a crime, it is a defense that the defendant reasonably believed the threatened charge to be true and that the sole purpose of the defendant was to compel or induce the victim to take reasonable action to make good the wrong which was the subject of the threatened charge.
(3) In a prosecution for theft by receiving, it is a defense that the defendant received, retained, concealed or disposed of the property with the intent of restoring it to the owner.
(4) It is a defense that the property involved was that of the defendant's spouse, unless the parties were not living together as husband and wife and were living in separate abodes at the time of the alleged theft.

164.043 Theft in the third degree *Amended 2009*
(1) A person commits the crime of theft in the third degree if:
   (a) ***By means other than extortion, the person*** commits theft as defined in ORS 164.015; and
   (b) The total value of the property in a single or an aggregate transaction is ***less than $100***.
(2) Theft in the third degree is a Class C misdemeanor.

164.045 Theft in the second degree *Amended 2009*
(1) A person commits the crime of theft in the second degree if:
   (a) ***By means other than extortion, the person*** commits theft as defined in ORS 164.015; and
   (b) The total value of the property in a single or aggregate transaction is ***$100 or more and less than $1,000***.
(2) Theft in the second degree is a Class A misdemeanor.

164.055 Theft in the first degree *Amended 2009*
(1) A person commits the crime of theft in the first degree if, by ***means*** other than extortion, the person commits theft as defined in ORS 164.015 and:
   (a) The total value of the property in a single or aggregate transaction is ***$1,000 or more***;

164.057

(b) The theft is committed during a riot, fire, explosion, catastrophe or other emergency in an area affected by the riot, fire, explosion, catastrophe or other emergency;
(c) The theft is theft by receiving committed by buying, selling, borrowing or lending on the security of the property;
(d) The subject of the theft is a firearm or explosive;
(e) The subject of the theft is a livestock animal, a companion animal or a wild animal removed from habitat or born of a wild animal removed from habitat, pursuant to ORS 497.308 (2)(c); or
(f) The subject of the theft is a precursor substance.

(2) As used in this section:
(a) "Companion animal" means a dog or cat possessed by a person, business or other entity for purposes of companionship, security, hunting, herding or providing assistance in relation to a physical disability.
(b) "Explosive" means a chemical compound, mixture or device that is commonly used or intended for the purpose of producing a chemical reaction resulting in a substantially instantaneous release of gas and heat, including but not limited to dynamite, blasting powder, nitroglycerin, blasting caps and nitrojelly, but excluding fireworks as defined in ORS 480.110 (1), black powder, smokeless powder, small arms ammunition and small arms ammunition primers.
(c) "Firearm" *has the meaning given that term in ORS 166.210.*
(d) "Livestock animal" means a ratite, psittacine, horse, gelding, mare, *filly*, stallion, colt, mule, ass, jenny, bull, steer, cow, calf, goat, sheep, lamb, llama, pig or hog.
(e) "Precursor substance" has the meaning given that term in ORS 475.940.

(3) Theft in the first degree is a Class C felony.

164.057 Aggravated theft in the first degree

(1) A person commits the crime of aggravated theft in the first degree, if:
(a) The person violates ORS 164.055 with respect to property, other than a motor vehicle used primarily for personal rather than commercial transportation; and
(b) The value of the property in a single or aggregate transaction is $10,000 or more.

(2) Aggravated theft in the first degree is a Class B felony.

164.065 Theft of lost, mislaid or misdelivered property

A person who comes into control of property of another that the person knows or has good reason to know to have been lost, mislaid or delivered under a mistake as to the nature or amount of the property or the identity of the recipient, commits theft if, with intent to deprive the owner thereof, the person fails to take reasonable measures to restore the property to the owner.

164.075 Theft by extortion

(1) A person commits theft by extortion when the person compels or induces another to deliver property to the person or to a third person by instilling in the other a fear that, if the property is not so delivered, the actor or a third person will in the future:

(a) Cause physical injury to some person;

(b) Cause damage to property;

(c) Engage in other conduct constituting a crime;

(d) Accuse some person of a crime or cause criminal charges to be instituted against the person;

(e) Expose a secret or publicize an asserted fact, whether true or false, tending to subject some person to hatred, contempt or ridicule;

(f) Cause or continue a strike, boycott or other collective action injurious to some person's business, except that such conduct is not considered extortion when the property is demanded or received for the benefit of the group in whose interest the actor purports to act;

(g) Testify or provide information or withhold testimony or information with respect to another's legal claim or defense;

(h) Use or abuse the position as a public servant by performing some act within or related to official duties, or by failing or refusing to perform an official duty, in such manner as to affect some person adversely; or

(i) Inflict any other harm that would not benefit the actor.

(2) Theft by extortion is a Class B felony.

164.085 Theft by deception

(1) A person, who obtains property of another thereby, commits theft by deception when, with intent to defraud, the person:

(a) Creates or confirms another's false impression of law, value, intention or other state of mind that the actor does not believe to be true;

(b) Fails to correct a false impression that the person previously created or confirmed;

(c) Prevents another from acquiring information pertinent to the disposition of the property involved;

(d) Sells or otherwise transfers or encumbers property, failing to disclose a lien, adverse claim or other legal impediment to the enjoyment of the property, whether such impediment is or is not valid, or is or is not a matter of official record; or

(e) Promises performance that the person does not intend to perform or knows will not be performed.

(2) "Deception" does not include falsity as to matters having no pecuniary significance, or representations unlikely to deceive ordinary persons in the group addressed. For purposes of this subsection, the theft of a companion animal, as defined in ORS 164.055, or a captive wild animal is a matter having pecuniary significance.

(3) In a prosecution for theft by deception, the defendant's intention or belief that a promise would not be performed may not be established by or inferred from the fact alone that such promise was not performed.

(4) In a prosecution for theft by deception committed by means of a bad check, it is prima facie evidence of knowledge that the check or order would not be honored if:

(a) The drawer has no account with the drawee at the time the check or order is drawn or uttered; or

(b) Payment is refused by the drawee for lack of funds, upon presentation within 30 days after the date of utterance, and the drawer fails to make good within 10 days after receiving notice of refusal.

164.095 Theft by receiving *Amended 2009*

(1) A person commits theft by receiving if the person receives, retains, conceals or disposes of property of another knowing or having good reason to know that the property was the subject of theft.

(2) It is a defense to a charge of violating subsection (1) of this section if:

(a) The person is a scrap metal business as defined in ORS 165.116 or an agent or employee of a scrap metal business;

(b) The person receives or retains metal property as defined in ORS 165.116; and

(c) The person makes a report in accordance with ORS 165.118 (3)(a).

(3) "Receiving" means acquiring possession, control or title, or lending on the security of the property.

164.098 Organized retail theft

(1) A person commits the crime of organized retail theft if, acting in concert with another person:

(a) The person violates ORS 164.015 or aids or abets the other person to violate ORS 164.015;

(b) The subject of the theft is merchandise and the merchandise is taken from a mercantile establishment; and

(c) The aggregate value of the merchandise taken within any 90-day period exceeds $5,000.

(2) As used in this section:

(a) "Merchandise" has the meaning given that term in ORS 30.870.

(b) "Mercantile establishment" has the meaning given that term in ORS 30.870.

(3) Organized retail theft is a Class B felony.

164.105 Definitions–Right of possession
Right of possession of property is as follows:
(1) A person who has obtained possession of property by theft or other illegal means shall be deemed to have a right of possession superior to that of another person who takes, obtains or withholds the property from that person by means of theft.
(2) A joint or common owner of property shall not be deemed to have a right of possession of the property superior to that of any other joint or common owner of the property.
(3) In the absence of a specific agreement to the contrary, a person in lawful possession of property shall be deemed to have a right of possession superior to that of a person having only a security interest in the property, even if legal title to the property lies with the holder of the security interest pursuant to a conditional sale contract or other security agreement.

164.115 Value of property
For the purposes of chapter 743, Oregon Laws 1971, the value of property shall be ascertained as follows:
(1) Except as otherwise specified in this section, value means the market value of the property at the time and place of the crime, or if such cannot reasonably be ascertained, the cost of replacement of the property within a reasonable time after the crime.
(2) Whether or not they have been issued or delivered, certain written instruments, not including those having a readily ascertainable market value, shall be evaluated as follows:
  (a) The value of an instrument constituting an evidence of debt, including, but not limited to, a check, draft or promissory note, shall be considered the amount due or collectible thereon or thereby.
  (b) The value of any other instrument which creates, releases, discharges or otherwise affects any valuable legal right, privilege or obligation shall be considered the greatest amount of economic loss which the owner might reasonably suffer because of the loss of the instrument.
(3) The value of a gambling chip, token, imitation currency or similar device is its face value.
(4) When the value of property cannot reasonably be ascertained, it shall be presumed to be an amount less than $50 in a case of theft, and less than $500 in any other case.
(5) The value of single theft transactions may be added together if the thefts were committed:
  (a) Against multiple victims by similar means within a 30-day period; or
  (b) Against the same victim, or two or more persons who are joint owners, within a 180-day period.

164.125 Theft of services   *Amended 2009*
(1) A person commits the crime of theft of services if:

(a) With intent to avoid payment therefor, the person obtains services that are available only for compensation, by force, threat, deception or other means to avoid payment for the services; or

(b) Having control over the disposition of labor or of business, commercial or industrial equipment or facilities of another, the person uses or diverts to the use of the person or a third person such labor, equipment or facilities with intent to derive for the person or the third person a commercial benefit to which the person or the third person is not entitled.

(2) As used in this section, "services" includes, but is not limited to, labor, professional services, toll facilities, transportation, communications service, entertainment, the supplying of food, lodging or other accommodations in hotels, restaurants or elsewhere, the supplying of equipment for use, and the supplying of commodities of a public utility nature such as gas, electricity, steam and water. "Communication service" includes, but is not limited to, use of telephone, computer and cable television systems.

(3) Absconding without payment or offer to pay for hotel, restaurant or other services for which compensation is customarily paid immediately upon the receiving of them is prima facie evidence that the services were obtained with intent to avoid payment therefor. Obtaining the use of any communication system the use of which is available only for compensation, including but not limited to telephone, computer and cable television systems, or obtaining the use of any services of a public utility nature, without payment or offer to pay for such use is prima facie evidence that the obtaining of the use of such system or the use of such services was gained with intent to avoid payment therefor.

(4) The value of single theft transactions may be added together if the thefts were committed:

(a) Against multiple victims by a similar means within a 30-day period; or

(b) Against the same victim, or two or more persons who are joint owners, within a 180-day period.

(5) Theft of services is:

(a) A Class C misdemeanor if the aggregate total value of services that are the subject of the theft is *less than $100*;

(b) A Class A misdemeanor if the aggregate total value of services that are the subject of the theft is *$100 or more and less than $1,000*;

(c) A Class C felony if the aggregate total value of services that are the subject of the theft is *$1,000* or more; and

(d) A Class B felony if the aggregate total value of services that are the subject of the theft is $10,000 or more.

164.135 Unauthorized use of vehicle

(1) A person commits the crime of unauthorized use of a vehicle when:

(a) The person takes, operates, exercises control over, rides in or otherwise uses another's vehicle, boat or aircraft without consent of the owner;

(b) Having custody of a vehicle, boat or aircraft pursuant to an agreement between the person or another and the owner thereof whereby the person or another is to perform for compensation a specific service for the owner involving the maintenance, repair or use of such vehicle, boat or aircraft, the person intentionally uses or operates it, without consent of the owner, for the person's own purpose in a manner constituting a gross deviation from the agreed purpose; or

(c) Having custody of a vehicle, boat or aircraft pursuant to an agreement with the owner thereof whereby such vehicle, boat or aircraft is to be returned to the owner at a specified time, the person knowingly retains or withholds possession thereof without consent of the owner for so lengthy a period beyond the specified time as to render such retention or possession a gross deviation from the agreement.

(2) Unauthorized use of a vehicle, boat or aircraft is a Class C felony.

(3) Subsection (1)(a) of this section does not apply to a person who rides in or otherwise uses a public transit vehicle, as defined in ORS 166.116, if the vehicle is being operated by an authorized operator within the scope of the operator's employment.

164.138 Criminal possession of a rented or leased motor vehicle

(1) A person commits the offense of criminal possession of a rented or leased motor vehicle if:

(a) After renting a motor vehicle from a commercial renter of motor vehicles under a written agreement that provides for the return of the motor vehicle to a particular place at a particular time, the person fails to return the motor vehicle as specified, is thereafter served in accordance with subsection (2) of this section with a written demand to return the motor vehicle and knowingly fails to return the motor vehicle within three calendar days from the date of the receipt or refusal of the demand; or

(b) After leasing a motor vehicle from a commercial lessor of motor vehicles under a written agreement that provides for periodic lease payments, the person fails to pay the lessor a periodic payment when due for a period of 45 days, is thereafter served with a written demand to return the motor vehicle in accordance with subsection (2) of this section and knowingly fails to return the motor vehicle within three calendar days from the date of the receipt or refusal of the demand.

(2)(a) Service of written demand under this section shall be accomplished by delivery through any commercial overnight service that can supply a delivery receipt. The demand shall be sent to the person who obtained the motor vehicle by rental or lease at the address stated in the rental or lease agreement and any other address of the person provided by the person to the renter or lessor. The person is responsible for providing correct current address information to the renter or lessor until the motor vehicle is returned.

(b) The person shall be considered to have refused the written demand if the commercial delivery service determines that the demand is not deliverable to the person at the address or addresses provided by the person.

(3) A bona fide contract dispute with the lessor or renter shall be an affirmative defense to a charge of criminal possession of a rented or leased motor vehicle.

(4) Criminal possession of a rented or leased motor vehicle is a Class C felony.

164.140 Criminal possession of rented or leased personal property

(1) A person is guilty of criminal possession of rented or leased personal property if:

(a) After renting an item of personal property from a commercial renter of personal property under a written agreement which provides for the return of the item to a particular place at a particular time, the person fails to return the item as specified, is thereafter served by mail with a written demand to return the item, and knowingly fails to return the item within 10 business days from the date of mailing of the demand; or

(b) After leasing an item of personal property from a commercial lessor of personal property under a written agreement which provides for periodic lease payments, the person fails to pay the lessor a periodic payment when due for a period of 45 days, is thereafter served by mail with a written demand to return the item, and knowingly fails to return the item within 10 business days from the date of mailing of the demand.

(2) Service of written demand under this section shall be accomplished by certified mail sent to the person who obtained the item of personal property by rental or lease, sent to the address stated in the rental or lease agreement and any other address of the person provided by the person to the renter or lessor. The person is responsible for providing correct current address information to the renter or lessor until the item of personal property is returned.

Amended 2009

(3) A bona fide contract dispute with the lessor or renter shall be an affirmative defense to a charge of criminal possession of rented or leased personal property.

(4) For purposes of this section, the value of property shall be ascertained as provided in ORS 164.115. Criminal possession of rented or leased personal property is:

(a) A Class A misdemeanor if the aggregate total value of the personal property not returned is under $500.

(b) A Class C felony if the aggregate total value of the personal property not returned is $500 or more.

164.160 Definitions–Mail-related offenses

As used in this section and ORS 164.162:

(1) "Authorized depository" means a mailbox, post office box or rural box used by postal customers to deposit outgoing mail or used by the Postal Service to deliver incoming mail.

(2) "Mail" means any letter, card, parcel or other material that:

(a) Is sent or delivered by means of the Postal Service;

(b) Has postage affixed by the postal customer or Postal Service or has been accepted for delivery by the Postal Service; or

(c) Is placed in any authorized depository or mail receptacle or given to any Postal Service employee for delivery.

(3) "Mail receptacle" means any location used by the Postal Service or postal customers to place outgoing mail or receive incoming mail.

(4) "Postage" means a Postal Service stamp, permit imprint, meter strip or other authorized indication of prepayment for service provided or authorized by the Postal Service for collection and delivery of mail.

(5) "Postal Service" means the United States Postal Service.

164.162 Mail theft or receipt of stolen mail
Amended 2009

(1) A person commits the crime of mail theft or receipt of stolen mail if the person intentionally:

(a) Takes or, by fraud or deception, obtains mail from a post office, postal station, mail receptacle, authorized depository or mail carrier;

(b) Takes from mail any article contained therein;

(c) Secretes, embezzles or destroys mail or any article contained therein;

(d) Takes or, by fraud or deception, obtains mail that has been delivered to or left for collection on or adjacent to a mail receptacle or authorized depository; or

(e) Buys, receives, conceals or possesses mail or any article contained therein knowing that the mail or article has been unlawfully taken or obtained.

[Note: The following subsection (2) is effective **UNTIL** 1/1/2012.]
(2) Mail theft or receipt of stolen mail is a *Class A misdemeanor.*
[Note: The following subsection (2) is **NOT** effective **UNTIL** 1/1/2012.]
(2) Mail theft or receipt of stolen mail is a *Class C felony.*

164.164 Defenses–Mail theft

(1) In a prosecution under ORS 164.162, it is a defense that the defendant acted under an honest claim of right in that:
  (a) The defendant was unaware that the property was that of another person;
  (b) The defendant reasonably believed that the defendant was entitled to the property involved or had a right to acquire or dispose of it as the defendant did; or
  (c) The property involved was that of the defendant's spouse, unless the parties were not living together as husband and wife and were living in separate abodes at the time of the alleged offense.
(2)(a) ORS 164.162 does not apply to employees charged with the operation of facilities listed in paragraph (b) of this subsection when the employees are carrying out their official duties to protect the safety and security of the facilities.
  (b) The facilities to which paragraph (a) of this subsection applies are juvenile detention facilities and local correctional facilities as defined in ORS 169.005, detention facilities as defined in ORS 419A.004, youth correction facilities as defined in ORS 420.005 and Department of Corrections institutions as defined in ORS 421.005.

164.205 Definitions–Burglary & trespass

As used in ORS 164.205 to 164.270, except as the context requires otherwise:
(1) "Building," in addition to its ordinary meaning, includes any booth, vehicle, boat, aircraft or other structure adapted for overnight accommodation of persons or for carrying on business therein. Where a building consists of separate units, including, but not limited to, separate apartments, offices or rented rooms, each unit is, in addition to being a part of such building, a separate building.
(2) "Dwelling" means a building which regularly or intermittently is occupied by a person lodging therein at night, whether or not a person is actually present.
(3) "Enter or remain unlawfully" means:
  (a) To enter or remain in or upon premises when the premises, at the time of such entry or remaining, are not open to the public or when the entrant is not otherwise licensed or privileged to do so;
  (b) To fail to leave premises that are open to the public after being lawfully directed to do so by the person in charge;
  (c) To enter premises that are open to the public after being lawfully directed not to enter the premises; or

(d) To enter or remain in a motor vehicle when the entrant is not authorized to do so.
(4) "Open to the public" means premises which by their physical nature, function, custom, usage, notice or lack thereof or other circumstances at the time would cause a reasonable person to believe that no permission to enter or remain is required.
(5) "Person in charge" means a person, a representative or employee of the person who has lawful control of premises by ownership, tenancy, official position or other legal relationship. "Person in charge" includes, but is not limited to the person, or holder of a position, designated as the person or position-holder in charge by the Governor, board, commission or governing body of any political subdivision of this state.
(6) "Premises" includes any building and any real property, whether privately or publicly owned.

164.215 Burglary in the second degree
(1) Except as otherwise provided in ORS 164.255, a person commits the crime of burglary in the second degree if the person enters or remains unlawfully in a building with intent to commit a crime therein.
(2) Burglary in the second degree is a Class C felony.

164.225 Burglary in the first degree
(1) A person commits the crime of burglary in the first degree if the person violates ORS 164.215 and the building is a dwelling, or if in effecting entry or while in a building or in immediate flight therefrom the person:
  (a) Is armed with a burglary tool or theft device as defined in ORS 164.235 or a deadly weapon;
  (b) Causes or attempts to cause physical injury to any person; or
  (c) Uses or threatens to use a dangerous weapon.
(2) Burglary in the first degree is a Class A felony.

164.235 Possession of burglary tool or theft device
(1) A person commits the crime of possession of a burglary tool or theft device if the person possesses a burglary tool or theft device and the person:
  (a) Intends to use the tool or device to commit or facilitate a forcible entry into premises or a theft by a physical taking; or
  (b) Knows that another person intends to use the tool or device to commit or facilitate a forcible entry into premises or a theft by a physical taking.

(2) For purposes of this section, "burglary tool or theft device" means an acetylene torch, electric arc, burning bar, thermal lance, oxygen lance or other similar device capable of burning through steel, concrete or other solid material, or nitroglycerine, dynamite, gunpowder or any other explosive, tool, instrument or other article adapted or designed for committing or facilitating a forcible entry into premises or theft by a physical taking.

(3) Possession of a burglary tool or theft device is a Class A misdemeanor.

164.243 Criminal trespass in the second degree by guest

A guest commits the crime of criminal trespass in the second degree if that guest intentionally remains unlawfully in a transient lodging after the departure date of the guest's reservation without the approval of the hotel-keeper. "Guest" means a person who is registered at a hotel and is assigned to transient lodging, and includes any individual accompanying the person.

164.245 Criminal trespass in the second degree

(1) A person commits the crime of criminal trespass in the second degree if the person enters or remains unlawfully in a motor vehicle or in upon premises.

(2) Criminal trespass in the second degree is a Class C misdemeanor.

164.255 Criminal trespass in the first degree

(1) A person commits the crime of criminal trespass in the first degree if the person:
  (a) Enters or remains unlawfully in a dwelling;
  (b) Having been denied future entry to a building pursuant to a merchant's notice of trespass, reenters the building during hours when the building is open to the public with the intent to commit theft therein;
  (c) Enters or remains unlawfully upon railroad yards, tracks, bridges or rights of way; or
  (d) Enters or remains unlawfully in or upon premises that have been determined to be not fit for use under ORS 453.855 to 453.912 [Illegal Drug Manufacturing cleanup].

(2) Subsection (1)(d) of this section does not apply to the owner of record of the premises if:
  (a) The owner notifies the law enforcement agency having jurisdiction over the premises that the owner intends to enter the premises;
  (b) The owner enters or remains on the premises for the purpose of inspecting or decontaminating the premises or lawfully removing items from the premises; and

(c) The owner has not been arrested for, charged with or convicted of a criminal offense that contributed to the determination that the premises are not fit for use.

(3) Criminal trespass in the first degree is a Class A misdemeanor.

164.265 Criminal trespass while in possession of firearm

(1) A person commits the crime of criminal trespass while in possession of a firearm who, while in possession of a firearm, enters or remains unlawfully in or upon premises.

(2) Criminal trespass while in possession of a firearm is a Class A misdemeanor.

164.270 Closure of premises to motor vehicles

(1) For purposes of ORS 164.245, a landowner or an agent of the landowner may close the privately owned premises of the landowner to motor-propelled vehicles by posting signs on or near the boundaries of the closed premises at the normal points of entry as follows:
  (a) Signs must be no smaller than eight inches in height and 11 inches in width;
  (b) Signs must contain the words "Closed to Motor-propelled Vehicles" or words to that effect in letters no less than one inch in height;
  (c) Signs must display the name, business address and phone number, if any, of the landowner or agent of the landowner; and
  (d) Signs must be posted at normal points of entry and be no further apart than 350 yards.

(2) A person violates ORS 164.245 if the person operates or rides upon or within a motor-propelled vehicle upon privately owned premises when the premises are posted as provided in this section and the person does not have written authorization to operate a motor-propelled vehicle upon the premises.

(3) Nothing contained in this section prevents emergency or law enforcement vehicles from entering upon land closed to motor-propelled vehicles.

164.272 Unlawful entry into motor vehicle

(1) A person commits the crime of unlawful entry into a motor vehicle if the person enters a motor vehicle, or any part of a motor vehicle, with the intent to commit a crime.

(2) Unlawful entry into a motor vehicle is a Class A misdemeanor.

(3) As used in this section, "enters" includes, but is not limited to, inserting:
  (a) Any part of the body; or
  (b) Any object connected with the body.

164.274 Definitions–Sports event trespass

As used in ORS 164.276 and 164.278:

(1) "Coach" means a person who instructs or trains members of a team or directs the strategy of a team participating in a sports event.

(2) "Inappropriate behavior" means:

(a) Engaging in fighting or in violent, tumultuous or threatening behavior;
(b) Violating the rules of conduct governing coaches, team players and spectators at a sports event;
(c) Publicly insulting another person by abusive words or gestures in a manner intended to provoke a violent response; or
(d) Intentionally subjecting another person to offensive physical contact.

(3) "Premises" has the meaning given that term in ORS 164.205.
(4) "Spectator" means any person, other than a team player or coach, who attends a sports event.
(5) "Sports official" has the meaning given that term in ORS 30.882.

164.276 Authority of sports official to eject persons

A sports official may order a coach, team player or spectator to leave the premises at which a sports event is taking place and at which the sports official is officiating if the coach, team player or spectator is engaging in inappropriate behavior.

164.278 Criminal trespass at sports event

(1) A person commits the crime of criminal trespass at a sports event if the person:
  (a) Is a coach, team player or spectator at a sports event;
  (b) Engages in inappropriate behavior;
  (c) Has been ordered by a sports official to leave the premises at which the sports event is taking place; and
  (d) Fails to leave the premises or returns to the premises during the period of time when reentry has been prohibited.

(2) Criminal trespass at a sports event is a Class C misdemeanor.

164.305 Definitions–Arson, criminal mischief & related offenses

As used in ORS 164.305 to 164.377, except as the context requires otherwise:
(1) "Protected property" means any structure, place or thing customarily occupied by people, including "public buildings" as defined by ORS 479.168 and "forestland," as defined by ORS 477.001.
(2) "Property of another" means property in which anyone other than the actor has a legal or equitable interest that the actor has no right to defeat or impair, even though the actor may also have such an interest in the property.

164.315 Arson in the second degree

(1) A person commits the crime of arson in the second degree if:
  (a) By starting a fire or causing an explosion, the person intentionally damages:
    (A) Any building of another that is not protected property; or

Amended 2009

  (B) Any property of another and the damages to the property exceed $750; or
 (b) By knowingly engaging in the manufacture of methamphetamine, the person causes fire or causes an explosion that damages property described in paragraph (a) of this subsection.
(2) Arson in the second degree is a Class C felony.

164.325 Arson in the first degree

(1) A person commits the crime of arson in the first degree if:
 (a) By starting a fire or causing an explosion, the person intentionally damages:
  (A) Protected property of another;
  (B) Any property, whether the property of the person or the property of another person, and such act recklessly places another person in danger of physical injury or protected property of another in danger of damage; or
  (C) Any property, whether the property of the person or the property of another person, and recklessly causes serious physical injury to a firefighter or peace officer acting in the line of duty relating to the fire; or
 (b) By knowingly engaging in the manufacture of methamphetamine, the person causes fire or causes an explosion that damages property described in paragraph (a) of this subsection.
(2) Arson in the first degree is a Class A felony.

164.335 Reckless burning

(1) A person commits the crime of reckless burning if the person recklessly damages property of another by fire or explosion.
(2) Reckless burning is a Class A misdemeanor.

164.345 Criminal mischief in the third degree

(1) A person commits the crime of criminal mischief in the third degree if, with intent to cause substantial inconvenience to the owner or to another person, and having no right to do so nor reasonable ground to believe that the person has such right, the person tampers or interferes with property of another.
(2) Criminal mischief in the third degree is a Class C misdemeanor.

164.354 Criminal mischief in the second degree
Amended 2009

(1) A person commits the crime of criminal mischief in the second degree if:

(a) The person violates ORS 164.345, and as a result thereof, damages property in an amount exceeding *$500*; or

(b) Having no right to do so nor reasonable ground to believe that the person has such right, the person intentionally damages property of another, or, the person recklessly damages property of another in an amount exceeding *$500*.

(2) Criminal mischief in the second degree is a Class A misdemeanor.

164.365 Criminal mischief in the first degree
Amended 2009

(1) A person commits the crime of criminal mischief in the first degree who, with intent to damage property, and having no right to do so nor reasonable ground to believe that the person has such right:

(a) Damages or destroys property of another:

   (A) In an amount exceeding *$1,000*;

   (B) By means of an explosive;

   (C) By starting a fire in an institution while the person is committed to and confined in the institution;

   (D) Which is a livestock animal as defined in ORS 164.055;

   (E) Which is the property of a public utility, telecommunications carrier, railroad, public transportation facility or medical facility used in direct service to the public; or

   (F) By intentionally interfering with, obstructing or adulterating in any manner the service of a public utility, telecommunications carrier, railroad, public transportation facility or medical facility; or

(b) Intentionally uses, manipulates, arranges or rearranges the property of a public utility, telecommunications carrier, railroad, public transportation facility or medical facility used in direct service to the public so as to interfere with its efficiency.

(2) As used in subsection (1) of this section:

   (a) "Institution" includes state and local correctional facilities, mental health facilities, juvenile detention facilities and state training schools.

   (b) "Medical facility" means a health care facility as defined in ORS 442.015, a licensed physician's office or anywhere a licensed medical practitioner provides health care services.

   (c) "Public utility" has the meaning provided for that term in ORS 757.005 and includes any cooperative, people's utility district or other municipal corporation providing an electric, gas, water or other utility service.

   (d) "Railroad" has the meaning provided for that term in ORS 824.020.

(e) "Public transportation facility" means any property, structure or equipment used for or in connection with the transportation of persons for hire by rail, air or bus, including any railroad cars, buses or airplanes used to carry out such transportation.

(f) "Telecommunications carrier" has the meaning given that term in ORS 133.721.

(3) Criminal mischief in the first degree is a Class C felony.

164.367 Value of damage–Aggregation

For purposes of ORS 164.345, 164.354 and 164.365, the value of damage done during single incidents of criminal mischief may be added together if the incidents of criminal mischief were committed:

(1) Against multiple victims in the same course of conduct; or

(2) Against the same victim, or two or more persons who are joint owners, within a 30-day period.

164.373 Tampering with cable television equipment

(1) A person commits the crime of tampering with cable television equipment if the person:

(a) Knowingly tampers or otherwise interferes with or connects to by any means, whether mechanical, electrical, acoustical or other means, any cable, wire or other device used for the distribution of cable television service, without authority of the provider of such service; or

(b) Knowingly permits another person to tamper or otherwise interfere with, or connect to by any means, whether mechanical, electrical, acoustical or other means, any cable, wire or other device used for the distribution of cable television service, such tampering, interfering or connecting being upon premises under the control of such first person or intended for the benefit of such first person, without authority of the provider of such service.

(2) Tampering with cable television equipment is a Class B misdemeanor.

164.377 Computer crime

(1) As used in this section:

(a) To "access" means to instruct, communicate with, store data in, retrieve data from or otherwise make use of any resources of a computer, computer system or computer network.

(b) "Computer" means, but is not limited to, an electronic, magnetic, optical electrochemical or other high-speed data processing device that performs logical, arithmetic or memory functions by the manipulations of electronic, magnetic or optical signals or impulses, and includes the components of a computer and all input, output, processing, storage, software or communication facilities that are connected or related to such a device in a system or network.

(c) "Computer network" means, but is not limited to, the interconnection of communication lines, including microwave or other means of electronic communication, with a computer through remote terminals or a complex consisting of two or more interconnected computers.

(d) "Computer program" means, but is not limited to, a series of instructions or statements, in a form acceptable to a computer, which permits the functioning of a computer system in a manner designed to provide appropriate products from or usage of such computer system.

(e) "Computer software" means, but is not limited to, computer programs, procedures and associated documentation concerned with the operation of a computer system.

(f) "Computer system" means, but is not limited to, a set of related, connected or unconnected, computer equipment, devices and software. "Computer system" also includes any computer, device or software owned or operated by the Oregon State Lottery or rented, owned or operated by another person or entity under contract to or at the direction of the Oregon State Lottery.

(g) "Data" means a representation of information, knowledge, facts, concepts, computer software, computer programs or instructions. "Data" may be in any form, in storage media, or as stored in the memory of the computer, or in transit, or presented on a display device. "Data" includes, but is not limited to, computer or human readable forms of numbers, text, stored voice, graphics and images.

(h) "Property" includes, but is not limited to, financial instruments, information, including electronically produced data, and computer software and programs in either computer or human readable form, intellectual property and any other tangible or intangible item of value.

(i) "Proprietary information" includes any scientific, technical or commercial information including any design, process, procedure, list of customers, list of suppliers, customers' records or business code or improvement thereof that is known only to limited individuals within an organization and is used in a business that the organization conducts. The information must have actual or potential commercial value and give the user of the information an opportunity to obtain a business advantage over competitors who do not know or use the information.

(j) "Services" include, but are not limited to, computer time, data processing and storage functions.

(2) Any person commits computer crime who knowingly accesses, attempts to access or uses, or attempts to use, any computer, computer system, computer network or any part thereof for the purpose of:

(a) Devising or executing any scheme or artifice to defraud;

(b) Obtaining money, property or services by means of false or fraudulent pretenses, representations or promises; or

(c) Committing theft, including, but not limited to, theft of proprietary information.

(3) Any person who knowingly and without authorization alters, damages or destroys any computer, computer system, computer network, or any computer software, program, documentation or data contained in such computer, computer system or computer network, commits computer crime.

(4) Any person who knowingly and without authorization uses, accesses or attempts to access any computer, computer system, computer network, or any computer software, program, documentation or data contained in such computer, computer system or computer network, commits computer crime.

(5)(a) A violation of the provisions of subsection (2) or (3) of this section shall be a Class C felony. Except as provided in paragraph (b) of this subsection, a violation of the provisions of subsection (4) of this section shall be a Class A misdemeanor.

(b) Any violation of this section relating to a computer, computer network, computer program, computer software, computer system or data owned or operated by the Oregon State Lottery or rented, owned or operated by another person or entity under contract to or at the direction of the Oregon State Lottery Commission shall be a Class C felony.

164.381 Definitions–Graffiti

As used in ORS 137.131, 164.381 to 164.386 and 419C.461:

(1) "Graffiti" means any inscriptions, words, figures or designs that are marked, etched, scratched, drawn, painted, pasted or otherwise affixed to the surface of property.

(2) "Graffiti implement" means paint, ink, chalk, dye or other substance or any instrument or article designed or adapted for spraying, marking, etching, scratching or carving surfaces.

164.383 Unlawfully applying graffiti

(1) A person commits the offense of unlawfully applying graffiti if the person, having no right to do so nor reasonable ground to believe that the person has such right, intentionally damages property of another by applying graffiti to the property.

(2) Unlawfully applying graffiti is a Class A violation. Upon a conviction for unlawfully applying graffiti, a court, in addition to any fine it imposes and pursuant to ORS 137.128 but notwithstanding ORS 137.129, may order the defendant to perform up to 100 hours of community service. The community service must include removing graffiti, either those that the defendant created or those created by another, or both.

(3) If the court orders community service, the community service must be completed within six months after entry of the order unless the person

shows good cause why community service cannot be completed within the six-month time period.

164.386 Unlawfully possessing graffiti implement

(1) A person commits the offense of unlawfully possessing a graffiti implement if the person possesses a graffiti implement with the intent of using the graffiti implement in violation of ORS 164.383.

(2) Unlawfully possessing a graffiti implement is a Class C violation. Upon a conviction for unlawfully possessing a graffiti implement, a court, in addition to any fine it imposes and pursuant to ORS 137.128 but notwithstanding ORS 137.129, may order the defendant to perform up to 50 hours of community service. The community service must include removing graffiti, either those that the defendant created or those created by another, or both.

(3) If the court orders community service, the community service must be completed within six months after entry of the order unless the person shows good cause why community service cannot be completed within the six-month time period.

164.388 Preemption–Graffiti

The provisions of ORS 137.131, 164.381 to 164.386 and 419C.461 are not intended to preempt any local regulation of graffiti or graffiti-related activities or any prosecution under ORS 164.345, 164.354 or 164.365.

164.395 Robbery in the third degree

(1) A person commits the crime of robbery in the third degree if in the course of committing or attempting to commit theft or unauthorized use of a vehicle as defined in ORS 164.135 the person uses or threatens the immediate use of physical force upon another person with the intent of:
  (a) Preventing or overcoming resistance to the taking of the property or to retention thereof immediately after the taking; or
  (b) Compelling the owner of such property or another person to deliver the property or to engage in other conduct which might aid in the commission of the theft or unauthorized use of a vehicle.

(2) Robbery in the third degree is a Class C felony.

164.405 Robbery in the second degree

(1) A person commits the crime of robbery in the second degree if the person violates ORS 164.395 and the person:
  (a) Represents by word or conduct that the person is armed with what purports to be a dangerous or deadly weapon; or
  (b) Is aided by another person actually present.

(2) Robbery in the second degree is a Class B felony.

164.415 Robbery in the first degree

(1) A person commits the crime of robbery in the first degree if the person violates ORS 164.395 and the person:
 (a) Is armed with a deadly weapon;
 (b) Uses or attempts to use a dangerous weapon; or
 (c) Causes or attempts to cause serious physical injury to any person.
(2) Robbery in the first degree is a Class A felony.

164.775 Littering in or near waters

(1) It is unlawful for any person to discard any glass, cans or other trash, rubbish, debris or litter on land within 100 yards of any of the waters of the state, as defined in ORS 468B.005, other than in receptacles provided for the purpose of holding such trash, rubbish, debris or litter.
(2) It is unlawful for any person to discard any glass, cans or other similar refuse in any waters of the state, as defined in ORS 468.700.
(3) In addition to and in lieu of the penalties provided for violation of any provision of this section, the court in which any individual is convicted of a violation of this section may order suspension of certain permits or licenses for a period not to exceed 90 days if the court finds that the violation occurred during or in connection with the exercise of the privilege granted by the permit or license. The permits and licenses to which this section applies are motor vehicle operator's permits or licenses, hunting licenses, fishing licenses or boat registrations.
(4)(a) Any person sentenced under subsection (6) of this section to pay a fine for violation of this section shall be permitted, in default of the payment of the fine, to work at clearing rubbish, trash and debris from the lands and waters described by subsections (1) and (2) of this section. Credit in compensation for such work shall be allowed at the rate of $25 for each day of work.
 (b) In any case, upon conviction, if punishment by imprisonment is imposed upon the defendant, the form of the sentence shall include that the defendant shall be punished by confinement at labor clearing rubbish, trash and debris from the lands and waters described by subsections (1) and (2) of this section, for not less than one day nor more than five days.
(5) A citation conforming to the requirements of ORS 133.066 shall be used for all violations of subsection (1) or (2) of this section in the state.
(6) Violation of this section is a Class B misdemeanor.
(7) In addition to and not in lieu of the criminal penalty authorized by subsection (6) of this section, the civil penalty authorized by ORS 468.140 may be imposed for violation of this section.
(8) Nothing in this section or ORS 164.785 prohibits the operation of a disposal site, as defined in ORS 459.005, for which a permit is required by the

Department of Environmental Quality, for which such a permit has been issued and which is being operated and maintained in accordance with the terms and conditions of such permit.

164.785 Placing offensive substances in waters, on highways or other property

(1) It is unlawful for any person, including a person in the possession or control of any land, to discard any dead animal carcass or part thereof, excrement, putrid, nauseous, noisome, decaying, deleterious or offensive substance into or in any other manner befoul, pollute or impair the quality of any spring, river, brook, creek, branch, well, irrigation drainage ditch, irrigation ditch, cistern or pond of water.

(2) It is unlawful for any person to place or cause to be placed any polluting substance listed in subsection (1) of this section into any road, street, alley, lane, railroad right of way, lot, field, meadow or common. It is unlawful for an owner thereof to knowingly permit any polluting substances to remain in any of the places described in this subsection to the injury of the health or to the annoyance of any citizen of this state. Every 24 hours after conviction for violation of this subsection during which the violator permits the polluting substances to remain is an additional offense against this subsection.

(3) Nothing in this section shall apply to the storage or spreading of manure or like substance for agricultural, silvicultural or horticultural purposes, except that no sewage sludge, septic tank or cesspool pumpings shall be used for these purposes unless treated and applied in a manner approved by the Department of Environmental Quality.

(4) Violation of this section is a Class A misdemeanor.

(5) The Department of Environmental Quality may impose the civil penalty authorized by ORS 468.140 for violation of this section.

164.805 Offensive littering

(1) A person commits the crime of offensive littering if the person creates an objectionable stench or degrades the beauty or appearance of property or detracts from the natural cleanliness or safety of property by intentionally:

(a) Discarding or depositing any rubbish, trash, garbage, debris or other refuse upon the land of another without permission of the owner, or upon any public way or in or upon any public transportation facility;

(b) Draining, or causing or permitting to be drained, sewage or the drainage from a cesspool, septic tank, recreational or camping vehicle waste holding tank or other contaminated source, upon the land of another without permission of the owner, or upon any public way; or

(c) Permitting any rubbish, trash, garbage, debris or other refuse to be thrown from a vehicle that the person is operating. This subsection does not apply to a person operating a vehicle transporting passengers for hire subject to regulation by the Interstate Commerce Commission or the Department of Transportation or a person operating a school bus described under ORS 801.460.

(2) As used in this section:

(a) "Public transportation facility" has the meaning given that term in ORS 164.365.

(b) "Public way" includes, but is not limited to, roads, streets, alleys, lanes, trails, beaches, parks and all recreational facilities operated by the state, a county or a local municipality for use by the general public.

(3) Offensive littering is a Class C misdemeanor.

164.857 Unlawfully transporting metal property
Added 2009

(1) A person commits the offense of unlawfully transporting metal property if the person transports metal property on a public highway or on premises open to the public with the intent to deliver the metal property to a scrap metal business and the person does not have a metal transportation certificate in the person's possession.

(2) A seller or transferor of metal property that has reason to believe that a buyer or transferee intends to obtain the metal property for delivery to a scrap metal business shall provide the buyer or transferee with a metal transportation certificate.

(3) A metal transportation certificate must include:

(a) The date the metal property was acquired and the amount and type of metal property that the person is transporting;

(b) The location where the metal property was loaded and the destination of the metal property;

(c) The name, address and telephone number of the seller or the transferor;

(d) The signature of the seller or transferor or the authorized agent of the seller or transferor; and

(e) The name, address and telephone number of the person transporting the metal property.

(4) The Department of State Police shall create a form that may serve as a metal transportation certificate and shall make the form available on the department's website.

(5) It is a defense to a charge of unlawfully transporting metal property that the person transporting the metal property is the owner of the property or an agent or employee of the owner of the property.
(6) Unlawfully transporting metal property is a Class C misdemeanor.

164.882 Unlawful operation of an audiovisual device

(1) A person commits the crime of unlawful operation of an audiovisual device if the person knowingly operates the audiovisual recording function of any device in a motion picture theater, while a motion picture is being exhibited, without the written consent of the motion picture theater owner.
(2) Unlawful operation of an audiovisual device is a Class B misdemeanor.
(3) The provisions of subsection (1) of this section do not apply to any activity undertaken in the course of bona fide law enforcement activity or necessary to the proper functioning of the criminal justice system.

164.885 Endangering aircraft in the first degree Amended 2009

(1) A person commits the crime of endangering aircraft *in the first degree* if the person knowingly:
 (a) Throws an object at, or drops an object upon, an aircraft;
 (b) Discharges a bow and arrow, gun, airgun or firearm at or toward an aircraft;
 (c) Tampers with *an* aircraft or *a part, system, machine or substance used to operate an aircraft in such* a manner as to impair the safety, efficiency or operation of *an* aircraft *without* the consent of the owner, operator or possessor of the aircraft; or
 (d) Places, sets, arms or causes to be discharged *a* spring gun, trap, explosive device or explosive material with the intent of damaging, destroying or discouraging the operation of *an* aircraft.
(2)(a) Except as provided in paragraph (b) of this subsection, a person commits the crime of endangering aircraft in the second degree if the person knowingly possesses a firearm or deadly weapon in a restricted access area of a commercial service airport that has at least 2 million passenger boardings per calendar year.
(b) Paragraph (a) of this subsection does not apply to a person authorized under federal law or an airport security program to possess a firearm or deadly weapon in a restricted access area.
(3)(a) Endangering aircraft *in the first degree* is a Class C felony.
(b) Endangering aircraft in the second degree is a Class A misdemeanor.

(4) As used in this section, "restricted access area" means an area of a commercial service airport that is:
(a) Designated as restricted in the airport security program approved by the federal Transportation Security Administration; and
(b) Marked at points of entry with signs giving notice that access to the area is restricted

164.887 Interference with agricultural operations
Note: Due to recent case law, please consult with your local prosecuting authority regarding the enforceability of this section.

164.889 Interference with agricultural research
(1) A person commits the crime of interference with agricultural research if the person knowingly:
  (a) Damages any property at an agricultural research facility with the intent to damage or hinder agricultural research or experimentation;
  (b) Obtains any property of an agricultural research facility with the intent to damage or hinder agricultural research or experimentation;
  (c) Obtains access to an agricultural research facility by misrepresentation with the intent to perform acts that would damage or hinder agricultural research or experimentation;
  (d) Enters an agricultural research facility with the intent to damage, alter, duplicate or obtain unauthorized possession of records, data, materials, equipment or specimens related to agricultural research or experimentation;
  (e) Without the authorization of the agricultural research facility, obtains or exercises control over records, data, materials, equipment or specimens of the agricultural research facility with the intent to destroy or conceal the records, data, materials, equipment or specimens; or
  (f) Releases or steals an animal from, or causes the death, injury or loss of an animal at, an agricultural research facility.
(2) Interference with agricultural research is a Class C felony.
(3) For purposes of this section:
  (a) "Agricultural research facility" means any structure or land, whether privately or publicly owned, leased or operated, that is being used for agricultural research or experimentation.
  (b) "Agricultural research or experimentation" means the lawful study, analysis or testing of plants or animals, or the use of plants or animals to conduct studies, analyses, testing or teaching, for the purpose of improving farming, forestry or animal husbandry.

(4) In addition to any other penalty imposed for violation of this section, a person convicted of interference with agricultural research is liable for:
  (a) Damages to real and personal property caused by acts constituting the violation; and
  (b) The costs of repeating an experiment, including the replacement of the records, data, equipment, specimens, labor and materials, if acts constituting the violation cause the failure of an experiment in progress or irreparably damage completed research or experimentation.

165.002 Definitions–Forgery & related offenses

As used in ORS 165.002 to 165.027, and 165.032 to 165.070, unless the context requires otherwise:

(1) "Written instrument" means any paper, document, instrument, article or electronic record containing written or printed matter or the equivalent thereof, whether complete or incomplete, used for the purpose of reciting, embodying, conveying or recording information or constituting a symbol or evidence of value, right, privilege or identification, which is capable of being used to the advantage or disadvantage of some person.

(2) "Complete written instrument" means one which purports to be a genuine written instrument fully drawn with respect to every essential feature thereof.

(3) "Incomplete written instrument" means one which contains some matter by way of content or authentication but which requires additional matter in order to render it a complete written instrument.

(4) To "falsely make" a written instrument means to make or draw a complete written instrument in its entirety, or an incomplete written instrument which purports to be an authentic creation of its ostensible maker, but which is not, either because the ostensible maker is fictitious or because, if real, the ostensible maker did not authorize the making or drawing thereof.

(5) To "falsely complete" a written instrument means to transform, by adding, inserting or changing matter, an incomplete written instrument into a complete one, without the authority of anyone entitled to grant it, so that the complete written instrument falsely appears or purports to be in all respects an authentic creation of its ostensible maker or authorized by the ostensible maker.

(6) To "falsely alter" a written instrument means to change, without authorization by anyone entitled to grant it, a written instrument, whether complete or incomplete, by means of erasure, obliteration, deletion, insertion of new matter, transposition of matter, or in any other manner, so that the instrument so altered falsely appears or purports to be in all respects an authentic creation of its ostensible maker or authorized by the ostensible maker.

(7) To "utter" means to issue, deliver, publish, circulate, disseminate, transfer or tender a written instrument or other object to another.

(8) "Forged instrument" means a written instrument which has been falsely made, completed or altered.

(9) "Electronic record" has the meaning given that term in ORS 84.004.

(10) "Signature" includes, but is not limited to, an electronic signature, as defined in ORS 84.004.

165.007 Forgery in the second degree

(1) A person commits the crime of forgery in the second degree if, with intent to injure or defraud, the person:
  (a) Falsely makes, completes or alters a written instrument; or
  (b) Utters a written instrument which the person knows to be forged.
(2) Forgery in the second degree is a Class A misdemeanor.

165.013 Forgery in the first degree

(1) A person commits the crime of forgery in the first degree if the person violates ORS 165.007:
  (a) And the written instrument is or purports to be any of the following:
    (A) Part of an issue of money, securities, postage or revenue stamps, or other valuable instruments issued by a government or governmental agency;
    (B) Part of an issue of stock, bonds or other instruments representing interests in or claims against any property or person;
    (C) A deed, will, codicil, contract or assignment;
    (D) A check for $1,000 or more, a credit card purchase slip for $1,000 or more, or a combination of checks and credit card purchase slips that, in the aggregate, total $1,000 or more, or any other commercial instrument or other document that does or may evidence, create, transfer, alter, terminate or otherwise affect a legal right, interest, obligation or status; or
    (E) A public record; or
  (b) By falsely making, completing or altering, or by uttering, at least 15 retail sales receipts, Universal Product Code labels, EAN-8 labels or EAN-13 labels or a combination of at least 15 retail sales receipts, Universal Product Code labels, EAN-8 labels or EAN-13 labels.
(2) The value of single check or credit card transactions may be added together under subsection (1)(a)(D) of this section if the transactions were committed:
  (a) Against multiple victims within a 30-day period; or
  (b) Against the same victim within a 180-day period.
(3) Forgery in the first degree is a Class C felony.

165.017 Criminal possession of a forged instrument in the second degree

(1) A person commits the crime of criminal possession of a forged instrument in the second degree if, knowing it to be forged and with intent to utter same, the person possesses a forged instrument.

(2) Criminal possession of a forged instrument in the second degree is a Class A misdemeanor.

165.022 Criminal possession of a forged instrument in the first degree

(1) A person commits the crime of criminal possession of a forged instrument in the first degree if, knowing it to be forged and with intent to utter same, the person possesses a forged instrument of the kind and in the amount specified in ORS 165.013 (1).

(2) Criminal possession of a forged instrument in the first degree is a Class C felony.

165.032 Criminal possession of a forgery device

(1) A person commits the crime of criminal possession of a forgery device if:

(a) The person makes or possesses with knowledge of its character any plate, die or other device, apparatus, equipment or article specifically designed for use in counterfeiting or otherwise forging written instruments; or

(b) With intent to use, or to aid or permit another to use, the same for purposes of forgery, the person makes or possesses any device, apparatus, equipment or article capable of or adaptable to such use.

(2) Criminal possession of a forgery device is a Class C felony.

165.037 Criminal simulation

(1) A person commits the crime of criminal simulation if:

(a) With intent to defraud, the person makes or alters any object in such a manner that it appears to have an antiquity, rarity, source or authorship that it does not in fact possess; or

(b) With knowledge of its true character and with intent to defraud, the person utters or possesses an object so simulated.

(2) Criminal simulation is a Class A misdemeanor.

165.042 Fraudulently obtaining a signature

(1) A person commits the crime of fraudulently obtaining a signature if, with intent to defraud or injure another, the person obtains

the signature of a person to a written instrument by knowingly misrepresenting any fact.

(2) Fraudulently obtaining a signature is a Class A misdemeanor.

165.055 Fraudulent use of a credit card
Amended 2009

(1) A person commits the crime of fraudulent use of a credit card if, with intent to injure or defraud, the person uses a credit card for the purpose of obtaining property or services with knowledge that:

(a) The card is stolen or forged;

(b) The card has been revoked or canceled; or

(c) For any other reason the use of the card is unauthorized by either the issuer or the person to whom the credit card is issued.

(2) "Credit card" means a card, booklet, credit card number or other identifying symbol or instrument evidencing an undertaking to pay for property or services delivered or rendered to or upon the order of a designated person or bearer.

(3) The value of single credit card transactions may be added together if the transactions were committed:

(a) Against multiple victims within a 30-day period; or

(b) Against the same victim within a 180-day period.

(4) Fraudulent use of a credit card is:

(a) A Class A misdemeanor if the aggregate total amount of property or services the person obtains or attempts to obtain is *less than $1,000*.

(b) A Class C felony if the aggregate total amount of property or services the person obtains or attempts to obtain is *$1,000* or more.

165.065 Negotiating a bad check

(1) A person commits the crime of negotiating a bad check if the person makes, draws or utters a check or similar sight order for the payment of money, knowing that it will not be honored by the drawee.

(2) For purposes of this section, unless the check or order is postdated, it is prima facie evidence of knowledge that the check or order would not be honored if:

(a) The drawer has no account with the drawee at the time the check or order is drawn or uttered; or

(b) Payment is refused by the drawee for lack of funds, upon presentation within 30 days after the date of utterance, and the drawer fails to make good within 10 days after receiving notice of refusal.

(3) Negotiating a bad check is:

(a) A Class A misdemeanor, except as provided in paragraph (b) of this subsection.

(b) Enhanced from a Class A misdemeanor to a Class C felony if at the time of sentencing it is established beyond a reasonable doubt that the person has been convicted in this state, within the preceding five years, of the crime of negotiating a bad check or of theft by deception by means of a bad check.

165.070 Possessing fraudulent communications device

(1) A person commits the crime of possessing a fraudulent communications device if the person:
  (a) Makes, possesses, sells, gives or otherwise transfers to another, or offers or advertises pictures or diagrams concerning an instrument, apparatus or device with intent that the same be used or with knowledge or reason to believe the same is intended to or may be used to avoid any lawful telephone or telegraph toll charge or to conceal the existence or place of origin or destination of any telephone or telegraph communication; or
  (b) Sells, gives or otherwise transfers to another or offers, or advertises plans or instructions for making or assembling an instrument, apparatus or device described in paragraph (a) of this subsection with knowledge or reason to believe that they may be used to make or assemble such instrument, apparatus or device.
(2) An instrument, apparatus, device, plans, instructions or written publication described in subsection (1) of this section may be seized under warrant or incident to a lawful arrest, and upon the conviction of a person under subsection (1) of this section, such instrument, apparatus, device, plans, instructions or written publication may be destroyed as contraband by the sheriff of the county in which such person was convicted or turned over to the person providing telephone or telegraph service in the territory in which the same was seized.
(3) Possessing a fraudulent communications device is a Class C felony.

165.072 Definitions–Payment card offenses

As used in this section and ORS 165.074, unless the context requires otherwise:
(1) "Cardholder" means a person to whom a payment card is issued or a person who is authorized to use the payment card.
(2) "Credit card" means a card, plate, booklet, credit card number, credit card account number or other identifying symbol, instrument or device that can be used to pay for, or to obtain on credit, goods or services.
(3) "Financial institution" means a financial institution as that term is defined in ORS 706.008.
(4) "Merchant" means:
  (a) An owner or operator of a retail mercantile establishment;

(b) An agent, employee, lessee, consignee, franchisee, officer, director or independent contractor of an owner or operator of a retail mercantile establishment; and

(c) A person who receives what the person believes to be a payment card or information from a payment card from a cardholder as the instrument for obtaining something of value from the merchant.

(5) "Payment card" means a credit card, charge card, debit card, stored value card or any card that is issued to a person and allows the user to obtain something of value from the merchant.

(6) "Payment card transaction" means a sale or other transaction or act in which a payment card is used to pay for, or to obtain on credit, goods or services.

(7) "Payment card transaction record" means any record or evidence of a payment card transaction, including, without limitation, any paper, sales draft, instrument or other writing and any electronic or magnetic transmission or record.

(8) "Person" does not include a financial institution or its authorized employee, representative or agent.

(9) "Previous conviction" has the meaning given that term in ORS 137.712.

(10) "Reencoder" means an electronic device that places encoded information from one payment card onto another payment card.

(11) "Scanning device" means an electronic device that used to access, read, scan, obtain, memorize or store, temporarily or permanently, information encoded on a payment card.

165.074 Payment card factoring

(1) A person commits the crime of unlawful factoring of a payment card transaction if the person intentionally or knowingly:

(a) Presents to or deposits with, or causes another to present to or deposit with, a financial institution for payment a payment card transaction record that is not the result of a payment card transaction between the cardholder and the person;

(b) Employs, solicits or otherwise causes a merchant to present to or deposit with a financial institution for payment a payment card transaction record that is not the result of a payment card transaction between the cardholder and the merchant;

(c) Employs, solicits or otherwise causes another to become a merchant for purposes of engaging in conduct made unlawful by this section;

(d) Uses a scanning device to access, read, scan, obtain, memorize or store information encoded on a payment card:

(A) Without the permission of the cardholder; or

(B) With the intent to defraud another person; or

(e) Uses a reencoder to place encoded information from one payment card onto another payment card:
(A) Without the permission of the cardholder of the payment card from which encoded information is being taken; or
(B) With the intention to defraud another person.
(2) Unlawful factoring of a payment card transaction is a Class C felony.
(3) Notwithstanding subsection (2) of this section, unlawful factoring of a payment card transaction is a Class B felony if the person has one or more previous convictions under this section.

165.107 Failing to maintain a metal purchase record   Amended 2009

(1) Before completing a transaction, a scrap metal business engaged in business in this state shall:

(a) Create a metal property record for the transaction at the time and in the location where the transaction occurs. The record must:

(A) Be accurate and written clearly and legibly in English;

(B) Be entered onto a standardized printed form or an electronic form that is securely stored and is capable of ready retrieval and printing; and

(C) Contain all of the following information:

(i) The signature of the individual with whom the scrap metal business conducts the transaction;

(ii) The time, date, location and monetary amount or other value of the transaction;

(iii) The name of the employee who conducts the transaction on behalf of the scrap metal business;

(iv) The name, street address and telephone number of the individual with whom the scrap metal business conducts the transaction;

(v) A description of, and the license number and issuing state shown on the license plate affixed to, the motor vehicle, if any, used to transport the individual who conducts, or the nonferrous metal property or private metal property that is the subject of, the transaction;

(vi) A photocopy of a current, valid driver license or other government-issued photo identification belonging to the individual with whom the scrap metal business conducts the transaction;

(vii) A photograph of, or video surveillance recording depicting, a recognizable facial image of the individual with whom the scrap metal business conducts the transaction; and

(viii) A general description of the nonferrous metal property or private metal property that constitutes the predominant part of the transaction. The description must include any identifiable marks on the property, if readily discernible, and must specify the weight, quantity or volume of the nonferrous metal property or private metal property and indicate the appropriate classification code from the current edition of the Institute of Scrap Recycling Industries' Scrap Specifications Circular,

or successor publication, for each separately classifiable component of the nonferrous metal property or private metal property.

(b) Require the individual with whom the scrap metal business conducts a transaction to sign and date a declaration printed in conspicuous type, either on the record described in this subsection or on a receipt issued to the individual with whom the scrap metal business conducts the transaction, that states:

I, _____, AFFIRM UNDER PENALTY OF LAW THAT THE PROPERTY I AM SELLING IN THIS TRANSACTION IS NOT, TO THE BEST OF MY KNOWLEDGE, STOLEN PROPERTY.

(c) Require the employee of the scrap metal business who conducts the transaction on behalf of the scrap metal business to witness the individual sign the declaration, and also to sign and date the declaration in a space provided for that purpose.

(d) For one year following the date of the transaction, keep a copy of the record and the signed and dated declaration described in this subsection. If the scrap metal business uses a video surveillance recording as part of the record kept in accordance with this subsection, the scrap metal business need not keep the video surveillance recording for one year, but shall retain the video surveillance recording for a minimum of 30 days following the date of the transaction. The scrap metal business shall at all times keep the copies at the current place of business for the scrap metal business.

(2) A scrap metal business engaged in business in this state may not do any of the following:

(a) Purchase or receive kegs or similar metallic containers used to store or dispense alcoholic beverages, except from a person that manufactures the kegs or containers or from a person licensed by the Oregon Liquor Control Commission under ORS 471.155.

(b) Conduct a transaction with an individual if the individual does not at the time of the transaction consent to the creation of the record described in subsection (1) of this section and produce for inspection a valid driver license or other government-issued photo identification that belongs to the individual.

(c) Conduct a transaction with an individual in which the scrap metal business pays the individual other than by mailing a nontransferable check for the amount of the transaction to the street address the individual provided under subsection (1) of this section not earlier than three business days after the date of the transaction. The check must be drawn on an

account that the scrap metal business maintains with a financial institution, as defined in ORS 706.008.

(d) Cash a check issued in payment for a transaction or release a check issued in payment for a transaction other than as provided in paragraph (c) of this subsection. If a check is returned as undelivered or undeliverable, the scrap metal business shall retain the check until the individual with whom the scrap metal business conducted the transaction provides a valid street address for the individual. If after 30 days following the date of the transaction the individual fails to provide a valid street address, the scrap metal business may cancel the check and the individual shall forfeit to the scrap metal business the amount due as payment.

(3) Before purchasing or receiving metal property from a commercial seller, a scrap metal business shall:

(a) Create and maintain a commercial account with the commercial seller. As part of the commercial account, the scrap metal business shall enter accurately, clearly and legibly in English onto a standardized printed form, or an electronic form that is securely stored and is capable of ready retrieval and printing, the following information:

(A) The full name of the commercial seller;

(B) The business address and telephone number of the commercial seller; and

(C) The full name of each employee, agent or other individual the commercial seller authorizes to deliver metal property to the scrap metal business.

(b) Record as part of the commercial account at the time the scrap metal business purchases or receives metal property from a commercial seller the following information:

(A) The time, date and location at which the commercial seller delivered the metal property for purchase or receipt;

(B) The monetary amount or other value of the metal property;

(C) A description of the type of metal property that constitutes the predominant part of the purchase or receipt; and

(D) The signature of the individual who delivered the metal property to the scrap metal business.

(4) A scrap metal business may require an individual from whom the business obtains metal property to provide the individual's thumbprint to the scrap metal business.

(5) A scrap metal business shall make all records and accounts required to be maintained under this section available to any peace officer on demand.

(6)(a) A scrap metal *business* that violates *a provision of subsections (1) to (3)* of this section shall pay a fine of $1,000.

Added 2009

(b) Notwithstanding paragraph (a) of this subsection, a scrap metal *business* that violates *a provision of subsections (1) to (3) of* this section shall pay a fine of $5,000 if the scrap metal *business* has at least three previous convictions for violations of *a provision of subsections (1) to (3) of* this section.
(7) The definitions in ORS 165.116 apply to this section.

165.116 Definitions–Metal property offenses
Added 2009

As used in ORS 164.857 and 165.116 to 165.124:
(1) "Commercial account" means an agreement or arrangement between a commercial seller and a scrap metal business for regularly or periodically selling, delivering, purchasing or receiving metal property.
(2) "Commercial metal property" means an item fabricated or containing parts made of metal or metal alloys that:
(a) Is used as, used in or used as part of:
  (A) A utility access cover or a cover for a utility meter;
  (B) A pole, fixture or component of a street light or traffic light;
  (C) A sign or marker located, with the permission of a governmental entity, alongside a street, road or bridge for the purpose of directing or controlling traffic or providing information to motorists;
  (D) A traffic safety device, including a guardrail for a highway, road or bridge;
  (E) A vase, plaque, marker, tablet, plate or other sign or ornament affixed to or in proximity to a historic site, grave, statue, monument or similar property accessible to members of the public;
  (F) An agricultural implement, including an irrigation wheel, sprinkler head or pipe;
  (G) A forestry implement or structure, including silvicultural equipment, gates, culverts and servicing and maintenance parts or supplies; or
  (H) A logging operation implement, including mechanical equipment, rigging equipment and servicing and maintenance parts or supplies;
(b) Bears the name of, or a serial or model number, logo or other device used by, a commercial seller to identify the commercial seller's property including, but not limited to, implements or equipment used by railroads and utilities that provide telephone, commercial mobile radio, cable television, electricity, water, natural gas or similar services;
(c) Consists of material used in building construction or other commercial construction, including:
  (A) Copper or aluminum pipe, tubing or wiring;
  (B) Aluminum gutters, downspouts, siding, decking, bleachers or risers; or
  (C) Aluminum or stainless steel fence panels made of one-inch tubing 42 inches long, with four-inch gaps; or
(d) Constitutes wire of a gauge typically used by utilities to provide electrical or telecommunications service.

Added 2009

(3) *"Commercial seller"* means a business entity, as defined in ORS **60.470**, or governmental entity that regularly or periodically sells or delivers metal property to a scrap metal business as part of the entity's business functions.

(4) *"Metal property"* means commercial metal property, nonferrous metal property or private metal property.

(5)(a) *"Nonferrous metal property"* means an item fabricated or containing parts made of or in an alloy with copper, brass, aluminum, bronze, lead, zinc or nickel.

(b) *"Nonferrous metal property"* does not include gold, silver or platinum that is used in the manufacture, repair, sale or resale of jewelry.

(6) *"Private metal property"* means a catalytic converter that has been removed from a vehicle and is offered for sale as an independent item, whether individually or as part of a bundle, bale or in other bulk form.

(7)(a) *"Scrap metal business"* means a person that is licensed to do business in this state or another state and that:

(A) Maintains a permanent or fixed place of business at which the person:

(i) Engages in the business of purchasing or receiving metal property;

(ii) Alters or prepares metal property the person receives for use in manufacturing other products; and

(iii) Owns, leases, rents, maintains or uses a device used in metal recycling, including a hydraulic baler, metal shearer or metal shredder;

(B) Maintains a permanent or fixed place of business at which the person engages in the business of purchasing or receiving metal property for the purpose of aggregation and sale to another scrap metal business; or

(C) Does not necessarily maintain a permanent or fixed place of business in this state but engages in the business of purchasing or receiving nonferrous metal property or private metal property for the purpose of aggregation and sale to another scrap metal business.

(b) *"Scrap metal business"* does not include a governmental entity that accepts metal property for recycling.

(8)(a) *"Transaction"* means a sale, purchase, receipt or trade of, or a contract, agreement or pledge to sell, purchase, receive or trade, private metal property or nonferrous metal property that occurs or forms between an individual and a scrap metal business.

(b) *"Transaction"* does not include:

(A) A transfer of metal property made without consideration; or

(B) A sale, purchase, receipt or trade of, or a contract, agreement or pledge to sell, purchase, receive or trade, private metal property or nonferrous metal property that occurs or forms between:

(i) A commercial seller or an authorized employee or agent of the commercial seller; and

(ii) A scrap metal business or an authorized employee or agent of the scrap metal business.

165.118 Metal property offenses *Added 2009*

(1) A person commits the offense of unlawfully altering metal property if the person, with intent to deceive a scrap metal business as to the ownership or origin of an item of metal property, knowingly removes, alters, renders unreadable or invisible or obliterates a name, logo, model or serial number, personal identification number or other mark or method that a manufacturer uses to identify the metal property.

(2) A person commits the offense of making a false statement on a metal property record if the person:

(a) Knowingly makes, causes or allows to be made a false entry or misstatement of material fact in a metal property record described in ORS 165.107; or

(b) Signs a declaration under ORS 165.107 knowing that the nonferrous metal property or private metal property that is the subject of a transaction is stolen.

(3) A scrap metal business or an agent or employee of a scrap metal business commits the offense of unlawfully purchasing or receiving metal property if the scrap metal business or agent or employee fails to report any of the following to a law enforcement agency within 24 hours:

(a) The purchase or receipt of metal property that the person knows or has good reason to know was the subject of theft.

(b) The purchase or receipt of metal property that the person knows or reasonably suspects has been unlawfully altered as described in subsection (1) of this section.

(c) The purchase or receipt of metallic wire from which insulation has been removed, unless the individual offering the wire for purchase or receipt can prove by appropriate documentation that the individual owns or is entitled to offer the wire for purchase or receipt and that the insulation has been removed by accident or was done by legitimate means or for a legitimate purpose. The scrap metal business shall retain a copy of the documentation provided.

(d) The purchase or receipt of commercial metal property from a person other than:

(A) A commercial seller that has a commercial account with the scrap metal business; or

(B) An individual who can produce written documentation or identification that proves that the individual is an employee, agent or other individual authorized by a commercial seller that has a commercial account with the scrap metal business to deliver commercial metal property for purchase or receipt.

(e) The purchase or receipt of metal property from an individual whom the scrap metal business knows or reasonably suspects:
  (A) Is under 16 years of age; or
  (B) Has, according to written or electronically transmitted information provided by a peace officer or law enforcement agency, been convicted within the past five years, as a principal, agent or accessory of a crime involving:
   (i) Drugs;
   (ii) Burglary, robbery or theft;
   (iii) Possession or receipt of stolen property;
   (iv) The manufacture, delivery or possession of, with intent to deliver, methamphetamine;
   (v) The manufacture, delivery or possession of, with intent to deliver, ephedrine or a salt, isomer or salt of an isomer of ephedrine;
   (vi) The manufacture, delivery or possession of, with intent to deliver, pseudoephedrine or a salt, isomer or salt of an isomer of pseudoephedrine; or
   (vii) Possession of anhydrous ammonia with intent to manufacture methamphetamine.
(4) Violation of a provision of subsections (1) to (3) of this section is a Class A misdemeanor.

165.124 Exceptions–Metal property offenses
Added 2009

(1) Except as provided in subsection (2) of this section, ORS 164.857, 165.107, do not apply to:
  (a) A person engaged in recycling beverage containers as defined in ORS 459A.700.
  (b) A person engaged in buying or selling used or empty food containers made of metal.
  (c) A person to whom a vehicle dealer certificate has been issued under ORS 822.020.
  (d) A person to whom a dismantler certificate has been issued under ORS 822.110.
  (e) A person to whom a towing business certificate has been issued under ORS 822.205.
(2) A person described in subsection (1)(c) to (e) of this section shall comply with and is subject to the penalty provided for violating a provision of ORS 164.857, 165.107, 165.116, 165.118 or 165.122, if the person purchases, receives or transports:
  (a) Private metal property; or
  (b) Commercial metal property or nonferrous metal property, that is not a motor vehicle or a part of a motor vehicle.

Amended 2009

165.535 Definitions–Obtaining contents of communications

As used in ORS 41.910, 133.723, 133.724, 165.540 and 165.545:

(1) "Conversation" means the transmission between two or more persons of an oral communication which is not a telecommunication or a radio communication.

(2) "Person" means any person as defined in ORS 174.100 and includes public officials and law enforcement officers of the state, county, municipal corporation or any other political subdivision of the state.

(3) "Radio communication" means the transmission by radio or other wireless methods of writing, signs, signals, pictures and sounds of all kinds, including all instrumentalities, facilities, equipment and services (including, among other things, the receipt, forwarding and delivering of communications) incidental to such transmission.

(4) "Telecommunication" means the transmission of writing, signs, signals, pictures and sounds of all kinds by aid of wire, cable or other similar connection between the points of origin and reception of such transmission, including all instrumentalities, facilities, equipment and services (including, among other things, the receipt, forwarding and delivering of communications) incidental to such transmission.

165.540 Obtaining contents of communications
Amended 2009

(1) Except as otherwise provided in ORS 133.724 or 133.726 or subsections (2) to (7) of this section, a person may not:

(a) Obtain or attempt to obtain the whole or any part of a telecommunication or a radio communication to which the person is not a participant, by means of any device, contrivance, machine or apparatus, whether electrical, mechanical, manual or otherwise, unless consent is given by at least one participant.

(b) Tamper with the wires, connections, boxes, fuses, circuits, lines or any other equipment or facilities of a telecommunication or radio communication company over which messages are transmitted, with the intent to obtain unlawfully the contents of a telecommunication or radio communication to which the person is not a participant.

(c) Obtain or attempt to obtain the whole or any part of a conversation by means of any device, contrivance, machine or apparatus, whether electrical, mechanical, manual or otherwise, if not all participants in the conversation are specifically informed that their conversation is being obtained.

(d) Obtain the whole or any part of a conversation, telecommunication or radio communication from any person, while knowing or having good reason to believe that the conversation, telecommunication or radio communication was initially obtained in a manner prohibited by this section.

(e) Use or attempt to use, or divulge to others, any conversation, telecommunication or radio communication obtained by any means prohibited by this section.

(2)(a) The prohibitions in subsection (1)(a), (b) and (c) of this section do not apply to:

(A) Officers, employees or agents of a telecommunication or radio communication company who perform the acts prohibited by subsection (1)(a), (b) and (c) of this section for the purpose of construction, maintenance or conducting of their telecommunication or radio communication service, facilities or equipment.

(B) Public officials in charge of and at jails, police premises, sheriffs' offices, Department of Corrections institutions and other penal or correctional institutions, except as to communications or conversations between an attorney and the client of the attorney.

(b) Officers, employees or agents of a telecommunication or radio communication company who obtain information under paragraph (a) of this subsection may not use or attempt to use, or divulge to others, the information except for the purpose of construction, maintenance, or conducting of their telecommunication or radio communication service, facilities or equipment.

(3) The prohibitions in subsection (1)(a), (b) or (c) of this section do not apply to subscribers or members of their family who perform the acts prohibited by subsection (1) of this section in their homes.

(4) The prohibitions in subsection (1)(a) of this section do not apply to the receiving or obtaining of the contents of any radio or television broadcast transmitted for the use of the general public.

(5) The prohibitions in subsection (1)(c) of this section do not apply to:

(a) A person who records a conversation during a felony that endangers human life;

(b) A person who, pursuant to ORS 133.400, records an interview conducted by a peace officer in a law enforcement facility;

(c) A law enforcement officer who is in uniform and displaying a badge and who is operating a vehicle-mounted video camera that records the scene in front of, within or surrounding a police vehicle, unless the officer has reasonable opportunity to inform participants in the conversation that the conversation is being obtained; or

(d) A law enforcement officer who, acting in the officer's official capacity, deploys an Electro-Muscular Disruption Technology device that contains

a built-in monitoring system capable of recording audio or video, for the duration of that deployment.

(6) The prohibitions in subsection (1)(c) of this section do not apply to persons who intercept or attempt to intercept with an unconcealed recording device the oral communications that are part of any of the following proceedings:

(a) Public or semipublic meetings such as hearings before governmental or quasi-governmental bodies, trials, press conferences, public speeches, rallies and sporting or other events;

(b) Regularly scheduled classes or similar educational activities in public or private institutions; or

(c) Private meetings or conferences if all others involved knew or reasonably should have known that the recording was being made.

(7) The prohibitions in subsection (1)(a), (c), (d) and (e) of this section do not apply to any:

(a) Radio communication that is transmitted by a station operating on an authorized frequency within the amateur or citizens bands; or

(b) Person who intercepts a radio communication that is transmitted by any governmental, law enforcement, civil defense or public safety communications system, including police and fire, readily accessible to the general public provided that the interception is not for purposes of illegal activity.

(8) Violation of subsection (1) or (2)(b) of this section is a Class A misdemeanor.

(9) As used in this section:

(a) "Electro-Muscular Disruption Technology device" means a device that uses a high-voltage, low power charge of electricity to induce involuntary muscle contractions intended to cause temporary incapacitation. "Electro-Muscular Disruption Technology device" includes devices commonly known as tasers.

(b) "Law enforcement officer" has the meaning given that term in ORS 133.726.

165.543 Interception of communications

(1) Except as provided in ORS 133.724 or as provided in ORS 165.540 (2)(a), any person who willfully intercepts, attempts to intercept or procures any other person to intercept or attempt to intercept any wire or oral communication where such person is not a party to the communication and where none of the parties to the communication has given prior consent to the interception, is guilty of a Class A misdemeanor.

(2) As used in this section, the terms "intercept" and "wire or oral communication" have the meanings provided under ORS 133.721.

165.570 Improper use of 911 emergency reporting system

(1) A person commits the crime of improper use of an emergency reporting system if the person knowingly:
  (a) Calls a 9-1-1 emergency reporting system or the School Safety Hotline for a purpose other than to report a situation that the person reasonably believes requires prompt service in order to preserve human life or property; or
  (b) Allows another person to use telephone equipment owned, rented or leased by or under the control of the person to call a 9-1-1 emergency reporting system or the School Safety Hotline for a purpose other than to report a situation that the other person reasonably believes requires prompt service in order to preserve human life or property.
(2) As used in this section:
  (a) "9-1-1 emergency reporting system" has the meaning given that term in ORS 401.710.
  (b) "School Safety Hotline" means the toll-free telephone line established under ORS 180.650.
(3) Improper use of an emergency reporting system is a Class A misdemeanor.

Note: Pursuant to ORS 401.710
"(16) "9-1-1 emergency reporting system" means a telephone service that provides the users of a public telephone system the ability to reach a primary public safety answering point by calling 9-1-1."

165.572 Interference with making a report

(1) A person commits the crime of interference with making a report if the person, by removing, damaging or interfering with a telephone line, telephone or similar communication equipment, intentionally prevents or hinders another person from making a report to a law enforcement agency, a law enforcement official, an agency charged with the duty of taking public safety reports or a 9-1-1 emergency reporting system.
(2) Interference with making a report is a Class A misdemeanor.

165.800 Identity theft

(1) A person commits the crime of identity theft if the person, with the intent to deceive or to defraud, obtains, possesses, transfers, creates, utters or converts to the person's own use the personal identification of another person.
(2) Identity theft is a Class C felony.

(3) It is an affirmative defense to violating subsection (1) of this section that the person charged with the offense:
  (a) Was under 21 years of age at the time of committing the offense and the person used the personal identification of another person solely for the purpose of purchasing alcohol;
  (b) Was under 18 years of age at the time of committing the offense and the person used the personal identification of another person solely for the purpose of purchasing tobacco products; or
  (c) Used the personal identification of another person solely for the purpose of misrepresenting the person's age to gain access to a:
    (A) Place the access to which is restricted based on age; or
    (B) Benefit based on age.
(4) As used in this section:
  (a) "Another person" means a real person, whether living or deceased, or an imaginary person.
  (b) "Personal identification" includes, but is not limited to, any written document or electronic data that does, or purports to, provide information concerning:
    (A) A person's name, address or telephone number;
    (B) A person's driving privileges;
    (C) A person's Social Security number or tax identification number;
    (D) A person's citizenship status or alien identification number;
    (E) A person's employment status, employer or place of employment;
    (F) The identification number assigned to a person by a person's employer;
    (G) The maiden name of a person or a person's mother;
    (H) The identifying number of a person's depository account at a "financial institution" or "trust company," as those terms are defined in ORS 706.008, or a credit card account;
    (I) A person's signature or a copy of a person's signature;
    (J) A person's electronic mail name, electronic mail signature, electronic mail address or electronic mail account;
    (K) A person's photograph;
    (L) A person's date of birth; and
    (M) A person's personal identification number.

165.803 Aggravated identity theft

(1) A person commits the crime of aggravated identity theft if:
  (a) The person violates ORS 165.800 in 10 or more separate incidents within a 180-day period;
  (b) The person violates ORS 165.800 and the person has a previous conviction for aggravated identity theft;
  (c) The person violates ORS 165.800 and the losses incurred in a single or aggregate transaction are $10,000 or more within a 180-day period; or

(d) The person violates ORS 165.800 and has in the person's custody, possession or control 10 or more pieces of personal identification from 10 or more different persons.
(2) Aggravated identity theft is a Class B felony.
(3) As used in this section, "previous conviction" includes:
 (a) Convictions occurring before, on or after January 1, 2008; and
 (b) Convictions entered in any other state or federal court for comparable offenses.
(4) The state shall plead in the accusatory instrument and prove beyond a reasonable doubt, as an element of the offense, the previous conviction for aggravated identity theft.

165.805 Misrepresentation of age by a minor

(1) A person commits the crime of misrepresentation of age by a minor if:
 (a) Being less than a certain, specified age, the person knowingly purports to be of any age other than the true age of the person with the intent of securing a right, benefit or privilege which by law is denied to persons under that certain, specified age; or
 (b) Being unmarried, the person knowingly represents that the person is married with the intent of securing a right, benefit or privilege which by law is denied to unmarried persons.
(2) Misrepresentation of age by a minor is a Class C misdemeanor.
(3) In addition to and not in lieu of any other penalty established by law, a person who, using a driver permit or license or other identification issued by the Department of Transportation of this state or its equivalent in another state, commits the crime of misrepresentation of age by a minor in order to purchase or consume alcoholic liquor may be required to perform community service and the court shall order that the person's driving privileges and right to apply for driving privileges be suspended for a period not to exceed one year. If a court has issued an order denying driving privileges under this section, the court, upon petition of the person, may withdraw the order at any time the court deems appropriate. The court notification to the department under this subsection may include a recommendation that the person be granted a hardship permit under ORS 807.240 if the person is otherwise eligible for the permit.
(4) The prohibitions of this section do not apply to any person acting under the direction of the Oregon Liquor Control Commission or under the direction of state or local law enforcement agencies for the purpose of investigating possible violations of laws prohibiting sales of alcoholic beverages to persons who are under a certain, specified age.
(5) The prohibitions of this section do not apply to a person under the age of 21 years who is acting under the direction of a licensee for the purpose of

investigating possible violations by employees of the licensee of laws prohibiting sales of alcoholic beverages to persons who are under the age of 21 years.

165.810 Unlawful possession of personal identification device

(1) A person commits the crime of unlawful possession of a personal identification device if the person possesses a personal identification device with the intent to use the device to commit a crime. As used in this subsection, "personal identification device" means a device that is used to manufacture or print:
  (a) A driver license or permit or an identification card issued by any state or the federal government;
  (b) An employee identification card issued by an employer; or
  (c) A credit or debit card.
(2) Unlawful possession of a personal identification device is a Class C felony.

165.813 Unlawful possession of fictitious identification

(1) A person commits the crime of unlawful possession of fictitious identification if the person possesses a personal identification card containing identification information for a fictitious person with the intent to use the personal identification card to commit a crime.
(2) Unlawful possession of fictitious identification is a Class C felony.
(3) It is an affirmative defense to violating subsection (1) of this section that the person charged with the offense:
  (a) Was under 21 years of age at the time of committing the offense and the person possessed the personal identification card solely for the purpose of enabling the person to purchase alcohol; or
  (b) Was under 18 years of age at the time of committing the offense and the person possessed the personal identification card solely for the purpose of enabling the person to purchase tobacco products.

166.015 Riot

(1) A person commits the crime of riot if while participating with five or more other persons the person engages in tumultuous and violent conduct and thereby intentionally or recklessly creates a grave risk of causing public alarm.
(2) Riot is a Class C felony.

166.023 Disorderly conduct in the first degree

(1) A person commits the crime of disorderly conduct in the first degree if, with intent to cause public inconvenience, annoyance or alarm, or knowingly creating a risk thereof, the person initiates or circulates a report, knowing it to be false:

(a) Concerning an alleged hazardous substance or an alleged or impending fire, explosion, catastrophe or other emergency; and
(b) Stating that the hazardous substance, fire, explosion, catastrophe or other emergency is located in or upon a school as defined in ORS 339.315.

(2)(a) Disorderly conduct in the first degree is a Class A misdemeanor.
(b) Notwithstanding paragraph (a) of this subsection, disorderly conduct in the first degree is a Class C felony if the defendant has at least one prior conviction for violating subsection (1) of this section.

166.025 Disorderly conduct in the second degree

(1) A person commits the crime of disorderly conduct in the second degree if, with intent to cause public inconvenience, annoyance or alarm, or recklessly creating a risk thereof, the person:
   (a) Engages in fighting or in violent, tumultuous or threatening behavior;
   (b) Makes unreasonable noise;
   (c) Disturbs any lawful assembly of persons without lawful authority;
   (d) Obstructs vehicular or pedestrian traffic on a public way;
   (e) Congregates with other persons in a public place and refuses to comply with a lawful order of the police to disperse;
   (f) Initiates or circulates a report, knowing it to be false, concerning an alleged or impending fire, explosion, crime, catastrophe or other emergency; or
   (g) Creates a hazardous or physically offensive condition by any act which the person is not licensed or privileged to do.

(2) Disorderly conduct in the second degree is a Class B misdemeanor.

166.065 Harassment   *Amended 2009*

(1) A person commits the crime of harassment if the person intentionally:
   (a) Harasses or annoys another person by:
      (A) Subjecting such other person to offensive physical contact; or
      (B) Publicly insulting such other person by abusive words or gestures in a manner intended and likely to provoke a violent response;
   (b) Subjects another to alarm by conveying a false report, known by the conveyor to be false, concerning death or serious physical injury to a person, which report reasonably would be expected to cause alarm; or

(c) Subjects another to alarm by conveying a telephonic, electronic or written threat to inflict serious physical injury on that person or to commit a felony involving the person or property of that person or any member of that person's family, which threat reasonably would be expected to cause alarm.

(2)(a) A person is criminally liable for harassment if the person knowingly permits any telephone or electronic device under the person's control to be used in violation of subsection (1) of this section.

(b) Harassment that is committed under the circumstances described in subsection (1)(c) of this section is committed in either the county in which the communication originated or the county in which the communication was received.

(3) Harassment is a Class B misdemeanor.

(4) Notwithstanding subsection (3) of this section, harassment is a Class A misdemeanor if a person violates:

(a) Subsection (1)(a)(A) of this section by subjecting another person to offensive physical contact and the offensive physical contact consists of touching the sexual or other intimate parts of the other person; or

(b) Subsection (1)(c) of this section and:

(A) The person has a previous conviction under subsection (1)(c) of this section and the victim of the current offense was the victim or a member of the family of the victim of the previous offense;

(B) At the time the offense was committed, the victim was protected by a stalking protective order, a restraining order as defined in ORS 24.190 or any other court order prohibiting the person from contacting the victim;

(C) At the time the offense was committed, the person reasonably believed the victim to be under 18 years of age and more than three years younger than the person; or

(D)(i) The person conveyed a threat to kill the other person or any member of the family of the other person;

(ii) The person expressed the intent to carry out the threat; and

(iii) A reasonable person would believe that the threat was likely to be followed by action.

(5) As used in this section, "electronic threat" means a threat conveyed by electronic mail, the Internet, a telephone text message or any other transmission of information by wire, radio, optical cable, cellular system, electromagnetic system or other similar means.

166.070 Aggravated harassment Added 2009

(1) A person commits the crime of aggravated harassment if the person, knowing that the other person is a:

(a) Staff member, knowingly propels saliva, blood, urine, semen, feces or other dangerous substance at the staff member while

the staff member is acting in the course of official duty or as a result of the staff member's official duties; or

(b) Public safety officer, knowingly propels blood, urine, semen or feces at the public safety officer while the public safety officer is acting in the course of official duty or as a result of the public safety officer's official duties.

(2) Aggravated harassment is a Class C felony. When a person is convicted of violating subsection (1)(a) of this section, in addition to any other sentence it may impose, the court shall impose a term of incarceration in a state correctional facility.

(3) As used in this section:

(a) "Public safety officer" means an emergency medical technician as defined in ORS 682.025 or a fire service professional, a parole and probation officer or a police officer as those terms are defined in ORS 181.610.

(b) "Staff member" has the meaning given that term in ORS 163.165.

166.075 Abuse of venerated objects

(1) A person commits the crime of abuse of venerated objects if the person intentionally abuses a public monument or structure, a place of worship or the national or state flag.

(2) As used in this section and ORS 166.085, "abuse" means to deface, damage, defile or otherwise physically mistreat in a manner likely to outrage public sensibilities.

(3) Abuse of venerated objects is a Class C misdemeanor.

166.076 Abuse of memorial to the dead

(1) A person commits the crime of abuse of a memorial to the dead if the person:

(a) Intentionally destroys, mutilates, defaces, injures or removes any:

(A) Tomb, monument, gravestone or other structure or thing placed as or designed for a memorial to the dead; or

(B) Fence, railing, curb or other thing intended for the protection or for the ornamentation of any structure or thing listed in subparagraph (A) of this paragraph;

(b) Intentionally destroys, mutilates, removes, cuts, breaks or injures any tree, shrub or plant within any structure listed in paragraph (a) of this subsection; or

(c) Buys, sells or transports any object listed in paragraph (a) of this subsection that was stolen from a historic cemetery knowing that the object is stolen.

(2) Abuse of a memorial to the dead is a Class A misdemeanor.

(3)(a) Notwithstanding ORS 161.635, the maximum fine that a court may impose for abuse of a memorial to the dead is $50,000 if:
  (A) The person violates subsection (1)(a) of this section and the object destroyed, mutilated, defaced, injured or removed is or was located in a historic cemetery; or
  (B) The person violates subsection (1)(c) of this section.
 (b) In addition to any other sentence a court may impose, if a defendant is convicted of violating this section under the circumstances described in paragraph (a)(A) of this subsection, the court shall consider ordering the defendant to pay restitution. The court shall base the amount of restitution on the historical value of the object destroyed, mutilated, defaced, injured or removed.
(4) This section does not apply to a person who is the burial right owner or that person's representative, an heir at law of the deceased, or a person having care, custody or control of a cemetery by virtue of law, contract or other legal right, if the person is acting within the scope of the person's legal capacity and the person's actions have the effect of maintaining, protecting or improving the tomb, monument, gravestone or other structure or thing placed as or designed for a memorial to the dead.
(5) As used in this section, "historic cemetery" means a cemetery that is listed with the Oregon Commission on Historic Cemeteries under ORS 97.782.

166.085 Abuse of corpse in the second degree

(1) A person commits the crime of abuse of corpse in the second degree if, except as otherwise authorized by law, the person intentionally:
  (a) Abuses a corpse; or
  (b) Disinters, removes or carries away a corpse.
(2) Abuse of corpse in the second degree is a Class C felony.
(3) As used in this section and ORS 166.087, "abuse of corpse" includes treatment of a corpse by any person in a manner not recognized by generally accepted standards of the community or treatment by a professional person in a manner not generally accepted as suitable practice by other members of the profession, as may be defined by rules applicable to the profession.

166.087 Abuse of corpse in the first degree

(1) A person commits the crime of abuse of corpse in the first degree if the person:
  (a) Engages in sexual activity with a corpse or involving a corpse; or
  (b) Dismembers, mutilates, cuts or strikes a corpse.
(2) Abuse of corpse in the first degree is a Class B felony.

166.090 Telephonic harassment

(1) A telephone caller commits the crime of telephonic harassment if the caller intentionally harasses or annoys another person:
  (a) By causing the telephone of the other person to ring, such caller having no communicative purpose;
  (b) By causing such other person's telephone to ring, knowing that the caller has been forbidden from so doing by a person exercising lawful authority over the receiving telephone; or
  (c) By sending to, or leaving at, the other person's telephone a text message, voice mail or any other message, knowing that the caller has been forbidden from so doing by a person exercising lawful authority over the receiving telephone.

(2) Telephonic harassment is a Class B misdemeanor.

(3) It is an affirmative defense to a charge of violating subsection (1) of this section that the caller is a debt collector, as defined in ORS 646.639, who engaged in the conduct proscribed by subsection (1) of this section while attempting to collect a debt. The affirmative defense created by this subsection does not apply if the debt collector committed the unlawful collection practice described in ORS 646.639 (2)(a) while engaged in the conduct proscribed by subsection (1) of this section.

166.116 Interfering with public transportation

(1) A person commits the crime of interfering with public transportation if the person:
  (a) Intentionally or knowingly enters or remains unlawfully in or on a public transit vehicle or public transit station;
  (b) Intentionally or knowingly interferes with the provision or use of public transportation services by, among other things, interfering with the movement of, or access to, public transit vehicles;
  (c) While in or on a public transit vehicle or public transit station, engages in disorderly conduct in the second degree as defined in ORS 166.025; or
  (d) Subjects a public transportation passenger, employee, agent or security officer or transit police officer to offensive physical contact.

(2) Interfering with public transportation is a Class A misdemeanor.

(3) As used in this section:
  (a) "Enter or remain unlawfully" has the meaning given that term in ORS 164.205.
  (b) "Public transit station" includes all facilities, structures, lands and rights of way that are owned, leased, held or used for the purposes of providing public transportation services.

(c) "Public transit vehicle" means a vehicle that is used for public transportation or operated by or under contract to any public body in order to provide public transportation.

(d) "Public transportation" means transportation provided by a city, county, special district or any other political subdivision or municipal or public corporation.

166.155 Intimidation in the second degree

(1) A person commits the crime of intimidation in the second degree if the person:

(a) Tampers or interferes with property, having no right to do so nor reasonable ground to believe that the person has such right, with the intent to cause substantial inconvenience to another because of the person's perception of the other's race, color, religion, sexual orientation or national origin;

(b) Intentionally subjects another to offensive physical contact because of the person's perception of the other's race, color, religion, sexual orientation or national origin; or

(c) Intentionally, because of the person's perception of race, color, religion, sexual orientation or national origin of another or of a member of the other's family, subjects the other person to alarm by threatening:

(A) To inflict serious physical injury upon or to commit a felony affecting the other person, or a member of the person's family; or

(B) To cause substantial damage to the property of the other person or of a member of the other person's family.

(2) Intimidation in the second degree is a Class A misdemeanor.

(3) For purposes of this section, "property" means any tangible personal property or real property.

166.165 Intimidation in the first degree

(1) Two or more persons acting together commit the crime of intimidation in the first degree, if the persons:

(a)(A) Intentionally, knowingly or recklessly cause physical injury to another person because of the actors' perception of that person's race, color, religion, sexual orientation or national origin; or

(B) With criminal negligence cause physical injury to another person by means of a deadly weapon because of the actors' perception of that person's race, color, religion, sexual orientation or national origin;

(b) Intentionally, because of the actors' perception of another person's race, color, religion, sexual orientation or national origin, place another person in fear of imminent serious physical injury; or

(c) Commit such acts as would constitute the crime of intimidation in the second degree, if undertaken by one person acting alone.

(2) Intimidation in the first degree is a Class C felony.

166.180 Negligently wounding another

Any person who, as a result of failure to use ordinary care under the circumstances, wounds any other person with a bullet or shot from any firearm, or with an arrow from any bow, shall be punished by imprisonment in the county jail for a period not to exceed six months, or by a fine not to exceed $500, or both. In addition, any person so convicted shall forfeit any license to hunt, obtained under the laws of this state, and shall be ineligible to obtain a license to hunt for a period of 10 years following the date of conviction.

166.190 Pointing firearm at another

Any person over the age of 12 years who, with or without malice, purposely points or aims any loaded or empty pistol, gun, revolver or other firearm, at or toward any other person within range of the firearm, except in self-defense, shall be fined upon conviction in any sum not less than $10 nor more than $500, or be imprisoned in the county jail not less than 10 days nor more than six months, or both. Justice courts have jurisdiction concurrent with the circuit court of the trial of violations of this section. When any person is charged before a justice court with violation of this section, the court shall, upon motion of the district attorney, at any time before trial, act as a committing magistrate, and if probable cause be established, hold such person to the grand jury.

166.210 Definitions–Weapons   Amended 2009

As used in ORS 166.250 to 166.270, 166.291 to 166.295 and 166.410 to 166.470:

(1) "Antique firearm" means:
  (a) Any firearm, including any firearm with a matchlock, flintlock, percussion cap or similar type of ignition system, manufactured in or before 1898; and
  (b) Any replica of any firearm described in paragraph (a) of this subsection if the replica:
    (A) Is not designed or redesigned for using rimfire or conventional centerfire fixed ammunition; or
    (B) Uses rimfire or conventional centerfire fixed ammunition that is no longer manufactured in the United States and that is not readily available in the ordinary channels of commercial trade.

(2) "Corrections officer" has the meaning given that term in ORS 181.610.
(3) "Firearm" means a weapon, by whatever name known, which is designed to expel a projectile by the action of powder.
(4) "Firearms silencer" means any device for silencing, muffling or diminishing the report of a firearm.
(5) "Handgun" means any pistol or revolver using a fixed cartridge containing a propellant charge, primer and projectile, and designed to be aimed or fired otherwise than from the shoulder.
(6) "Machine gun" means a weapon of any description by whatever name known, loaded or unloaded, which is designed or modified to allow two or more shots to be fired by a single pressure on the trigger device.
(7) "Minor" means a person under 18 years of age.
(8) "Offense" has the meaning given that term in ORS 161.505.
(9) "Parole and probation officer" has the meaning given that term in ORS 181.610.
(10) "Peace officer" has the meaning given that term in ORS 133.005.
(11) "Short-barreled rifle" means a rifle having one or more barrels less than 16 inches in length and any weapon made from a rifle if the weapon has an overall length of less than 26 inches.
(12) "Short-barreled shotgun" means a shotgun having one or more barrels less than 18 inches in length and any weapon made from a shotgun if the weapon has an overall length of less than 26 inches.

Note: *The 2009 amendments to this section consisted solely of deletions in subsection (3).*

166.220 Unlawful use of weapon *Amended 2009*

(1) A person commits the crime of unlawful use of a weapon if the person:
  (a) Attempts to use unlawfully against another, or carries or possesses with intent to use unlawfully against another, any dangerous or deadly weapon as defined in ORS 161.015; or
  (b) Intentionally discharges a firearm, blowgun, bow and arrow, crossbow or explosive device within the city limits of any city or within residential areas within urban growth boundaries at or in the direction of any person, building, structure or vehicle within the range of the weapon without having legal authority for such discharge.
(2) This section does not apply to:
  (a) Police officers or military personnel in the lawful performance of their official duties;
  (b) Persons lawfully defending life or property as provided in ORS 161.219;
  (c) Persons discharging firearms, blowguns, bows and arrows, crossbows or explosive devices upon public or private shooting ranges, shooting galleries or other areas designated and built for the purpose of target shooting; or

(d) Persons lawfully engaged in hunting in compliance with rules and regulations adopted by the State Department of Fish and Wildlife ; *or*

(e) An employee of the United States Department of Agriculture, acting within the scope of employment, discharging a firearm in the course of the lawful taking of wildlife.

(3) Unlawful use of a weapon is a Class C felony.

166.240 Carrying a concealed weapon

(1) Except as provided in subsection (2) of this section, any person who carries concealed upon the person any knife having a blade that projects or swings into position by force of a spring or by centrifugal force, any dirk, dagger, ice pick, slungshot, metal knuckles or any similar instrument by the use of which injury could be inflicted upon the person or property of any other person, commits a Class B misdemeanor.

(2) Nothing in subsection (1) of this section applies to any peace officer as defined in ORS 133.005, whose duty it is to serve process or make arrests. Justice courts have concurrent jurisdiction to try any person charged with violating any of the provisions of subsection (1) of this section.

166.250 Unlawful possession of firearms
Amended 2009

(1) Except as otherwise provided in this section or ORS 166.260, 166.270, 166.274, 166.291, 166.292 or 166.410 to 166.470 *or section 5, chapter 826, Oregon Laws 2009*[1], a person commits the crime of unlawful possession of a firearm if the person knowingly:

(a) Carries any firearm concealed upon the person;

(b) Possesses a handgun that is concealed and readily accessible to the person within any vehicle; or

(c) Possesses a firearm and:
 (A) Is under 18 years of age;
 (B)(i) While a minor, was found to be within the jurisdiction of the juvenile court for having committed an act which, if committed by an adult, would constitute a felony or a misdemeanor involving violence, as defined in ORS 166.470; and
  (ii) Was discharged from the jurisdiction of the juvenile court within four years prior to being charged under this section;
 (C) Has been convicted of a felony;
 (D) Was committed to the *Oregon Health Authority* under ORS 426.130; or

(E) Was found to be mentally ill and subject to an order under ORS 426.130 that the person be prohibited from purchasing or possessing a firearm as a result of that mental illness; *or*

(F) Has been found guilty except for insanity under ORS 161.295 of a felony.

(2) This section does not prohibit:

(a) A minor, who is not otherwise prohibited under subsection (1)(c) of this section, from possessing a firearm:

(A) Other than a handgun, if the firearm was transferred to the minor by the minor's parent or guardian or by another person with the consent of the minor's parent or guardian; or

(B) Temporarily for hunting, target practice or any other lawful purpose; or

(b) Any citizen of the United States over the age of 18 years who resides in or is temporarily sojourning within this state, and who is not within the excepted classes prescribed by ORS 166.270 and subsection (1) of this section, from owning, possessing or keeping within the person's place of residence or place of business any handgun, and no permit or license to purchase, own, possess or keep any such firearm at the person's place of residence or place of business is required of any such citizen. As used in this subsection, "residence" includes a recreational vessel or recreational vehicle while used, for whatever period of time, as residential quarters.

(3) Firearms carried openly in belt holsters are not concealed within the meaning of this section.

(4)(a) Except as provided in paragraph (b) of this subsection, a handgun is readily accessible within the meaning of this section if the handgun is within the passenger compartment of the vehicle.

(b) If a vehicle has no storage location that is outside the passenger compartment of the vehicle, a handgun is not readily accessible within the meaning of this section if:

(A) The handgun is stored in a closed and locked glove compartment, center console or other container; and

(B) The key is not inserted into the lock, if the glove compartment, center console or other container unlocks with a key.

(5) Unlawful possession of a firearm is a Class A misdemeanor.

[1] **Note:** The phrase "*or section 5, chapter 826, Oregon Laws 2009*" in section (1) is **NOT** effective **UNTIL** a rule is adopted by the Psychiatric Review Board to implement section 5, chapter 826, Oregon Laws 2009. The phrase, if it becomes effective, is repealed as of 1/2/2012. Section 5, chapter 826, Oregon Laws 2009 pertains to petition for relief from being barred from transporting, shipping, possessing or receiving a firearm for persons under the authority of the PSRB.

166.260 Exemptions–Unlawful possession of firearms *Amended 2009*

(1) ORS 166.250 does not apply to or affect:

(a) Sheriffs, constables, marshals, *parole and probation officers*, police officers, whether active or honorably retired, or other duly appointed peace officers.

(b) Any person summoned by any such officer to assist in making arrests or preserving the peace, while said person so summoned is actually engaged in assisting the officer.

(c) The possession or transportation by any merchant of unloaded firearms as merchandise.

(d) Active or reserve members of the Army, Navy, Air Force, Coast Guard or Marine Corps of the United States, or of the National Guard, when on duty.

(e) Organizations which are by law authorized to purchase or receive weapons described in ORS 166.250 from the United States, or from this state.

(f) Duly authorized military or civil organizations while parading, or the members thereof when going to and from the places of meeting of their organization.

(g) A corrections officer while transporting or accompanying an individual convicted of or arrested for an offense and confined in a place of incarceration or detention while outside the confines of the place of incarceration or detention.

(h) A person who is licensed under ORS 166.291 and 166.292 to carry a concealed handgun.

(2) It is an affirmative defense to a charge of violating ORS 166.250 (1) (c)(C) that the person has been granted relief from the disability under ORS 166.274.

(3) Except for persons who are otherwise prohibited from possessing a firearm under ORS 166.250 (1)(c) or 166.270, ORS 166.250 does not apply to or affect:

(a) Members of any club or organization, for the purpose of practicing shooting at targets upon the established target ranges, whether public or private, while such members are using any of the firearms referred to in ORS 166.250 upon such target ranges, or while going to and from such ranges.

(b) Licensed hunters or fishermen while engaged in hunting or fishing, or while going to or returning from a hunting or fishing expedition.

(4) The exceptions listed in subsection (1)(b) to (h) of this section constitute affirmative defenses to a charge of violating ORS 166.250.

166.262 Limitation on officer's authority to arrest for violating ORS 166.250 or 166.370

A peace officer may not arrest or charge a person for violating ORS 166.250 (1) (a) or (b) or 166.370 (1) if the person has in the person's immediate possession a valid license to carry a firearm as provided in ORS 166.291 and 166.292.

166.270 Possession of a weapon by a felon Amended 2009

(1) Any person who has been convicted of a felony under the law of this state or any other state, or who has been convicted of a felony under the laws of the Government of the United States,

who owns or has in the person's possession or under the person's custody or control any firearm commits the crime of felon in possession of a firearm.

(2) Any person who has been convicted of a felony under the law of this state or any other state, or who has been convicted of a felony under the laws of the Government of the United States, who owns or has in the person's possession or under the person's custody or control any instrument or weapon having a blade that projects or swings into position by force of a spring or by centrifugal force or any blackjack, slungshot, sandclub, sandbag, sap glove metal knuckles ***or an Electro-Muscular Disruption Technology device as defined in ORS 165.540***, or who carries a dirk, dagger or stiletto, commits the crime of felon in possession of a restricted weapon.

(3) For the purposes of this section, a person "has been convicted of a felony" if, at the time of conviction for an offense, that offense was a felony under the law of the jurisdiction in which it was committed. Such conviction shall not be deemed a conviction of a felony if:
  (a) The court declared the conviction to be a misdemeanor at the time of judgment; or
  (b) The offense was possession of marijuana and the conviction was prior to January 1, 1972.

(4) Subsection (1) of this section does not apply to any person who has been:
  (a) Convicted of only one felony under the law of this state or any other state, or who has been convicted of only one felony under the laws of the United States, which felony did not involve criminal homicide, as defined in ORS 163.005, or the possession or use of a firearm or a weapon having a blade that projects or swings into position by force of a spring or by centrifugal force, and who has been discharged from imprisonment, parole or probation for said offense for a period of 15 years prior to the date of alleged violation of subsection (1) of this section; or
  (b) Granted relief from the disability under 18 U.S.C. 925(c) ***or ORS 166.274*** or has had the person's record expunged under the laws of this state or equivalent laws of another jurisdiction.

(5) Felon in possession of a firearm is a Class C felony. Felon in possession of a restricted weapon is a Class A misdemeanor.

166.272 Unlawful possession of machine guns, short-barreled firearms and firearms silencers

(1) A person commits the crime of unlawful possession of a machine gun, short-barreled rifle, short-barreled shotgun or firearms silencer if the person knowingly possesses any machine gun, short-barreled rifle, short-barreled shotgun or firearms silencer.

(2) Unlawful possession of a machine gun, short-barreled rifle, short-barreled shotgun or firearms silencer is a Class B felony.

(3) A peace officer may not arrest or charge a person for violating subsection (1) of this section if the person has in the person's immediate possession documentation showing that the machine gun, short-barreled rifle, short-barreled shotgun or firearms silencer is registered as required under federal law.

(4) It is an affirmative defense to a charge of violating subsection (1) of this section that the machine gun, short-barreled rifle, short-barreled shotgun or firearms silencer was registered as required under federal law.

166.275 Unlawful possession of weapons by inmates of institutions

Any person committed to any institution who, while under the jurisdiction of any institution or while being conveyed to or from any institution, possesses or carries upon the person, or has under the custody or control of the person any dangerous instrument, or any weapon including but not limited to any blackjack, slingshot, billy, sand club, metal knuckles, explosive substance, dirk, dagger, sharp instrument, pistol, revolver or other firearm without lawful authority, is guilty of a felony and upon conviction thereof shall be punished by imprisonment in the custody of the Department of Corrections for a term not more than 20 years.

166.350 Unlawful possession of armor piercing ammunition

(1) A person commits the crime of unlawful possession of armor piercing ammunition if the person:

(a) Makes, sells, buys or possesses any handgun ammunition the bullet or projectile of which is coated with Teflon or any chemical compound with properties similar to Teflon and which is intended to penetrate soft body armor, such person having the intent that the ammunition be used in the commission of a felony; or

(b) Carries any ammunition described in paragraph (a) of this subsection while committing any felony during which the person or any accomplice of the person is armed with a firearm.

(2) As used in this section, "handgun ammunition" means ammunition principally for use in pistols or revolvers notwithstanding that the ammunition can be used in some rifles.

(3) Unlawful possession of armor piercing ammunition is a Class A misdemeanor.

166.360 Definitions–Weapon in public building

As used in ORS 166.360 to 166.380, unless the context requires otherwise:

(1) "Capitol building" means the Capitol, the State Office Building, the State Library Building, the Labor and Industries Building, the State Transportation Building, the Agriculture Building or the Public Service Building and includes any new buildings which may be constructed on the same grounds as an addition to the group of buildings listed in this subsection.

(2) "Court facility" means a courthouse or that portion of any other building occupied by a circuit court, the Court of Appeals, the Supreme Court or the Oregon Tax Court or occupied by personnel related to the operations of those courts, or in which activities related to the operations of those courts take place.

(3) "Loaded firearm" means:
  (a) A breech-loading firearm in which there is an unexpended cartridge or shell in or attached to the firearm including but not limited to, in a chamber, magazine or clip which is attached to the firearm.
  (b) A muzzle-loading firearm which is capped or primed and has a powder charge and ball, shot or projectile in the barrel or cylinder.

(4) "Public building" means a hospital, a capitol building, a public or private school, as defined in ORS 339.315, a college or university, a city hall or the residence of any state official elected by the state at large, and the grounds adjacent to each such building. The term also includes that portion of any other building occupied by an agency of the state or a municipal corporation, as defined in ORS 297.405, other than a court facility.

(5) "Weapon" means:
  (a) A firearm;
  (b) Any dirk, dagger, ice pick, slingshot, metal knuckles or any similar instrument or a knife other than an ordinary pocket knife, the use of which could inflict injury upon a person or property;
  (c) Mace, tear gas, pepper mace or any similar deleterious agent as defined in ORS 163.211;
  (d) An electrical stun gun or any similar instrument;
  (e) A tear gas weapon as defined in ORS 163.211;
  (f) A club, bat, baton, billy club, bludgeon, knobkerrie, nunchaku, nightstick, truncheon or any similar instrument, the use of which could inflict injury upon a person or property; or
  (g) A dangerous or deadly weapon as those terms are defined in ORS 161.015.

166.370 Possession of firearm or dangerous weapon in public building or court— Discharging firearm at school *Amended 2009*

(1) Any person who intentionally possesses a loaded or unloaded firearm or any other instrument used as a dangerous weapon, while in or on a public building, shall upon conviction be guilty of a Class C felony.

(2)(a) Except as otherwise provided in paragraph (b) of this subsection, a person who intentionally possesses:

(A) A firearm in a court facility is guilty, upon conviction, of a Class C felony. A person who intentionally possesses a firearm in a court facility shall surrender the firearm to a law enforcement officer.

(B) A weapon, other than a firearm, in a court facility may be required to surrender the weapon to a law enforcement officer or to immediately remove it from the court facility. A person who fails to comply with this subparagraph is guilty, upon conviction, of a Class C felony.

(b) The presiding judge of a judicial district may enter an order permitting the possession of specified weapons in a court facility.

(3) Subsection (1) of this section does not apply to:

(a) A sheriff, police officer, other duly appointed peace officers or a corrections officer while acting within the scope of employment.

(b) A person summoned by a peace officer to assist in making an arrest or preserving the peace, while the summoned person is engaged in assisting the officer.

(c) An active or reserve member of the military forces of this state or the United States, when engaged in the performance of duty.

(d) A person who is licensed under ORS 166.291 and 166.292 to carry a concealed handgun.

(e) A person who is authorized by the officer or agency that controls the public building to possess a firearm or dangerous weapon in that public building.

(f) An employee of the United States Department of Agriculture, acting within the scope of employment, who possesses a firearm in the course of the lawful taking of wildlife.

(g) Possession of a firearm on school property if the firearm:

(A) Is possessed by a person who is not otherwise prohibited from possessing the firearm; and

(B) Is unloaded and locked in a motor vehicle.

(4) The exceptions listed in subsection (3)(b) *to (g)* of this section constitute affirmative defenses to a charge of violating subsection (1) of this section.

(5)(a) Any person who knowingly, or with reckless disregard for the safety of another, discharges or attempts to discharge a firearm at a place that the person knows is a school shall upon conviction be guilty of a Class C felony.

(b) Paragraph (a) of this subsection does not apply to the discharge of a firearm:

(A) As part of a program approved by a school in the school by an individual who is participating in the program;

(B) By a law enforcement officer acting in the officer's official capacity; *or*

(C) By an employee of the United States Department of Agriculture, acting within the scope of employment, in the course of the lawful taking of wildlife.

(6) Any weapon carried in violation of this section is subject to the forfeiture provisions of ORS 166.279.
(7) Notwithstanding the fact that a person's conduct in a single criminal episode constitutes a violation of both subsections (1) and (5) of this section, the district attorney may charge the person with only one of the offenses.
(8) As used in this section, "dangerous weapon" means a dangerous weapon as that term is defined in ORS 161.015.

166.380 Examination of firearm by officer

(1) A peace officer may examine a firearm possessed by anyone on the person while in or on a public building to determine whether the firearm is a loaded firearm.
(2) Refusal by a person to allow the examination authorized by subsection (1) of this section constitutes reason to believe that the person has committed a crime and the peace officer may make an arrest pursuant to ORS 133.310.

166.382 Unlawful possession of destructive device

(1) A person commits the crime of unlawful possession of a destructive device if the person possesses:
  (a) Any of the following devices with an explosive, incendiary or poison gas component:
    (A) Bomb;
    (B) Grenade;
    (C) Rocket having a propellant charge of more than four ounces;
    (D) Missile having an explosive or incendiary charge of more than one-quarter ounce; or
    (E) Mine; or
  (b) Any combination of parts either designed or intended for use in converting any device into any destructive device described in paragraph (a) of this subsection and from which a destructive device may be readily assembled.
(2) As used in this section:
  (a) "Destructive device" does not include any device which is designed primarily or redesigned primarily for use as a signaling, pyrotechnic, line throwing, safety or similar device.
  (b) "Possess" has the meaning given that term in ORS 161.015.
(3) This section does not apply to:
  (a) Persons who possess explosives as provided in ORS 480.200 to 480.290.
  (b) The possession of an explosive by a member of the Armed Forces of the United States while on active duty and engaged in the performance of official duties or by a member of a regularly organized fire or police department of a public agency while engaged in the performance of official duties.

(c) The possession of an explosive in the course of transportation by way of railroad, water, highway or air while under the jurisdiction of, or in conformity with, regulations adopted by the United States Department of Transportation.

(d) The possession, sale, transfer or manufacture of an explosive by a person acting in accordance with the provisions of any applicable federal law or regulation that provides substantially the same requirements as the comparable provisions of ORS 480.200 to 480.290.

(4) Possession of a destructive device is a Class C felony.

166.384 Unlawful manufacture of destructive device

(1) A person commits the crime of unlawful manufacture of a destructive device if the person assembles, produces or otherwise manufactures:

(a) A destructive device, as defined in ORS 166.382; or

(b) A pyrotechnic device containing two or more grains of pyrotechnic charge in violation of chapter 10, Title 18 of the United States Code.

(2) Unlawful manufacture of a destructive device is a Class C felony.

166.385 Possession of hoax destructive device

(1) A person commits the crime of possession of a hoax destructive device if the person knowingly places another person in fear of serious physical injury by:

(a) Possessing, manufacturing, selling, delivering, placing or causing to be placed a hoax destructive device; or

(b) Sending a hoax destructive device to another person.

(2) Possession of a hoax destructive device is a Class A misdemeanor.

(3) Notwithstanding subsection (2) of this section, possession of a hoax destructive device is a Class C felony if a person possesses, or threatens to use, a hoax destructive device while the person is committing or attempting to commit a felony.

(4) As used in this section, "hoax destructive device" means an object that reasonably appears, under the circumstances:

(a) To be a destructive device, as described in ORS 166.382 (1)(a), or an explosive, as defined in ORS 166.660, but is an inoperative imitation of a destructive device or explosive; or

(b) To contain a destructive device, as described in ORS 166.382 (1)(a), or an explosive, as defined in ORS 166.660.

166.425 Unlawful purchase of firearm

(1) A person commits the crime of unlawfully purchasing a firearm if the person, knowing that the person is prohibited by state or

federal law from owning or possessing the firearm or having the firearm under the person's custody or control, purchases or attempts to purchase the firearm.

(2) Unlawfully purchasing a firearm is a Class A misdemeanor.

166.429 Firearms used in felony

Any person who, with intent to commit a felony or who knows or reasonably should know that a felony will be committed with the firearm, ships, transports, receives, sells or otherwise furnishes any firearm in the furtherance of the felony is guilty of a Class B felony.

166.438 Transfer of firearms at gun shows

(1) A transferor other than a gun dealer may not transfer a firearm at a gun show unless the transferor:
  (a)(A) Requests a criminal background check under ORS 166.436 prior to completing the transfer;
   (B) Receives notification that the recipient is qualified to complete the transfer; and
   (C) Has the recipient complete the form described in ORS 166.441; or
  (b) Completes the transfer through a gun dealer.
(2) The transferor shall retain the completed form referred to in subsection (1) of this section for at least five years and shall make the completed form available to law enforcement agencies for the purpose of criminal investigations.
(3) A person who organizes a gun show shall post in a prominent place at the gun show a notice explaining the requirements of subsections (1) and (2) of this section. The person shall provide the form required by subsection (1) of this section to any person transferring a firearm at the gun show.
(4) Subsection (1) of this section does not apply if the transferee is licensed as a dealer under 18 U.S.C. 923.
(5)(a) Failure to comply with the requirements of subsection (1), (2) or (3) of this section is a Class A misdemeanor.
  (b) Notwithstanding paragraph (a) of this subsection, failure to comply with the requirements of subsection (1), (2) or (3) of this section is a Class C felony if the person has two or more previous convictions under this section.
(6) It is an affirmative defense to a charge of violating subsection (1) or (3) of this section that the person did not know, or reasonably could not know, that more than 25 firearms were at the site and available for transfer.

166.450 Alteration, removal or obliteration of the identification number of a firearm

Any person who intentionally alters, removes or obliterates the identification number of any firearm for an unlawful purpose, shall be punished upon conviction by imprisonment in the custody of the Department of Corrections for not more than five years. Possession of any such firearm is presumptive evidence that the possessor has altered, removed or obliterated the identification number.

166.460 Exceptions–Antique firearms Amended 2009

(1) ORS 166.250, 166.260, 166.291 to 166.295, 166.410, 166.412, 166.425, 166.434, 166.438 and 166.450 do not apply to antique firearms.

(2) Notwithstanding the provisions of subsection (1) of this section, possession of an antique firearm by a person described in ORS 166.250 (1)(c)(B) *to (D) or (F)* constitutes a violation of ORS 166.250.

166.470 Sale/transfer of firearm Amended 2009

(1) Unless relief has been granted under ORS 166.274 *or section 5, chapter 826, Oregon Laws 2009*[1] *or* 18 U.S.C. 925(c) or the expunction laws of this state or an equivalent law of another jurisdiction, a person may not intentionally sell, deliver or otherwise transfer any firearm when the transferor knows or reasonably should know that the recipient:

(a) Is under 18 years of age;

(b) Has been convicted of a felony;

(c) Has any outstanding felony warrants for arrest;

(d) Is free on any form of pretrial release for a felony;

(e) Was committed to the *Oregon Health Authority* under ORS 426.130;

(f) After January 1, 1990, was found to be mentally ill and subject to an order under ORS 426.130 that the person be prohibited from purchasing or possessing a firearm as a result of that mental illness;

(g) Has been convicted of a misdemeanor involving violence or found guilty, except for insanity under ORS 161.295, of a misdemeanor involving violence within the previous four years. As used in this paragraph, "misdemeanor involving violence" means a misdemeanor described in ORS 163.160 [Assault IV], 163.187 [Strangulation], 163.190 [Menacing], 163.195 [Reckless endangering] or 166.155 (1)(b); or

(h) *Has been found guilty except for insanity under ORS 161.295 of a felony.*

(2) A person may not sell, deliver or otherwise transfer any firearm that the person knows or reasonably should know is stolen.

(3) Subsection (1)(a) of this section does not prohibit:

(a) The parent or guardian, or another person with the consent of the parent or guardian, of a minor from transferring to the minor a firearm, other than a handgun; or

(b) The temporary transfer of any firearm to a minor for hunting, target practice or any other lawful purpose.

(4) Violation of this section is a Class A misdemeanor.

[1] **Note:** Refer to the note under 166.250.

166.480 Sale or other transfer of explosives to children

Any person who sells, exchanges, barters or gives to any child, under the age of 14 years, any explosive article or substance, other than an ordinary firecracker containing not more than 10 grains of gunpowder or who sells, exchanges, barters or gives to any such child, any instrument or apparatus, the chief utility of which is the fact that it is used, or is ordinarily capable of being used, as an article or device to increase the force or intensity of any explosive, or to direct or control the discharge of any such explosive, is guilty of a misdemeanor.

166.630 Discharging weapon on or across highway, ocean shore recreation area or public utility facility   *Amended 2009*

(1) Except as provided in ORS 166.220, any person is guilty of a violation who discharges or attempts to discharge any blowgun, bow and arrow, crossbow, air rifle or firearm:

(a) Upon or across any highway, railroad right of way or other public road in this state, or upon or across the ocean shore within the state recreation area as defined in ORS 390.605.

(b) At any public or railroad sign or signal or an electric power, communication, petroleum or natural gas transmission or distribution facility of a public utility, telecommunications utility or railroad within range of the weapon.

(2) Any blowgun, bow and arrow, crossbow, air rifle or firearm in the possession of the person that was used in committing a violation of this section may be confiscated and forfeited to the State of Oregon. This section does not prevent:

(a) The discharge of firearms by peace officers in the performance of their duty or by military personnel within the confines of a military reservation.

(b) The discharge of firearms by an employee of the United States Department of Agriculture acting within the scope of employment in the course of the lawful taking of wildlife.

(3) The hunting license revocation provided in ORS 497.415 is in addition to and not in lieu of the penalty and forfeiture provided in subsections (1) and (2) of this section.

(4) As used in this section:

(a) "Public sign" includes all signs, signals and markings placed or erected by authority of a public body.

(b) "Public utility" has the meaning given that term in ORS 164.365 (2).

(c) "Railroad" has the meaning given that term in ORS 824.020.

166.635 Discharging weapon or throwing objects at trains

(1) A person shall not knowingly throw an object at, drop an object on, or discharge a bow and arrow, air rifle, rifle, gun, revolver or other firearm at a railroad train, a person on a railroad train or a commodity being transported on a railroad train. This subsection does not prevent a peace officer or a railroad employee from performing the duty of a peace officer or railroad employee.

(2) Violation of subsection (1) of this section is a misdemeanor.

166.638 Discharging weapon across airport operational surfaces

(1) Any person who knowingly or recklessly discharges any bow and arrow, gun, air gun or other firearm upon or across any airport operational surface commits a Class A misdemeanor. Any bow and arrow, gun, air gun or other firearm in the possession of the person that was used in committing a violation of this section may be confiscated and forfeited to the State of Oregon, and the clear proceeds shall be deposited with the State Treasury in the Common School Fund.

(2) As used in subsection (1) of this section, "airport operational surface" means any surface of land or water developed, posted or marked so as to give an observer reasonable notice that the surface is developed for the purpose of storing, parking, taxiing or operating aircraft, or any surface of land or water when actually being used for such purpose.

(3) Subsection (1) of this section does not prohibit the discharge of firearms by peace officers in the performance of their duty or by military personnel within the confines of a military reservation, or otherwise lawful hunting, wildlife control or other discharging of firearms done with the consent of the proprietor, manager or custodian of the airport operational surface.

(4) The hunting license revocation provided in ORS 497.415 is in addition to and not in lieu of the penalty provided in subsection (1) of this section.

166.641 Definitions–Body armor offenses

As used in this section and ORS 166.642 and 166.643:

(1) "Body armor" means any clothing or equipment designed in whole or in part to minimize the risk of injury from a deadly weapon.

(2) "Deadly weapon" has the meaning given that term in ORS 161.015.
(3) "Misdemeanor involving violence" has the meaning given that term in ORS 166.470.

166.642 Felon in possession of body armor

(1) A person commits the crime of felon in possession of body armor if the person:
  (a) Has been convicted of a felony or misdemeanor involving violence under the law of any state or the United States; and
  (b) Knowingly is in possession or control of body armor.
(2) Felon in possession of body armor is a Class C felony.
(3) For purposes of subsection (1) of this section, a person who has been found to be within the jurisdiction of a juvenile court for having committed an act that would constitute a felony or misdemeanor involving violence has been convicted of a felony or misdemeanor involving violence.
(4) Subsection (1) of this section does not apply to:
  (a) A person who is wearing body armor provided by a peace officer for the person's safety or protection while the person is being transported or accompanied by a peace officer; or
  (b) A person who has been convicted of only one felony under the law of this state or any other state, or who has been convicted of only one felony under the law of the United States, which felony did not involve criminal homicide, as defined in ORS 163.005, and who has been discharged from imprisonment, parole or probation for the offense for a period of 15 years prior to the date of the alleged violation of subsection (1) of this section.
(5) It is an affirmative defense to a charge of violating subsection (1) of this section that a protective order or restraining order has been entered to the benefit of the person. The affirmative defense created by this subsection is not available if the person possesses the body armor while committing or attempting to commit a crime.

166.643 Unlawful possession of body armor

(1) A person commits the crime of unlawful possession of body armor if the person, while committing or attempting to commit a felony or misdemeanor involving violence, knowingly:
  (a) Wears body armor; and
  (b) Possesses a deadly weapon.
(2) Unlawful possession of body armor is a Class B felony.

166.649 Throwing an object off an overpass in the second degree

(1) A person commits the crime of throwing an object off an overpass in the second degree if the person:
  (a) With criminal negligence throws an object off an overpass; and

(b) Knows, or reasonably should have known, that the object was of a type or size to cause damage to any person or vehicle that the object might hit.

(2) Throwing an object off an overpass in the second degree is a Class A misdemeanor.

(3) As used in this section and ORS 166.651, "overpass" means a structure carrying a roadway or pedestrian pathway over a roadway.

166.651 Throwing an object off an overpass in the first degree

(1) A person commits the crime of throwing an object off an overpass in the first degree if the person:
  (a) Recklessly throws an object off an overpass; and
  (b) Knows, or reasonably should have known, that the object was of a type or size to cause damage to any person or vehicle that the object might hit.

(2) Throwing an object off an overpass in the first degree is a Class C felony.

167.002 Definitions–Prostitution

As used in ORS 167.002 to 167.027, unless the context requires otherwise:
(1) "Place of prostitution" means any place where prostitution is practiced.
(2) "Prostitute" means a male or female person who engages in sexual conduct or sexual contact for a fee.
(3) "Prostitution enterprise" means an arrangement whereby two or more prostitutes are organized to conduct prostitution activities.
(4) "Sexual conduct" means sexual intercourse or deviate sexual intercourse.
(5) "Sexual contact" means any touching of the sexual organs or other intimate parts of a person not married to the actor for the purpose of arousing or gratifying the sexual desire of either party.

167.007 Prostitution

(1) A person commits the crime of prostitution if:
  (a) The person engages in or offers or agrees to engage in sexual conduct or sexual contact in return for a fee; or
  (b) The person pays or offers or agrees to pay a fee to engage in sexual conduct or sexual contact.

(2) Prostitution is a Class A misdemeanor.

167.012 Promoting prostitution

(1) A person commits the crime of promoting prostitution if, with intent to promote prostitution, the person knowingly:
  (a) Owns, controls, manages, supervises or otherwise maintains a place of prostitution or a prostitution enterprise; or

(b) Induces or causes a person to engage in prostitution or to remain in a place of prostitution; or

(c) Receives or agrees to receive money or other property, other than as a prostitute being compensated for personally rendered prostitution services, pursuant to an agreement or understanding that the money or other property is derived from a prostitution activity; or

(d) Engages in any conduct that institutes, aids or facilitates an act or enterprise of prostitution.

(2) Promoting prostitution is a Class C felony.

167.017 Compelling prostitution

(1) A person commits the crime of compelling prostitution if the person knowingly:

(a) Uses force or intimidation to compel another to engage in prostitution; or

(b) Induces or causes a person under 18 years of age to engage in prostitution; or

(c) Induces or causes the spouse, child or stepchild of the person to engage in prostitution.

(2) Compelling prostitution is a Class B felony.

167.057 Luring a minor

(1) A person commits the crime of luring a minor if the person:

(a) Furnishes to, or uses with, a minor a visual representation or explicit verbal description or narrative account of sexual conduct; and

(b) Furnishes or uses the representation, description or account for the purpose of:

(A) Arousing or satisfying the sexual desires of the person or the minor; or

(B) Inducing the minor to engage in sexual conduct.

(2) A person is not liable to prosecution for violating subsection (1) of this section if the person furnishes or uses a representation, description or account of sexual conduct that forms merely an incidental part of an otherwise nonoffending whole and serves some purpose other than titillation.

(3) In a prosecution under subsection (1) of this section, it is an affirmative defense:

(a) That the representation, description or account was furnished or used for the purpose of psychological or medical treatment and was furnished by a treatment provider or by another person acting on behalf of the treatment provider;

(b) That the defendant had reasonable cause to believe that the person to whom the representation, description or account was furnished or with whom the representation, description or account was used was not a minor; or

(c) That the defendant was less than three years older than the minor at the time of the alleged offense.

(4) In a prosecution under subsection (1) of this section, it is not a defense that the person to whom the representation, description or account was furnished or with whom the representation, description or account was used was not a minor but was a law enforcement officer posing as a minor.

(5) Luring a minor is a Class C felony.

167.060 Definitions–Obscenity

As used in ORS 167.060 to 167.095, unless the context requires otherwise:

(1) "Advertising purposes" means purposes of propagandizing in connection with the commercial sale of a product or type of product, the commercial offering of a service, or the commercial exhibition of an entertainment.

(2) "Displays publicly" means the exposing, placing, posting, exhibiting, or in any fashion displaying in any location, whether public or private, an item in such a manner that it may be readily seen and its content or character distinguished by normal unaided vision viewing it from a public thoroughfare, depot or vehicle.

(3) "Furnishes" means to sell, give, rent, loan or otherwise provide.

(4) "Minor" means an unmarried person under 18 years of age.

(5) "Nudity" means uncovered, or less than opaquely covered, post-pubertal human genitals, pubic areas, the post-pubertal human female breast below a point immediately above the top of the areola, or the covered human male genitals in a discernibly turgid state. For purposes of this definition, a female breast is considered uncovered if the nipple only or the nipple and areola only are covered.

(6) "Obscene performance" means a play, motion picture, dance, show or other presentation, whether pictured, animated or live, performed before an audience and which in whole or in part depicts or reveals nudity, sexual conduct, sexual excitement or sadomasochistic abuse, or which includes obscenities or explicit verbal descriptions or narrative accounts of sexual conduct.

(7) "Obscenities" means those slang words currently generally rejected for regular use in mixed society, that are used to refer to genitals, female breasts, sexual conduct or excretory functions or products, either that have no other meaning or that in context are clearly used for their bodily, sexual or excretory meaning.

(8) "Public thoroughfare, depot or vehicle" means any street, highway, park, depot or transportation platform, or other place, whether indoors or out, or any vehicle for public transportation, owned or operated by government, either directly or through a public corporation or authority, or owned or operated by any agency of public transportation that is designed for the use, enjoyment or transportation of the general public.

(9) "Sadomasochistic abuse" means flagellation or torture by or upon a person who is nude or clad in undergarments or in revealing or bizarre costume, or the condition of being fettered, bound or otherwise physically restrained on the part of one so clothed.

(10) "Sexual conduct" means human masturbation, sexual intercourse, or any touching of the genitals, pubic areas or buttocks of the human male or female, or the breasts of the female, whether alone or between members of the same or opposite sex or between humans and animals in an act of apparent sexual stimulation or gratification.

(11) "Sexual excitement" means the condition of human male or female genitals or the breasts of the female when in a state of sexual stimulation, or the sensual experiences of humans engaging in or witnessing sexual conduct or nudity.

167.062 Sadomasochistic abuse or sexual conduct in live show

Note: Due to recent case law, please consult with your local prosecuting authority regarding the enforceability of this section.

167.075 Exhibiting an obscene performance to a minor

(1) A person commits the crime of exhibiting an obscene performance to a minor if the minor is unaccompanied by the parent or lawful guardian of the minor, and for a monetary consideration or other valuable commodity or service, the person knowingly or recklessly:

(a) Exhibits an obscene performance to the minor; or

(b) Sells an admission ticket or other means to gain entrance to an obscene performance to the minor; or

(c) Permits the admission of the minor to premises whereon there is exhibited an obscene performance.

(2) No employee is liable to prosecution under this section or under any city or home-rule county ordinance for exhibiting or possessing with intent to exhibit any obscene motion picture provided the employee is acting within the scope of regular employment at a showing open to the public.

(3) As used in this section, "employee" means any person regularly employed by the owner or operator of a motion picture theater if the person has no financial interest other than salary or wages in the ownership or operation of the motion picture theater, no financial interest in or control over the selection of the motion pictures shown in the theater, and is working within the motion picture theater where the person is regularly employed, but does not include a manager of the motion picture theater.

(4) Exhibiting an obscene performance to a minor is a Class A misdemeanor. Notwithstanding ORS 161.635 and 161.655, a person convicted under this section may be sentenced to pay a fine, fixed by the court, not exceeding $10,000.

167.080 Displaying obscene material to minor

(1) A person commits the crime of displaying obscene materials to minors if, being the owner, operator or manager of a business or acting in a managerial capacity, the person knowingly or recklessly permits a minor who is not accompanied by the parent or lawful guardian of the minor to enter or remain on the premises, if in that part of the premises where the minor is so permitted to be, there is visibly displayed:

(a) Any picture, photograph, drawing, sculpture or other visual representation or image of a person or portion of the human body that depicts nudity, sexual conduct, sexual excitement or sadomasochistic abuse; or

(b) Any book, magazine, paperback, pamphlet or other written or printed matter, however reproduced, that reveals a person or portion of the human body that depicts nudity, sexual conduct, sexual excitement or sadomasochistic abuse.

(2) Displaying obscene materials to minors is a Class A misdemeanor. Notwithstanding ORS 161.635 and 161.655, a person convicted under this section may be sentenced to pay a fine, fixed by the court, not exceeding $10,000.

167.085 Defenses–Obscenity

In any prosecution under ORS 167.075 and 167.080, it is an affirmative defense for the defendant to prove:

(1) That the defendant was in a parental or guardianship relationship with the minor;

(2) That the defendant was a bona fide school, museum or public library, or was acting in the course of employment as an employee of such organization or of a retail outlet affiliated with and serving the educational purpose of such organization;

(3) That the defendant was charged with furnishing, showing, exhibiting or displaying an item, those portions of which might otherwise be contraband forming merely an incidental part of an otherwise nonoffending whole, and serving some purpose therein other than titillation; or

(4) That the defendant had reasonable cause to believe that the person involved was not a minor.

167.090 Publicly displaying nudity or sex for advertising purposes

(1) A person commits the crime of publicly displaying nudity or sex for advertising purposes if, for advertising purposes, the person knowingly:
  (a) Displays publicly or causes to be displayed publicly a picture, photograph, drawing, sculpture or other visual representation or image of a person or portion of the human body that depicts nudity, sadomasochistic abuse, sexual conduct or sexual excitement, or any page, poster or other written or printed matter bearing such representation or a verbal description or narrative account of such items or activities, or any obscenities; or
  (b) Permits any display described in this section on premises owned, rented or operated by the person.
(2) Publicly displaying nudity or sex for advertising purposes is a Class A misdemeanor.

167.095 Defenses–Publicly displaying nudity

In any prosecution for violation of ORS 167.090, it shall be an affirmative defense for the defendant to prove:
(1) That the public display, even though in connection with a commercial venture, was primarily for artistic purposes or as a public service; or
(2) That the public display was of nudity, exhibited by a bona fide art, antique or similar gallery or exhibition, and visible in a normal display setting.

167.108 Definitions–Internet gambling

As used in ORS 167.109 and 167.112:
(1) "Credit" and "credit card" have the meaning given those terms under the federal Consumer Credit Protection Act (P.L. 90-321, 82 Stat. 146, 15 U.S.C. 1601).
(2) "Electronic funds transfer" has the meaning given that term in ORS 293.525.
(3) "Financial institution" has the meaning given that term in ORS 706.008.
(4) "Money transmission" has the meaning given that term in ORS 717.200.

167.109 Internet gambling

(1) A person engaged in an Internet gambling business may not knowingly accept, in connection with the participation of another person in unlawful gambling using the Internet:
  (a) Credit, or the proceeds of credit, extended to or on behalf of such other person, including credit extended through the use of a credit card;
  (b) An electronic funds transfer or funds transmitted by or through a money transmission business, or the proceeds of an electronic

funds transfer or money transmission service, from or on behalf of the other person;

(c) Any check, draft or similar instrument that is drawn by or on behalf of the other person and is drawn on or payable at or through any financial institution; or

(d) The proceeds of any other form of financial transaction that involves a financial institution as a payor or financial intermediary on behalf of or for the benefit of the other person.

(2) Violation of subsection (1) of this section is a Class C felony.

167.117 Definitions–Gambling

As used in ORS 167.108 to 167.164 and 464.270 to 464.530, unless the context requires otherwise:

(1) "Bingo or lotto" means a game, played with cards bearing lines of numbers, in which a player covers or uncovers a number selected from a container, and which is won by a player who is present during the game and who first covers or uncovers the selected numbers in a designated combination, sequence or pattern.

(2) "Bookmaker" means a person who unlawfully accepts a bet from a member of the public upon the outcome of a future contingent event and who charges or accepts a percentage, fee or vigorish on the wager.

(3) "Bookmaking" means promoting gambling by unlawfully accepting bets from members of the public as a business, rather than in a casual or personal fashion, upon the outcomes of future contingent events.

(4) "Casino game" means any of the traditional gambling-based games commonly known as dice, faro, monte, roulette, fan-tan, twenty-one, blackjack, Texas hold-'em, seven-and-a-half, big injun, klondike, craps, poker, chuck-a-luck, Chinese chuck-a-luck (dai shu), wheel of fortune, chemin de fer, baccarat, pai gow, beat the banker, panquinqui, red dog, acey-deucey, or any other gambling-based game similar in form or content.

(5)(a) "Charitable, fraternal or religious organization" means any person that is:

(A) Organized and existing for charitable, benevolent, eleemosynary, humane, patriotic, religious, philanthropic, recreational, social, educational, civic, fraternal or other nonprofit purposes; and

(B) Exempt from payment of federal income taxes because of its charitable, fraternal or religious purposes.

(b) The fact that contributions to an organization profiting from a contest of chance do not qualify for a charitable deduction for tax purposes or that the organization is not otherwise exempt from payment of federal income taxes pursuant to the Internal Revenue Code of 1986, as amended, constitutes prima facie evidence that the organization is not a bona fide charitable, fraternal or religious organization.

(6) "Contest of chance" means any contest, game, gaming scheme or gaming device in which the outcome depends in a material degree upon an

element of chance, notwithstanding that skill of the contestants may also be a factor therein.

(7) "Gambling" means that a person stakes or risks something of value upon the outcome of a contest of chance or a future contingent event not under the control or influence of the person, upon an agreement or understanding that the person or someone else will receive something of value in the event of a certain outcome. "Gambling" does not include:

(a) Bona fide business transactions valid under the law of contracts for the purchase or sale at a future date of securities or commodities, and agreements to compensate for loss caused by the happening of chance, including but not limited to contracts of indemnity or guaranty and life, health or accident insurance.

(b) Engaging in contests of chance under the following conditions:
  (A) The contest is played for some token other than money;
  (B) An individual contestant may not purchase more than $100 worth of tokens for use in the contest during any 24-hour period;
  (C) The tokens may be exchanged only for property other than money;
  (D) Except when the tokens are exchanged for a beverage or merchandise to be consumed on the premises, the tokens are not redeemable on the premises where the contest is conducted or within 50 miles thereof; and
  (E) Except for charitable, fraternal or religious organizations, no person who conducts the contest as owner, agent or employee profits in any manner from operation of the contest.

(c) Social games.

(d) Bingo, lotto or raffle games or Monte Carlo events operated in compliance with ORS 167.118, by a charitable, fraternal or religious organization licensed pursuant to ORS 167.118, 464.250 to 464.380 and 464.420 to 464.530 to operate such games.

(8) "Gambling device" means any device, machine, paraphernalia or equipment that is used or usable in the playing phases of unlawful gambling, whether it consists of gambling between persons or gambling by a person involving the playing of a machine. Lottery tickets, policy slips and other items used in the playing phases of lottery and policy schemes are not gambling devices within this definition. Amusement devices other than gray machines, that do not return to the operator or player thereof anything but free additional games or plays, shall not be considered to be gambling devices.

(9)(a) "Gray machine" means any electrical or electromechanical device, whether or not it is in working order or some act of manipulation, repair, adjustment or modification is required to render it operational, that:
  (A) Awards credits or contains or is readily adaptable to contain, a circuit, meter or switch capable of removing or recording the removal of credits earned by a player, other than removal during the course of continuous play; or
  (B) Plays, emulates or simulates a casino game, bingo or keno.

(b) A device is no less a gray machine because, apart from its use or adaptability as such, it may also sell or deliver something of value on the basis other than chance.

(c) "Gray machine" does not include:

(A) Any device commonly known as a personal computer, including any device designed and marketed solely for home entertainment, when used privately and not for a fee and not used to facilitate any form of gambling;

(B) Any device operated under the authority of the Oregon State Lottery;

(C) Any device manufactured or serviced but not operated in Oregon by a manufacturer who has been approved under rules adopted by the Oregon State Lottery Commission;

(D) A slot machine;

(E) Any device authorized by the Oregon State Lottery Commission for:

(i) Display and demonstration purposes only at trade shows; or

(ii) Training and testing purposes by the Department of State Police; or

(F) Any device used to operate bingo in compliance with ORS 167.118 by a charitable, fraternal or religious organization licensed to operate bingo pursuant to ORS 167.118, 464.250 to 464.380 and 464.420 to 464.530.

(10) "Handle" means the total amount of money and other things of value bet on the bingo, lotto or raffle games, the value of raffle chances sold or the total amount collected from the sale of imitation money during Monte Carlo events.

(11) "Internet" means an interactive computer service or system or an information service, system or access software provider that provides or enables computer access by multiple users to a computer server and includes, but is not limited to, an information service, system or access software provider that provides access to a network system commonly known as the Internet, or any comparable system or service and also includes, but is not limited to a World Wide Web page, newsgroup, message board, mailing list or chat area on any interactive computer service or system or other on-line service.

(12) "Lottery" or "policy" means an unlawful gambling scheme in which:

(a) The players pay or agree to pay something of value for chances, represented and differentiated by numbers or by combinations of numbers or by some other medium, one or more of which chances are to be designated the winning ones;

(b) The winning chances are to be determined by a drawing or by some other method; and

(c) The holders of the winning chances are to receive something of value.

(13) "Monte Carlo event" means a gambling event at which wagers are placed with imitation money upon contests of chance in which players compete against other players or against the house. As used in this subsection, "imitation money" includes imitation currency, chips or tokens.

(14) "Numbers scheme or enterprise" means a form of lottery in which the winning chances or plays are not determined upon the basis of a drawing or other act on the part of persons conducting or connected with the scheme,

but upon the basis of the outcome of a future contingent event otherwise unrelated to the particular scheme.
(15) "Operating expenses" means those expenses incurred in the operation of a bingo, lotto or raffle game, including only the following:
  (a) Salaries, employee benefits, workers' compensation coverage and state and federal employee taxes;
  (b) Security services;
  (c) Legal and accounting services;
  (d) Supplies and inventory;
  (e) Rent, repairs, utilities, water, sewer and garbage;
  (f) Insurance;
  (g) Equipment;
  (h) Printing and promotions;
  (i) Postage and shipping;
  (j) Janitorial services and supplies; and
  (k) Leasehold improvements.
(16) "Player" means a person who engages in any form of gambling solely as a contestant or bettor, without receiving or becoming entitled to receive any profit therefrom other than personal gambling winnings, and without otherwise rendering any material assistance to the establishment, conduct or operation of the particular gambling activity. A person who gambles at a social game of chance on equal terms with the other participants therein is a person who does not otherwise render material assistance to the establishment, conduct or operation thereof by performing, without fee or remuneration, acts directed toward the arrangement or facilitation of the game, such as inviting persons to play, permitting the use of premises therefor and supplying cards or other equipment used therein. A person who engages in bookmaking is not a player.
(17) "Profits from unlawful gambling" means that a person, acting other than solely as a player, accepts or receives money or other property pursuant to an agreement or understanding with another person whereby the person participates or is to participate in the proceeds of unlawful gambling.
(18) "Promotes unlawful gambling" means that a person, acting other than solely as a player, engages in conduct that materially aids any form of unlawful gambling. Conduct of this nature includes, but is not limited to, conduct directed toward the creation or establishment of the particular game, contest, scheme, device or activity involved, toward the acquisition or maintenance of premises, paraphernalia, equipment or apparatus therefor, toward the solicitation or inducement of persons to participate therein, toward the conduct of the playing phases thereof, toward the arrangement of any of its financial or recording phases or toward any other phase of its operation. A person promotes unlawful gambling if, having control or right of control over premises being used with the knowledge of the person for purposes of unlawful gambling, the person permits the unlawful gambling to occur or continue or makes no effort to prevent its occurrence or continuation.

(19) "Raffle" means a lottery operated by a charitable, fraternal or religious organization wherein the players pay something of value for chances, represented by numbers or combinations thereof or by some other medium, one or more of which chances are to be designated the winning ones or determined by a drawing and the player holding the winning chance is to receive something of value.

(20)(a) "Slot machine" means a gambling device that as a result of the insertion of a coin or other object operates, either completely automatically, or with the aid of some physical act by the player, in such a manner that, depending upon elements of chance, it may eject something of value or otherwise entitle the player to something of value. A device so constructed or readily adaptable or convertible to such use is no less a slot machine because it is not in working order or because some mechanical act of manipulation or repair is required to accomplish its adaptation, conversion or workability. Nor is it any less a slot machine because apart from its use or adaptability as such it may also sell or deliver something of value on the basis other than chance.

(b) "Slot machine" does not include any device authorized by the Oregon State Lottery Commission for:

(A) Display and demonstration purposes only at trade shows; or

(B) Training and testing purposes by the Department of State Police.

(21) "Social game" means:

(a) A game, other than a lottery, between players in a private home where no house player, house bank or house odds exist and there is no house income from the operation of the social game; and

(b) If authorized pursuant to ORS 167.121, a game, other than a lottery, between players in a private business, private club or place of public accommodation where no house player, house bank or house odds exist and there is no house income from the operation of the social game.

(22) "Something of value" means any money or property, any token, object or article exchangeable for money or property, or any form of credit or promise directly or indirectly contemplating transfer of money or property or of any interest therein.

(23) "Trade show" means an exhibit of products and services that is:

(a) Not open to the public; and

(b) Of limited duration.

(24) "Unlawful" means not specifically authorized by law.

167.118 Bingo, lotto, raffles or Monte Carlo events by charitable, fraternal or religious organizations

(1) When a charitable, fraternal or religious organization is licensed by the Department of Justice to conduct bingo, lotto or raffle games or Monte Carlo events, only the organization itself or an employee thereof authorized by the department shall receive money or property or otherwise directly profit from the operation of the games, except that:

(a) The organization operating the games may present a prize of money or other property to any player not involved in the administration or management of the games.

(b) An organization licensed to conduct Monte Carlo events may contract with a licensed supplier of Monte Carlo event equipment to operate the event, including the provision of equipment, supplies and personnel, provided that the licensed supplier is paid a fixed fee to conduct the event and the imitation money is sold to players by employees or volunteers of the licensed charitable, fraternal or religious organization.

(c) A person may sell, rent or lease equipment, including electronic equipment, proprietary computer software and real property to a licensed charitable, fraternal or religious organization. Rent or lease payments must be made in compliance with the provisions of ORS 464.510.

(d) An organization licensed by the department may act as an escrow agent to receive money or property to be awarded as prizes.

(2) A charitable, fraternal or religious organization may not operate bingo, lotto or raffle games or Monte Carlo events except at such locations and upon such days and for such periods of time as the department authorizes pursuant to this section and ORS 464.250 to 464.380, 464.420 and 464.450 to 464.530.

(3)(a) An organization licensed by the department to operate bingo or lotto games may not award a prize exceeding $2,500 in value in any one game. An organization licensed by the department to operate a Monte Carlo event may not present any prize of money, or a cash equivalent, to any player.

(b) Notwithstanding any provision of this chapter [Ch. 167] to the contrary, a bingo licensee may operate two games per year with a prize not to exceed $10,000 per game and, if approved by the department, may also participate in a linked progressive game involving only Oregon licensees, without regard to the number of games or the size of the prize awarded.

(4) Each charitable, fraternal or religious organization that maintains, conducts or operates any bingo, lotto or raffle game or Monte Carlo event under license of the department must operate such games in accordance with rules adopted by the department.

(5) It is unlawful for a licensee to permit the operating expenses of the games to exceed 18 percent of the annual handle of its bingo, lotto and raffle operation.

(6) It is unlawful for a charitable, fraternal or religious organization licensed by the department to operate bingo, lotto or raffle games if:

(a) The handle of the games and events exceeds $250,000 in a year; and

(b) The games and events do not generate for the organization's purposes, after the cost of prizes and operating expenses are deducted from the handle, an amount that equals or exceeds five percent of the handle.

167.122 Unlawful gambling in the second degree

(1) A person commits the crime of unlawful gambling in the second degree if the person knowingly:

(a) Places a bet with a bookmaker; or

(b) Participates or engages in unlawful gambling as a player.

(2) Unlawful gambling in the second degree is a Class A misdemeanor.

167.127 Unlawful gambling in the first degree

(1) A person commits the crime of unlawful gambling in the first degree if the person knowingly promotes or profits from unlawful gambling.

(2) Unlawful gambling in the first degree is a Class C felony.

167.132 Possession of gambling records in the second degree

(1) A person commits the crime of possession of gambling records in the second degree if, with knowledge of the contents thereof, the person possesses any writing, paper, instrument or article:
  (a) Of a kind commonly used in the operation or promotion of a bookmaking scheme or enterprise; or
  (b) Of a kind commonly used in the operation, promotion or playing of a lottery or numbers scheme or enterprise.

(2) Possession of gambling records in the second degree is a Class A misdemeanor.

167.137 Possession of gambling records in the first degree

(1) A person commits the crime of possession of gambling records in the first degree if, with knowledge of the contents thereof, the person possesses any writing, paper, instrument or article:
  (a) Of a kind commonly used in the operation or promotion of a bookmaking scheme or enterprise, and constituting, reflecting or representing more than five bets totaling more than $500; or
  (b) Of a kind commonly used in the operation, promotion or playing of a lottery or numbers scheme or enterprise, and constituting, reflecting or representing more than 500 plays or chances therein.

(2) Possession of gambling records in the first degree is a Class C felony.

167.142 Defenses–Possession of gambling records

In any prosecution under ORS 167.132 or 167.137 it is a defense if the writing, paper, instrument or article possessed by the defendant is neither used nor intended to be used in the operation or promotion of a bookmaking scheme or enterprise, or in the operation, promotion or playing of a lottery or numbers scheme or enterprise.

167.147 Possession of a gambling device

(1) A person commits the crime of possession of a gambling device if, with knowledge of the character thereof, the person manufactures, sells, transports, places or possesses, or conducts or negotiates a transaction affecting or designed to affect ownership, custody or use of:
  (a) A slot machine; or
  (b) Any other gambling device, believing that the device is to be used in promoting unlawful gambling activity.
(2) Possession of a gambling device is a Class A misdemeanor.
(3) It is a defense to a charge of possession of a gambling device if the slot machine or gambling device that caused the charge to be brought was manufactured:
  (a) Prior to 1900 and is not operated for purposes of unlawful gambling; or
  (b) More than 25 years before the date on which the charge was brought and:
    (A) Is located in a private residence;
    (B) Is not operated for the purposes of unlawful gambling; and
    (C) Has permanently affixed to it by the manufacturer, the manufacturer's name and either the date of manufacture or the serial number.

167.167 Cheating

(1) A person commits the crime of cheating if the person, while in the course of participating or attempting to participate in any legal or illegal gambling activity, directly or indirectly:
  (a) Employs or attempts to employ any device, scheme or artifice to defraud any other participant or any operator;
  (b) Engages in any act, practice or course of operation that operates or would operate as a fraud or deceit upon any other participant or any operator;
  (c) Engages in any act, practice or course of operation with the intent of cheating any other participant or the operator to gain an advantage in the game over the other participant or operator; or
  (d) Causes, aids, abets or conspires with another person to cause any other person to violate paragraphs (a) to (c) of this subsection.
(2) As used in this section, "deceit," "defraud" and "fraud" are not limited to common law deceit or fraud.
(3) Cheating is a Class C felony.

167.203 Definitions–Controlled substance offenses

As used in ORS 167.212 to 167.252, unless the context requires otherwise:

(1) "Apothecary" means a pharmacist, as defined by ORS 689.005, and where the context so requires, the owner of a store or other place of business where controlled substances are compounded or dispensed by a licensed pharmacist.

(2) "Controlled substance" and "manufacture" have the meaning given those terms by ORS 475.005.

(3) "Official written order" means an order written on a form provided for that purpose by the United States Commissioner of Internal Revenue, under any laws of the United States making provision therefor, if such order form is not provided, then on an official form provided for that purpose by the State Board of Pharmacy.

(4) "Practitioner" has the meaning given that term by ORS 475.005.

(5) "Wholesaler" means a person who supplies controlled substances that the wholesaler has not produced or prepared, on official written orders, but not on prescriptions.

(6) "Unlawfully" means in violation of any provision of ORS 475.005 to 475.285 and 475.840 to 475.980.

167.212 Tampering with drug records

(1) A person commits the crime of tampering with drug records if the person knowingly:

(a) Alters, defaces or removes a controlled substance label affixed by a manufacturer, wholesaler or apothecary, except that it shall not be unlawful for an apothecary to remove or deface such a label for the purpose of filling prescriptions;

(b) Affixes a false or forged label to a package or receptacle containing controlled substances;

(c) Makes or utters a false or forged prescription or false or forged official written order for controlled substances; or

(d) Makes a false statement in any controlled substance prescription, order, report or record required by ORS 475.005 to 475.285 and 475.840 to 475.980.

(2) Tampering with drug records is a Class C felony.

167.222 Frequenting place where controlled substances are used

(1) A person commits the offense of frequenting a place where controlled substances are used if the person keeps, maintains, frequents, or remains at a place, while knowingly permitting persons to use controlled substances in such place or to keep or sell them in violation of ORS 475.005 to 475.285 and 475.840 to 475.980.

(2) Frequenting a place where controlled substances are used is a Class A misdemeanor.

(3) Notwithstanding subsection (2) of this section, if the conviction is for knowingly maintaining, frequenting or remaining at a place where less than one avoirdupois ounce of the dried leaves, stems, and flowers of the plant Cannabis family Moraceae is found at the time of the offense under this section, frequenting a place where controlled substances are used is a Class D violation.

(4) As used in this section, "frequents" means repeatedly or habitually visits, goes to or resorts to.

167.238 Prima facie evidence–Drug offenses

(1) Proof of unlawful manufacture, cultivation, transportation or possession of a controlled substance is prima facie evidence of knowledge of its character.

(2) Proof of possession of a controlled substance not in the container in which it was originally delivered, sold or dispensed, when a prescription or order of a practitioner is required under the provisions of ORS 475.005 to 475.285 and 475.840 to 475.980 is prima facie evidence that the possession is unlawful unless the possessor also has in possession a label prepared by the pharmacist for the drug dispensed or the possessor is authorized by ORS 475.005 to 475.285 and 475.840 to 475.980 to possess the controlled substance.

167.262 Using minor in controlled substance offense

(1) It is unlawful for an adult to knowingly use as an aider or abettor or to knowingly solicit, force, compel, coerce or employ a minor, with or without compensation to the minor:

 (a) To manufacture a controlled substance; or

 (b) To transport, carry, sell, give away, prepare for sale or otherwise distribute a controlled substance.

(2)(a) Except as otherwise provided in paragraph (b) of this subsection, violation of this section is a Class A felony.

 (b) Violation of this section is a Class A misdemeanor if the violation involves delivery for no consideration of less than five grams of marijuana.

167.310 Definitions–Animal offenses
Amended 2009

As used in ORS 167.310 to 167.351:

(1) "Animal" means any nonhuman mammal, bird, reptile, amphibian or fish.

(2) "Domestic animal" means an animal, other than livestock *or equines*, that is owned or possessed by a person.

(3) "Equine" means a horse, pony, donkey, mule, hinny, zebra or a hybrid of any of these animals.

(4) "Good animal husbandry" includes, but is not limited to, the dehorning of cattle, the docking of horses, sheep or swine, and the castration or neutering of livestock, according to accepted practices of veterinary medicine or animal husbandry.

167.312

(5) "Law enforcement animal" means a dog or horse used in law enforcement work under the control of a corrections officer, parole and probation officer, police officer or youth correction officer, as those terms are defined in ORS 181.610, who has successfully completed at least 360 hours of training in the care and use of a law enforcement animal, or who has passed the demonstration of minimum standards established by the Oregon Police Canine Association or other accredited and recognized animal handling organization.

(6) "Livestock" has the meaning provided in ORS 609.125.

(7) "Minimum care" means care sufficient to preserve the health and well-being of an animal and, except for emergencies or circumstances beyond the reasonable control of the owner, includes, but is not limited to, the following requirements:
  (a) Food of sufficient quantity and quality to allow for normal growth or maintenance of body weight.
  (b) Open or adequate access to potable water in sufficient quantity to satisfy the animal's needs. Access to snow or ice is not adequate access to potable water.
  (c) For a domestic animal other than a dog engaged in herding or protecting livestock, access to a barn, dog house or other enclosed structure sufficient to protect the animal from wind, rain, snow or sun and that has adequate bedding to protect against cold and dampness.
  (d) Veterinary care deemed necessary by a reasonably prudent person to relieve distress from injury, neglect or disease.
  (e) For a domestic animal, continuous access to an area:
    (A) With adequate space for exercise necessary for the health of the animal;
    (B) With air temperature suitable for the animal; and
    (C) Kept reasonably clean and free from excess waste or other contaminants that could affect the animal's health.
  (f) For a livestock animal that cannot walk or stand without assistance:
    (A) Humane euthanasia; or
    (B) The provision of immediate and ongoing care to restore the animal to an ambulatory state.

(8) "Physical injury" means physical trauma, impairment of physical condition or substantial pain.

(9) "Physical trauma" means fractures, cuts, punctures, bruises, burns or other wounds.

(10) "Possess" has the meaning provided in ORS 161.015.

(11) "Serious physical injury" means physical injury that creates a substantial risk of death or that causes protracted disfigurement, protracted impairment of health or protracted loss or impairment of the function of a limb or bodily organ.

167.312 Research and animal interference

(1) A person commits the crime of research and animal interference if the person:

(a) With the intent to interfere with research, releases, steals or otherwise causes the death, injury or loss of any animal at or from an animal research facility.

(b) With the intent to interfere with research, damages, vandalizes or steals any property in or on an animal research facility.

(c) With the intent to interfere with research, obtains access to an animal research facility to perform acts not authorized by that facility.

(d) Obtains or exerts unauthorized control over records, data, materials, equipment or animals of any animal research facility with the intent to interfere with research by concealing, abandoning or destroying such records, data, materials, equipment or animals.

(e) With the intent to interfere with research, possesses or uses equipment or animals that the person reasonably believes have been obtained by theft or deception from an animal research facility or without the authorization of an animal research facility.

(2) For the purposes of this section, "animal research facility" means any facility engaging in legal scientific research or teaching involving the use of animals.

(3) Research and animal interference is a:
  (a) Class C felony if damage to the animal research facility is $2,500 or more; or
  (b) Class A misdemeanor if there is no damage to the facility or if damage to the animal research facility is less than $2,500.

(4) Determination of damages to an animal research facility shall be made by the court. In making its determination, the court shall consider the reasonable costs of:
  (a) Replacing lost, injured or destroyed animals;
  (b) Restoring the animal research facility to the approximate condition of the facility before the damage occurred; and
  (c) Replacing damaged or missing records, data, material or equipment.

(5) In addition to any other penalty imposed for violation of this section, a person convicted of such violation is liable:
  (a) To the owner of the animal for damages, including the costs of restoring the animal to confinement and to its health condition prior to commission of the acts constituting the violation;
  (b) For damages to real and personal property caused by acts constituting the violation; and
  (c) For the costs of repeating an experiment, including the replacement of the animals, labor and materials, if acts constituting the violation cause the failure of an experiment.

167.315 Animal abuse in the second degree

(1) A person commits the crime of animal abuse in the second degree if, except as otherwise authorized by law, the person intentionally, knowingly or recklessly causes physical injury to an animal.
(2) Any practice of good animal husbandry is not a violation of this section.
(3) Animal abuse in the second degree is a Class B misdemeanor.

167.320 Animal abuse in the first degree

(1) A person commits the crime of animal abuse in the first degree if, except as otherwise authorized by law, the person intentionally, knowingly or recklessly:
   (a) Causes serious physical injury to an animal; or
   (b) Cruelly causes the death of an animal.
(2) Any practice of good animal husbandry is not a violation of this section.
(3) Animal abuse in the first degree is a Class A misdemeanor.
(4) Notwithstanding subsection (3) of this section, animal abuse in the first degree is a Class C felony if:
   (a) The person committing the animal abuse has previously been convicted of two or more of the following offenses:
      (A) Any offense under ORS 163.160, 163.165, 163.175, 163.185 or 163.187 or the equivalent laws of another jurisdiction, if the offense involved domestic violence as defined in ORS 135.230 or the offense was committed against a minor child; or
      (B) Any offense under this section or ORS 167.322, or the equivalent laws of another jurisdiction; or
   (b) The person knowingly commits the animal abuse in the immediate presence of a minor child. For purposes of this paragraph, a minor child is in the immediate presence of animal abuse if the abuse is seen or directly perceived in any other manner by the minor child.

167.322 Aggravated animal abuse in the first degree

(1) A person commits the crime of aggravated animal abuse in the first degree if the person:
   (a) Maliciously kills an animal; or
   (b) Intentionally or knowingly tortures an animal.
(2) Aggravated animal abuse in the first degree is a Class C felony.
(3) As used in this section:
   (a) "Maliciously" means intentionally acting with a depravity of mind and reckless and wanton disregard of life.
   (b) "Torture" means an action taken for the primary purpose of inflicting pain.

167.325 Animal neglect in the second degree

(1) A person commits the crime of animal neglect in the second degree if, except as otherwise authorized by law, the person intentionally, knowingly, recklessly or with criminal negligence fails to provide minimum care for an animal in such person's custody or control.

(2) Animal neglect in the second degree is a Class B misdemeanor.

167.330 Animal neglect in the first degree

(1) A person commits the crime of animal neglect in the first degree if, except as otherwise authorized by law, the person intentionally, knowingly, recklessly or with criminal negligence fails to provide minimum care for an animal in the person's custody or control and the failure to provide care results in serious physical injury or death to the animal.

(2) Animal neglect in the first degree is a Class A misdemeanor.

167.332 Domestic animal possession restrictions *Amended 2009*

(1) In addition to any other penalty imposed by law, a person convicted of violating ORS 167.315, 167.325, 167.330, *167.333,* 167.340 *or 167.355* or of a misdemeanor under ORS 167.320, may not possess a domestic animal for a period of five years following entry of the conviction.

(2) In addition to any other penalty imposed by law, a person convicted of violating ORS 167.322, *167.365 or 167.428* or of a felony under ORS 167.320, may not possess a domestic animal for a period of 15 years following entry of the conviction.

(3) A person who possesses a domestic animal in violation of this section commits a Class C misdemeanor. When a person is convicted of possessing a domestic animal in violation of this section, the court may order the removal of domestic animals from the person's residence.

167.333 Sexual assault of animal

(1) A person commits the crime of sexual assault of an animal if the person:

(a) Touches or contacts, or causes an object or another person to touch or contact, the mouth, anus or sex organs of an animal or animal carcass for the purpose of arousing or gratifying the sexual desire of a person; or

(b) Causes an animal or animal carcass to touch or contact the mouth, anus or sex organs of a person for the purpose of arousing or gratifying the sexual desire of a person.

(2) Subsection (1) of this section does not apply to the use of products derived from animals.

(3) Sexual assault of an animal is a Class A misdemeanor.

167.335 Exemptions–Animal offenses

Unless gross negligence can be shown, the provisions of ORS 167.315 to 167.333 do not apply to:

(1) The treatment of livestock being transported by owner or common carrier;
(2) Animals involved in rodeos or similar exhibitions;
(3) Commercially grown poultry;
(4) Animals subject to good animal husbandry practices;
(5) The killing of livestock according to the provisions of ORS 603.065;
(6) Animals subject to good veterinary practices as described in ORS 686.030;
(7) Lawful fishing, hunting and trapping activities;
(8) Wildlife management practices under color of law;
(9) Lawful scientific or agricultural research or teaching that involves the use of animals;
(10) Reasonable activities undertaken in connection with the control of vermin or pests; and
(11) Reasonable handling and training techniques.

167.337 Interfering with law enforcement animal
Amended 2009

(1) A person commits the crime of interfering with a law enforcement animal if the person intentionally or knowingly injures or attempts to injure an animal the person knows or reasonably should know is a law enforcement animal while the law enforcement animal is being used in the lawful discharge of its duty.

(2) Interfering with a law enforcement animal is a Class A misdemeanor.

(3) When a person is convicted of interfering with a law enforcement animal, in addition to any other sentence the court may impose, the court shall impose a fine in the amount of $500.

167.339 Assaulting law enforcement animal
Amended 2009

(1) A person commits the crime of assaulting a law enforcement animal if:

(a) The person knowingly causes serious physical injury to or the death of a law enforcement animal, knowing that the animal is a law enforcement animal; and

(b) The injury or death occurs while the law enforcement animal is being used in the lawful discharge of the animal's duties.

(2) Assaulting a law enforcement animal is a Class C felony.

(3) When a person is convicted of assaulting a law enforcement animal, in addition to any other sentence the court may impose, the court shall impose a fine in the amount of $1,000.

167.340 Animal abandonment   *Amended 2009*

(1) A person commits the crime of animal abandonment if the person intentionally, knowingly, recklessly or with criminal negligence leaves a domestic animal *or an equine* at a location without providing *minimum* care.

(2) It is no defense to the crime defined in subsection (1) of this section that the defendant abandoned the animal at or near an animal shelter, veterinary clinic or other place of shelter if the defendant did not make reasonable arrangements for the care of the animal.

(3) Animal abandonment is a Class B misdemeanor.

167.352 Interfering with assistance, search and rescue or therapy animal

(1) A person commits the crime of interfering with an assistance, a search and rescue or a therapy animal if the person intentionally or knowingly:

(a) Injures or attempts to injure an animal the person knows or reasonably should know is an assistance animal, a search and rescue animal or a therapy animal;

(b) Interferes with an assistance animal while the assistance animal is being used to provide assistance to a person with a physical impairment; or

(c) Interferes with a search and rescue animal or a therapy animal while the animal is being used for search and rescue or therapy purposes.

(2) As used in this section, "assistance animal" and "person with a physical impairment" have the meanings given those terms in ORS 346.680.

(3) As used in this section and ORS 30.822:

(a) "Search and rescue animal" means that the animal has been professionally trained for, and is actively used for, search and rescue purposes.

(b) "Therapy animal" means that the animal has been professionally trained for, and is actively used for, therapy purposes.

(4) Interfering with an assistance, a search and rescue or a therapy animal is a Class A misdemeanor.

167.355 Involvement in animal fighting Amended 2009

(1) A person commits the crime of involvement in animal fighting if the person:
  (a) Owns or trains an animal with the intention that the animal engage in an exhibition of fighting;
  (b) Promotes, conducts, participates in or is present as a spectator at an exhibition of fighting or preparations thereto;
  (c) Keeps or uses, or in any way is connected with or interested in the management of, or receives money for the admission of any person to any place kept or used for the purpose of an exhibition of fighting; or
  (d) Knowingly suffers or permits any place over which the person has possession or control to be occupied, kept or used for the purpose of an exhibition of fighting.
(2) For purposes of this section:
  (a) "Animal" means any bird, reptile, amphibian, fish or nonhuman mammal, other than a dog or a fighting bird as defined in ORS 167.426.
  (b) "Exhibition of fighting" means a public or private display of combat between two or more animals in which the fighting, killing, maiming or injuring of animals is a significant feature. "Exhibition of fighting" does not include demonstrations of the hunting or tracking skills of an animal or the lawful use of animals for hunting, tracking or self-protection.
(3) Involvement in animal fighting is a *Class C felony*.

167.360 Definitions–Dogfighting Amended 2008

As used in ORS 167.360 to 167.375:
(1) "Breaking stick" means a device designed for insertion behind the molars of a dog for the purpose of breaking the dog's grip on another animal or object.
(2) "Cat mill" means a device that rotates around a central support with one arm designed to secure a dog and one arm designed to secure a cat, rabbit or other small animal beyond the grasp of the dog.
(3) "Dogfight" means a fight, arranged by any person, between two or more dogs the purpose or probable result of which fight is the infliction of injury by one dog upon another.
(4) "Dogfighting paraphernalia" means:
  (a) A breaking stick;
  (b) A springpole;
  (c) A cat mill;
  (d) A treadmill;
  (e) A fighting pit;
  (f) A leather or mesh collar with a strap more than two inches in width;
  (g) A weighted or unweighted chain collar weighing 10 pounds or more; or

(h) An unprescribed veterinary medicine that is a prescription drug as defined in ORS 689.005.

(5) "Fighting dog" means a dog that is intentionally bred or trained to be used in, or that is actually used in, a dogfight. A dog does not constitute a fighting dog solely on account of its breed.

(6) "Fighting pit" means a walled area designed to contain a dogfight.

(7) "Springpole" means a biting surface attached to a stretchable device, suspended at a height sufficient to prevent a dog from reaching the biting surface while touching the ground.

(8) "Treadmill" means:
  (a) A carpet mill made of narrow sections of carpet;
  (b) A modified electric treadmill for the purpose of conditioning dogs; or
  (c) A slat mill with a running surface constructed of slats made of wood, fiberglass, plastic or other similar material.

Note: *This section was amended in the 2008 Special Session.*

167.365 Dogfighting

(1) A person commits the crime of dogfighting if the person knowingly does any of the following:
  (a) Owns, possesses, keeps, breeds, trains, buys, sells or offers to sell a fighting dog, including but not limited to any advertisement by the person to sell such a dog.
  (b) Promotes, conducts or participates in, or performs any service in the furtherance of, an exhibition of dogfighting, including but not limited to refereeing of a dogfight, handling of dogs at a dogfight, transportation of spectators to a dogfight, organizing a dogfight, advertising a dogfight, providing or serving as a stakes holder for any money wagered on a fight.
  (c) Keeps, uses or manages, or accepts payment of admission to, any place kept or used for the purpose of dogfighting.
  (d) Suffers or permits any place over which the person has possession or control to be occupied, kept or used for the purpose of an exhibition of dogfighting.

(2) Dogfighting is a Class C felony.

167.370 Participation in dogfighting
Amended 2008

(1) A person commits the crime of participation in dogfighting if the person knowingly:
  (a) Attends or has paid admission at any place for the purpose of viewing or betting upon a dogfight.

(b) Advertises or otherwise offers to sell equipment *that the person knows or reasonably should know will be used* for the *purpose of* training and handling a fighting dog.
(2) Participation in dogfighting is a *Class C felony*.
Note: *This section was amended in the 2008 Special Session.*

167.372 Possessing dogfighting paraphernalia Amended 2008

(1) A person commits the crime of possessing dogfighting paraphernalia if the person owns or possesses dogfighting paraphernalia with the intent that the paraphernalia be used to train a dog as a fighting dog or be used in the furtherance of a dogfight.
(2) Possessing dogfighting paraphernalia is a *Class C felony*.
Note: *This section was amended in the 2008 Special Session.*

167.385 Unauthorized use of livestock animal

(1) A person commits the crime of unauthorized use of a livestock animal when the person knowingly:
  (a) Takes, appropriates, obtains or withholds a livestock animal from the owner thereof or derives benefit from a livestock animal without the consent of the owner of the animal; or
  (b) Takes or holds a livestock animal and thereby obtains the use of the animal to breed, bear or raise offspring without the consent of the owner of the animal.
(2) Except as otherwise provided by law, offspring born to a female livestock animal or hatched from the egg of a female livestock animal belong to the owner of the female livestock animal until the owner transfers ownership of the offspring.
(3) As used in this section, "livestock animal" has the same meaning given that term in ORS 164.055.
(4) Unauthorized use of a livestock animal is a Class A misdemeanor.
(5) In addition to any criminal sanctions, if a defendant is convicted of the crime of unauthorized use of a livestock animal under this section, the court shall order the defendant to pay restitution to the owner of the animal.

167.387 Definitions–Interference with livestock production

As used in this section and ORS 167.388:
(1) "Livestock" has the meaning given in ORS 609.125.
(2) "Livestock production facility" means:
  (a) Any facility or organization engaged in animal breeding, production or processing; or
  (b) Any facility or institution whose primary purpose is to impound estray animals, as that term is defined in ORS 607.007.

167.388 Interference with livestock production

(1) A person commits the crime of interference with livestock production when the person, with the intent to interfere with livestock production:
  (a) Takes, appropriates, obtains or withholds livestock from the owner thereof, or causes the loss, death or injury of any livestock maintained at a livestock production facility;
  (b) Damages, vandalizes or steals any property located on a livestock production facility; or
  (c) Obtains access to a livestock production facility to perform any act contained in this subsection or any other act not authorized by the livestock production facility.
(2) The crime of interference with livestock production is:
  (a) A Class C felony if damage to the livestock production facility is $2,500 or more; or
  (b) A Class A misdemeanor if there is no damage to the livestock production facility or if damage to the facility is less than $2,500.
(3) Determination of damages to a livestock production facility shall be made by the court. In making its determination, the court shall consider the reasonable costs of:
  (a) Replacing lost, injured or destroyed livestock;
  (b) Restoring the livestock production facility to the approximate condition of the facility before the damage occurred; and
  (c) Replacing damaged or missing records, data, material, equipment or substances used in the breeding and production of livestock.
(4) In addition to any criminal sanctions, if a defendant is convicted of the crime of interference with livestock production under subsection (1) of this section, the court shall order the defendant to pay restitution to the owner of the animal or the owner of the livestock production facility.

Note: For the purposes of this section, pursuant to ORS 167.387 and 609.125; "'livestock' means ratites, psittacines, horses, mules, jackasses, cattle, llamas, alpacas, sheep, goats, swine, domesticated fowl and any fur-bearing animal bred and maintained commercially or otherwise, within pens, cages and hutches."

167.400 Tobacco possession by minors

(1) It is unlawful for any person under 18 years of age to possess tobacco products, as defined in ORS 431.840.
(2) Any person who violates subsection (1) of this section commits a Class D violation.

167.401 Tobacco purchase by minors

(1) Except as provided in subsection (4) of this section, no person under 18 years of age shall purchase, attempt to purchase or

acquire tobacco products as defined in ORS 431.840. Except when such minor is in a private residence accompanied by the parent or guardian of the minor and with the consent of such parent or guardian, no person under 18 years of age shall have personal possession of tobacco products.

(2) Any person who violates subsection (1) of this section commits a violation.

(3)(a) In lieu of any other penalty established by law, a person who is convicted for the first time of a violation of subsection (1) of this section may be ordered to participate in a tobacco education program or a tobacco use cessation program or to perform community service related to diseases associated with consumption of tobacco products. A person may be ordered to participate in such a program only once.

(b) In addition to and not in lieu of any other penalty established by law, a person who is convicted of a second violation of subsection (1) of this section through misrepresentation of age may be required to participate in a tobacco education or a tobacco use cessation program or to perform community service related to diseases associated with the consumption of tobacco products, and the court shall order that the person's driving privileges and right to apply for driving privileges be suspended for a period not to exceed one year. If a court has issued an order denying driving privileges under this subsection, the court, upon petition of the person, may withdraw the order at any time the court deems appropriate. The court notification to the Department of Transportation under this subsection may include a recommendation that the person be granted a hardship permit under ORS 807.240 if the person is otherwise eligible for the permit.

(4) A minor acting under the supervision of an adult may purchase, attempt to purchase or acquire tobacco products for the purpose of testing compliance with a federal law, state statute, local law or retailer management policy limiting or regulating the delivery of tobacco products to minors.

167.426 Definitions–Cockfighting

As used in ORS 167.426 to 167.439:

(1) "Cockfight" means a fight between two or more birds that is arranged by a person and that has the purpose or probable result of one bird inflicting injury to another bird.

(2) "Constructive possession" means an exercise of dominion and control over the location and treatment of property without taking physical possession of the property.

(3) "Fighting bird" means a bird that is intentionally reared or trained for use in, or that actually is used in, a cockfight.

(4) "Gaff" means an artificial steel spur designed for attachment to the leg of a fighting bird in replacement of the bird's natural spurs.

(5) "Slasher" means a steel weapon resembling a curved knife blade designed for attachment to the foot of a fighting bird.

Amended 2009

167.428 Cockfighting

(1) A person commits the crime of cockfighting if the person knowingly:
  (a) Owns, possesses, keeps, rears, trains, buys, sells or advertises or otherwise offers to sell a fighting bird.
  (b) Promotes or participates in, or performs services in furtherance of, the conducting of a cockfight. As used in this paragraph, "services in furtherance" includes, but is not limited to, transporting spectators to a cockfight, handling fighting birds, organizing, advertising or refereeing a cockfight and providing, or acting as stakeholder for, money wagered on a cockfight.
  (c) Keeps, uses or manages, or accepts payment of admission to, a place for the conducting of a cockfight.
  (d) Suffers or permits a place in the possession or control of the person to be occupied, kept or used for the conducting of a cockfight.
  (e) Manufactures, buys, sells, barters, exchanges, possesses, advertises or otherwise offers to sell a gaff, slasher or other sharp implement designed for attachment to a fighting bird with the intent that the gaff, slasher or other sharp implement be used in cockfighting.

(2) Subsection (1)(a) of this section does not apply to the owning, possessing, keeping, rearing, buying, selling, advertising or otherwise offering for sale of a bird for purposes other than training the bird as a fighting bird, using or intending to use the bird in cockfighting or supplying the bird knowing that the bird is intended to be used in cockfighting.

(3) Cockfighting is a Class C felony.

167.431 Participation in cockfighting
Amended 2009

(1) A person commits the crime of participation in cockfighting if the person knowingly:
  (a) Attends a cockfight or pays admission at any location to view or bet on a cockfight; or
  (b) Manufactures, buys, sells, barters, exchanges, possesses, advertises or otherwise offers to sell equipment with the intent that the equipment be used in training or handling a fighting bird or for enhancing the fighting ability of a fighting bird. This paragraph does not apply to a gaff, slasher or other sharp implement designed for attachment to a fighting bird.

(2) Participation in cockfighting is a ***Class C felony***.

167.808 Possession and use of inhalants

(1) For the purposes of this section:
  (a) "Inhalant" means any glue, cement or other substance that is capable of causing intoxication and that contains one or more of the following chemical compounds:
    (A) Acetone;
    (B) Amyl acetate;
    (C) Benzol or benzene;
    (D) Butane;
    (E) Butyl acetate;
    (F) Butyl alcohol;
    (G) Carbon tetrachloride;
    (H) Chloroform;
    (I) Cyclohexanone;
    (J) Difluoroethane;
    (K) Ethanol or ethyl alcohol;
    (L) Ethyl acetate;
    (M) Hexane;
    (N) Isopropanol or isopropyl alcohol;
    (O) Isopropyl acetate;
    (P) Methyl cellosolve acetate;
    (Q) Methyl ethyl ketone;
    (R) Methyl isobutyl ketone;
    (S) Nitrous oxide;
    (T) Toluol or toluene;
    (U) Trichloroethylene;
    (V) Tricresyl phosphate;
    (W) Xylol or xylene; or
    (X) Any other solvent, material, substance, chemical or combination thereof having the property of releasing toxic vapors or fumes.
  (b) "Intoxication" means any mental or physical impairment or incapacity.
(2) It is unlawful for a person to possess any inhalant if the person intends to use the inhalant for the purpose of inducing intoxication in the person who possesses the inhalant or for the purpose of inducing intoxication in any other person.
(3) A person may not use any inhalant for the purpose of inducing intoxication in the person using the inhalant or for the purpose of inducing intoxication in any other person.
(4) The prohibitions of this section do not apply to any substance that:
  (a) Has been prescribed by a health practitioner, as described in ORS 31.740, and that is used in the manner prescribed by the health practitioner; or
  (b) Is administered or used under the supervision of a health practitioner, as described in ORS 31.740.

(5)(a) Any person who violates this section commits a violation. Violation of this section is punishable by a fine of not more than $300. In addition to or in lieu of a fine, a juvenile court may require that a minor who engages in conduct prohibited by this section be provided with treatment and counseling.
  (b) Notwithstanding paragraph (a) of this subsection, a second or subsequent violation of this section by a person is a Class B misdemeanor. If a juvenile court finds that a minor has engaged in conduct prohibited by this section on a second or subsequent occasion, the court shall require that the minor receive treatment and counseling.

167.810 Creating a hazard

(1) A person commits the crime of creating a hazard if:
  (a) The person intentionally maintains or leaves in a place accessible to children a container with a compartment of more than one and one-half cubic feet capacity and a door or lid which locks or fastens automatically when closed and which cannot easily be opened from the inside; or
  (b) Being the owner or otherwise having possession of property upon which there is a well, cistern, cesspool, excavation or other hole of a depth of four feet or more and a top width of 12 inches or more, the owner intentionally fails or refuses to cover or fence it with a suitable protective construction.
(2) Creating a hazard is a Class B misdemeanor.

167.830 Employment of minors in place of public entertainment

Except as provided in ORS 167.840, any person operating or conducting a place of public amusement or entertainment, who employs or allows a child under the age of 18 years to conduct or assist in conducting any public dance, including but not limited to dancing by the child as a public performance, or to assist in or furnish music for public dancing, commits a Class D violation.

167.840 Application of ORS 167.830 limited

(1) ORS 167.830 does not apply if:
  (a) Alcoholic beverages are not permitted to be dispensed or consumed in the place of public amusement or entertainment open to the individuals attending the public dance;
  (b) Alcoholic beverages are not permitted to be dispensed or consumed in any place connected by an entrance to the place of public amusement or entertainment;
  (c) Applicable laws, regulations and ordinances for the protection of children under the age of 18 years are observed in the conduct of the dance; and

(d) At least one responsible adult is present at all times during the public dance to see that applicable laws, regulations and ordinances for the protection of children under 18 years of age are observed.

(2) ORS 167.830 does not apply if the child has the written permission of the judge of the juvenile court, for the county in which the child resides, to conduct or assist in conducting the public dance. The judge of the juvenile court shall grant such permission only if:

(a) The parents or legal guardians of the child have consented to the child's participation in such activity; and

(b) The judge has found that participation in such activity will not be inconsistent with the health, safety and morals of the child.

(3) This section is not intended to make lawful any activity that is prohibited within a political subdivision of this state by ordinance or other regulation of the political subdivision.

(4) The requirements of this section are in addition to, and not in lieu of, the requirements of ORS 653.315.

181.594 Definitions–Sex offender registration
Amended 2009

As used in *this section and* ORS 181.595, 181.596, 181.597, 181.603, *181.826, 181.830 and 181.833*:

(1) "Another United States court" means a federal court, a military court, the tribal court of a federally recognized Indian tribe or a court of:

(a) A state other than Oregon;

(b) The District of Columbia;

(c) The Commonwealth of Puerto Rico;

(d) Guam;

(e) American Samoa;

(f) The Commonwealth of the Northern Mariana Islands; or

(g) The United States Virgin Islands.

(2) "Attends" means is enrolled on a full-time or part-time basis.

(3)(a) "Correctional facility" means any place used for the confinement of persons:

(A) Charged with or convicted of a crime or otherwise confined under a court order.

(B) Found to be within the jurisdiction of the juvenile court for having committed an act that if committed by an adult would constitute a crime.

(b) "Correctional facility" applies to a state hospital or a secure intensive community inpatient facility only as to persons detained therein charged with or convicted of a crime, or detained therein after being found guilty except for insanity under ORS 161.290 to 161.370.

(4) "Institution of higher education" means a public or private educational institution that provides a program of post-secondary education.

(5) "Sex crime" means:

(a) Rape in any degree;

(b) Sodomy in any degree;

(c) Unlawful sexual penetration in any degree;
(d) Sexual abuse in any degree;
(e) Incest with a child victim;
(f) Using a child in a display of sexually explicit conduct;
(g) Encouraging child sexual abuse in any degree;
(h) Transporting child pornography into the state;
(i) Paying for viewing a child's sexually explicit conduct;
(j) Compelling prostitution;
(k) Promoting prostitution;
(L) Kidnapping in the first degree if the victim was under 18 years of age;
(m) Contributing to the sexual delinquency of a minor;
(n) Sexual misconduct if the offender is at least 18 years of age;
(o) Possession of materials depicting sexually explicit conduct of a child in the first degree;
(p) Kidnapping in the second degree if the victim was under 18 years of age, except by a parent or by a person found to be within the jurisdiction of the juvenile court;
(q) Online sexual corruption of a child in any degree if the offender reasonably believed the child to be more than five years younger than the offender;
(r) Any attempt to commit any of the crimes set forth in paragraphs (a) to (q) of this subsection;
(s) Burglary, when committed with intent to commit any of the offenses listed in paragraphs (a) to (q) or (t) of this subsection; or
(t) Public indecency or private indecency, if the person has a prior conviction for a crime listed in this subsection.

(6) "Sex offender" means a person who:
(a) Has been convicted of a sex crime;
(b) Has been found guilty except for insanity of a sex crime;
(c) Has been found to be within the jurisdiction of the juvenile court for having committed an act that if committed by an adult would constitute a sex crime;
(d) Is paroled to this state under ORS 144.610 after being convicted in another **United States court** of a crime that would constitute a sex crime if committed in this state; **or**
(e) Is paroled to or otherwise placed in this state after having been found by another United States court to have committed an act while the person was under 18 years of age that would constitute a sex crime if committed in this state by an adult.

(7) "Works" or "carries on a vocation" means full-time or part-time employment for more than 14 days within one calendar year whether financially compensated, volunteered or for the purpose of governmental or educational benefit.

181.599 Failure to report as sex offender
Amended 2009

(1) A person who is required to report as a sex offender **under ORS 181.595, 181.596 or 181.597** and who has knowledge of the

reporting requirement commits the crime of failure to report as a sex offender if the person:
(a) *Fails to* make the initial report to *an* agency;
(b) *Fails to* report when the person works at, carries on a vocation at or attends an institution of higher education;
(c) *Fails to* report following a change of school enrollment or employment status, including enrollment, employment or vocation status at an institution of higher education;
(d) Moves to a new residence and fails to report the move and the person's new address;
(e) Fails to make an annual report;
(f) Fails to provide complete and accurate information;
(g) Fails to sign the sex offender registration form as required; or
(h) Fails to submit to fingerprinting or to having a photograph taken of the person's face, identifying scars, marks or tattoos.
(2) Except as otherwise provided in subsection (3) of this section, failure to report as a sex offender is a Class A misdemeanor.
(3) Failure to report as a sex offender is a Class C felony if the person violates:
(a) Subsection (1)(a) of this section; or
(b) Subsection (1)(b), *(c), (d) or (g)* of this section and the crime for which the person is required to report is a felony.
(4) A person who fails to sign and return an address verification form as required by ORS 181.598 (2) commits a violation.

471.410 Providing liquor to minor or intoxicated person–Allowing consumption by minor Amended 2009

(1) *A person may not* sell, give or otherwise make available any alcoholic liquor to any person who is visibly intoxicated.
(2) No one other than the person's parent or guardian *may* sell, give or otherwise make available any alcoholic liquor to a person under the age of 21 years. *A parent or guardian may give or otherwise make alcoholic liquor available to a person under the age of 21 years only if the person is in a private residence and is accompanied by the parent or guardian.* A person violates this subsection who sells, gives or otherwise makes available alcoholic liquor to a person with the knowledge that the person to whom the liquor is made available will violate this subsection.
(3)*(a) A* person who exercises control over private real property may *not* knowingly allow any other person under the age of 21 years who is not a child or minor ward of the person to consume

Amended 2009

alcoholic liquor on the property, or allow any other person under the age of 21 years who is not a child or minor ward of the person to remain on the property if the person under the age of 21 years consumes alcoholic liquor on the property.

(b) This subsection:

*(A) **Applies** only to a person who is present and in control of the location at the time the consumption occurs;*

*(B) **Does** not apply to the owner of rental property, or the agent of an owner of rental property, unless the consumption occurs in the individual unit in which the owner or agent resides; **and***

(C) Does not apply to a person who exercises control over a private residence if the liquor consumed by the person under the age of 21 years is supplied only by an accompanying parent or guardian.

(4) This section does not apply to sacramental wine given or provided as part of a religious rite or service.

(5) Except as provided in subsection (6) of this section, a person who violates subsection (1) or (2) of this section commits a Class A misdemeanor. Upon violation of subsection (2) of this section, the court shall impose at least a mandatory minimum sentence as follows:

(a) Upon a first conviction, a fine of *at least $500*.

(b) Upon a second conviction, a fine of *at least $1,000*.

(c) Upon a third or subsequent conviction, a fine of *at least $1,500* and not less than 30 days of imprisonment.

(6)(a) A person who violates subsection (2) of this section is subject to a mandatory minimum penalty under this subsection if the person does not act knowingly or intentionally and:

(A) Is licensed or appointed under this chapter [Ch. 471]*; or*

(B) Is an employee of a person licensed or appointed under this chapter and holds a valid service permit or has attended a program approved by the Oregon Liquor Control Commission that provides training to avoid violations of this section.

(b) For a person described in paragraph (a) of this subsection:

(A) A first conviction is a Class A violation. The court shall impose a mandatory fine of not less than $350.

(B) A second conviction is a Class A violation. The court shall impose a mandatory fine of not less than $720.

(C) A third conviction is a Class A misdemeanor. The court shall impose a mandatory fine of not less than $1,000.

(D) A fourth or subsequent conviction is a Class A misdemeanor. The court shall impose a mandatory fine of not less than $1,000 and a mandatory sentence of not less than 30 days of imprisonment.

(7) The court may waive an amount that is at least $200 but not more than one-third of the fine imposed under subsection (5) of this section, if the violator performs at least 30 hours of community service.

(8) Except as provided in subsection (7) of this section, the court may not waive or suspend imposition or execution of the mandatory minimum sentence required by subsection (5) or (6) of this section. In addition to the mandatory sentence, the court may require the violator to make restitution for any damages to property where the alcoholic liquor was illegally consumed or may require participation in volunteer service to a community service agency.

(9) A person who violates subsection (3) of this section commits a violation. Upon violation of subsection (3) of this section, the court shall impose at least a mandatory minimum fine as follows:
 (a) Upon a first conviction, a fine of $350.
 (b) Upon a second or subsequent conviction, a fine of $1,000.

(10) Nothing in this section prohibits any licensee under this chapter [Ch. 471] from allowing a person who is visibly intoxicated from remaining on the licensed premises so long as the person is not sold or served any alcoholic liquor.

471.430 Purchase or possession of liquor or entry of licensed premises by minor
Amended 2009

(1) A person under 21 years *of age* may not attempt to purchase, purchase or acquire alcoholic beverages. Except when such minor is in a private residence accompanied by the parent or guardian of the minor and with such parent's or guardian's consent, a person under 21 years *of age* may not have personal possession of alcoholic beverages.

(2) For the purposes of this section, personal possession of alcoholic beverages includes the acceptance or consumption of a bottle of such beverages, or any portion thereof or a drink of such beverages. However, this section does not prohibit the acceptance or consumption by any person of sacramental wine as part of a religious rite or service.

(3) Except as authorized by rule or as necessitated in an emergency, a person under 21 years *of age* may not enter or attempt to enter any portion of a licensed premises that is posted or otherwise identified as being prohibited to the use of minors.

(4)(a) Except as provided in paragraph (b) of this subsection, a person who violates subsection (1) or (3) of this section commits a Class B violation.
 (b) A person commits a Class A violation if the person violates subsection (1) of this section by reason of personal possession of alcoholic beverages while the person is operating a motor vehicle, as defined in ORS 801.360.

(5) In addition to and not in lieu of any other penalty established by law, a person under 21 years *of age* who violates subsection (1) of this section through misrepresentation of age may be required to perform commu-

nity service and the court shall order that the person's driving privileges and right to apply for driving privileges be suspended for a period not to exceed one year. If a court has issued an order denying driving privileges under this section, the court, upon petition of the person, may withdraw the order at any time the court deems appropriate. The court notification to the Department of Transportation under this subsection may include a recommendation that the person be granted a hardship permit under ORS 807.240 if the person is otherwise eligible for the permit.

(6) If a person cited under this section is at least 13 years of age but less than 21 years of age at the time the person is found in default under ORS 153.102 or 419C.472 for failure to appear, in addition to and in lieu of any other penalty, the court shall issue notice under ORS 809.220 to the department for the department to suspend the person's driving privileges under ORS 809.280 (5).

(7) In addition to and not in lieu of any penalty established by law, the court may order a person who violates this section to undergo assessment and treatment as provided in ORS 471.432. The court shall order a person to undergo assessment and treatment as provided in ORS 471.432 if the person has previously been found to have violated this section.

(8) The prohibitions of this section do not apply to a person under 21 years *of age* who is acting under the direction of the Oregon Liquor Control Commission or under the direction of state or local law enforcement agencies for the purpose of investigating possible violations of laws prohibiting sales of alcoholic beverages to persons who are under 21 years *of age*.

(9) The prohibitions of this section do not apply to a person under 21 years *of age* who is acting under the direction of a licensee for the purpose of investigating possible violations by employees of the licensee of laws prohibiting sales of alcoholic beverages to persons who are under 21 years *of age*.

475.005 Definitions–Controlled substance offenses *Amended 2009*

As used in ORS 475.005 to 475.285 and 475.840 to 475.980, unless the context requires otherwise:

(1) "Abuse" means the repetitive excessive use of a drug short of dependence, without legal or medical supervision, which may have a detrimental effect on the individual or society.

(2) "Administer" means the direct application of a controlled substance, whether by injection, inhalation, ingestion or any other means, to the body of a patient or research subject by:

(a) A practitioner or an authorized agent thereof; or

(b) The patient or research subject at the direction of the practitioner.

(3) "Administration" means the Drug Enforcement Administration of the United States Department of Justice, or its successor agency.

(4) "Agent" means an authorized person who acts on behalf of or at the direction of a manufacturer, distributor or dispenser. It does not include

a common or contract carrier, public warehouseman or employee of the carrier or warehouseman.

(5) "Board" means the State Board of Pharmacy.

(6) "Controlled substance":

  (**a**) Means a drug or its immediate precursor classified in Schedules I through V under the federal Controlled Substances Act, 21 U.S.C. 811 to 812, as modified under ORS 475.035. The use of the term "precursor" in this ***paragraph*** does not control and is not controlled by the use of the term "precursor" in ORS 475.840 to 475.980.

  (**b**) **Does not mean industrial hemp, as defined in ORS 571.300, or industrial hemp commodities or products.**

(7) "Counterfeit substance" means a controlled substance or its container or labeling, which, without authorization, bears the trademark, trade name, or other identifying mark, imprint, number or device, or any likeness thereof, of a manufacturer, distributor or dispenser other than the person who in fact manufactured, delivered or dispensed the substance.

(8) "Deliver" or "delivery" means the actual, constructive or attempted transfer, other than by administering or dispensing, from one person to another of a controlled substance, whether or not there is an agency relationship.

(9) "Device" means instruments, apparatus or contrivances, including their components, parts or accessories, intended:

  (a) For use in the diagnosis, cure, mitigation, treatment or prevention of disease in humans or animals; or

  (b) To affect the structure of any function of the body of humans or animals.

(10) "Dispense" means to deliver a controlled substance to an ultimate user or research subject by or pursuant to the lawful order of a practitioner, and includes the prescribing, administering, packaging, labeling or compounding necessary to prepare the substance for that delivery.

(11) "Dispenser" means a practitioner who dispenses.

(12) "Distributor" means a person who delivers.

(13) "Drug" means:

  (a) Substances recognized as drugs in the official United States Pharmacopoeia, official Homeopathic Pharmacopoeia of the United States or official National Formulary, or any supplement to any of them;

  (b) Substances intended for use in the diagnosis, cure, mitigation, treatment or prevention of disease in humans or animals;

  (c) Substances (other than food) intended to affect the structure or any function of the body of humans or animals; and

  (d) Substances intended for use as a component of any article specified in paragraph (a), (b) or (c) of this subsection; however, the term does not include devices or their components, parts or accessories.

(14) "Electronically transmitted" or "electronic transmission" means a communication sent or received through technological apparatuses, including computer terminals or other equipment or mechanisms linked by telephone or microwave relays, or any similar apparatus having electrical, digital, magnetic, wireless, optical, electromagnetic or similar capabilities.

(15) "Manufacture" means the production, preparation, propagation, compounding, conversion or processing of a controlled substance, either directly or indirectly by extraction from substances of natural origin, or independently by means of chemical synthesis, or by a combination of extraction and chemical synthesis, and includes any packaging or repackaging of the substance or labeling or relabeling of its container, except that this term does not include the preparation or compounding of a controlled substance:
  (a) By a practitioner as an incident to administering or dispensing of a controlled substance in the course of professional practice; or
  (b) By a practitioner, or by an authorized agent under the practitioner's supervision, for the purpose of, or as an incident to, research, teaching or chemical analysis and not for sale.
(16) "Marijuana":
  (a) Except as provided in this subsection, means all parts of the plant Cannabis family Moraceae, whether growing or not; the resin extracted from any part of the plant; and every compound, manufacture, salt, derivative, mixture, or preparation of the plant or its resin.
  (b) Does not *mean* the mature stalks of the plant, fiber produced from the stalks, oil or cake made from the seeds of the plant, any other compound, manufacture, salt, derivative, mixture, or preparation of the mature stalks (except the resin extracted therefrom); fiber, oil, or cake, or the sterilized seed of the plant which is incapable of germination.
  (c) Does not mean industrial hemp, as defined in ORS 571.300, or industrial hemp commodities or products.
(17) "Person" includes a government subdivision or agency, business trust, estate, trust or any other legal entity.
(18) "Practitioner" means physician, dentist, veterinarian, scientific investigator, certified nurse practitioner, physician assistant or other person licensed, registered or otherwise permitted by law to dispense, conduct research with respect to or to administer a controlled substance in the course of professional practice or research in this state but does not include a pharmacist or a pharmacy.
(19) "Prescription" means a written, oral or electronically transmitted direction, given by a practitioner for the preparation and use of a drug. When the context requires, "prescription" also means the drug prepared under such written, oral or electronically transmitted direction. Any label affixed to a drug prepared under written, oral or electronically transmitted direction shall prominently display a warning that the removal thereof is prohibited by law.
(20) "Production" includes the manufacture, planting, cultivation, growing or harvesting of a controlled substance.
(21) "Research" means an activity conducted by the person registered with the federal Drug Enforcement Administration pursuant to a protocol approved by the United States Food and Drug Administration.
(22) "Ultimate user" means a person who lawfully possesses a controlled substance for the use of the person or for the use of a member of the household

of the person or for administering to an animal owned by the person or by a member of the household of the person.

475.035 Schedule I Drugs

[Drug schedules are established pursuant to 475.035, by the Board of Pharmacy. The following information is excerpted from Board of Pharmacy Rules. For a complete list of this schedule, see 21 CFR 1308.11, and 855-080-0021 in a full text edition of the Board of Pharmacy Rules; or on our CD edition.]

(c)(11) Heroin
(d) Hallucinogenic substances.
  (11) 3,4-methylenedioxymethamphetamine (MDMA)
  (21) Lysergic acid diethylamide [LSD]
  (22) Marihuana
  (23) Mescaline
  (25) Peyote
  (28) Psilocybin
  (30) Tetrahydrocannabinols
(e)(1) gamma-hydroxybutyric acid

Note:
1. Pursuant to Oregon Laws 2009 Ch. 898 § 2 and 4, the State Board of Pharmacy shall classify marijuana as a controlled substance in Schedule II, III, IV or V by 6/30/2010.
2. Pursuant to Oregon Laws 2009 Ch. 898 § 3 and 4, the State Board of Pharmacy shall classify methamphetamine as a crontolled substance in Schedule I by 6/30/2010.
3. Pursuant to Oregon Laws 2009 Ch. 898 § 3; methamphetamine, its salts, isomers and salts of its isomers shall be classified as a controlled substance in Schedule II for purposes of currently accepted medical use in treatment in the United States and currently accepted medical use with severe restrictions within the meaning of 21 U.S.C. 812(b)(2).

475.035 Schedule II Drugs

[Drug schedules are established pursuant to 475.035, by the Board of Pharmacy. The following information is excerpted from Board of Pharmacy Rules. For a complete list of this schedule, see 21 CFR 1308.12, and 855-080-0022 in a full text edition of the Board of Pharmacy Rules; or on our CD edition.]

(b)(4) Coca leaves (9040) and any salt, compound, derivative or preparation of coca leaves (including cocaine (9041) and ecgonine (9180) and their salts, isomers, derivatives and salts of isomers and derivatives), and any salt, compound, derivative, or preparation thereof which is chemically equivalent or identical with any of these substances, except that the substances shall not include decocainized coca leaves or extraction of coca leaves, which extractions do not contain cocaine or ecgonine.
(c)(10) Methadone
(d) Stimulants.
  (1) Amphetamine, its salts, optical isomers, and salts of its optical isomers.
  (2) Methamphetamine, its salts, isomers, and salts of its isomers.

Amended 2009

Note:
1. Pursuant to Oregon Laws 2009 Ch. 898 § 2 and 4, the State Board of Pharmacy shall classify marijuana as a controlled substance in Schedule II, III, IV or V by 6/30/2010.
2. Pursuant to Oregon Laws 2009 Ch. 898 § 3 and 4, the State Board of Pharmacy shall classify methamphetamine as a controlled substance in Schedule I by 6/30/2010.
3. Pursuant to Oregon Laws 2009 Ch. 898 § 3; methamphetamine, its salts, isomers and salts of its isomers shall be classified as a controlled substance in Schedule II for purposes of currently accepted medical use in treatment in the United States and currently accepted medical use with severe restrictions within the meaning of 21 U.S.C. 812(b)(2).

475.035 Schedule IV Drugs

[Drug schedules are established pursuant to 475.035, by the Board of Pharmacy. The following information is excerpted from Board of Pharmacy Rules. For a complete list of this schedule, see 21 CFR 1308.14, and 855-080-0024 in a full text edition of the Board of Pharmacy Rules; or on our CD edition.]
(c)(21) Flunitrazepam

475.302 Definitions–Medical marijuana
Amended 2009

As used in ORS 475.300 to 475.346:
(1) "Attending physician" means a physician licensed under ORS chapter 677 who has primary responsibility for the care and treatment of a person diagnosed with a debilitating medical condition.
(2) "Authority" means the Oregon Health Authority.
(3) "Debilitating medical condition" means:
  (a) Cancer, glaucoma, agitation due to Alzheimer's disease, positive status for human immunodeficiency virus or acquired immune deficiency syndrome, or treatment for these conditions;
  (b) A medical condition or treatment for a medical condition that produces, for a specific patient, one or more of the following:
    (A) Cachexia;
    (B) Severe pain;
    (C) Severe nausea;
    (D) Seizures, including but not limited to seizures caused by epilepsy; or
    (E) Persistent muscle spasms, including but not limited to spasms caused by multiple sclerosis; or
  (c) Any other medical condition or treatment for a medical condition adopted by the *authority* by rule or approved by the *authority* pursuant to a petition submitted pursuant to ORS 475.334.
(4) "Delivery" has the meaning given that term in ORS 475.005. "Delivery" does not include transfer of marijuana by a registry identification cardholder to another registry identification cardholder if no consideration is paid for the transfer.

(5) "Designated primary caregiver" means an individual 18 years of age or older who has significant responsibility for managing the well-being of a person who has been diagnosed with a debilitating medical condition and who is designated as such on that person's application for a registry identification card or in other written notification to the ***authority***. "Designated primary caregiver" does not include the person's attending physician.

(6) "Marijuana" has the meaning given that term in ORS 475.005.

(7) "Marijuana grow site" means a location where marijuana is produced for use by a registry identification cardholder and that is registered under the provisions of ORS 475.304.

(8) "Medical use of marijuana" means the production, possession, delivery, or administration of marijuana, or paraphernalia used to administer marijuana, as necessary for the exclusive benefit of a person to mitigate the symptoms or effects of the person's debilitating medical condition.

(9) "Production" has the meaning given that term in ORS 475.005.

(10) "Registry identification card" means a document issued by the ***authority*** that identifies a person authorized to engage in the medical use of marijuana and the person's designated primary caregiver, if any.

(11) "Usable marijuana" means the dried leaves and flowers of the plant Cannabis family Moraceae, and any mixture or preparation thereof, that are appropriate for medical use as allowed in ORS 475.300 to 475.346. "Usable marijuana" does not include the seeds, stalks and roots of the plant.

(12) "Written documentation" means a statement signed by the attending physician of a person diagnosed with a debilitating medical condition or copies of the person's relevant medical records.

475.316 Limitations on medical marijuana immunity *Amended 2009*

(1) No person authorized to possess, deliver or produce marijuana for medical use pursuant to ORS 475.300 to 475.346 shall be excepted from the criminal laws of this state or shall be deemed to have established an affirmative defense to criminal charges of which possession, delivery or production of marijuana is an element if the person, in connection with the facts giving rise to such charges:

(a) Drives under the influence of marijuana as provided in ORS 813.010;

(b) Engages in the medical use of marijuana in a public place as that term is defined in ORS 161.015, or in public view or in a correctional facility as defined in ORS 162.135 (2) or youth correction facility as defined in ORS 162.135 (6);

(c) Delivers marijuana to any individual who the person knows is not in possession of a registry identification card;

(d) Delivers marijuana for consideration to any individual, even if the individual is in possession of a registry identification card;

(e) Manufactures or produces marijuana at a place other than a marijuana grow site authorized under ORS 475.304; or

(f) Manufactures or produces marijuana at more than one address.

(2) In addition to any other penalty allowed by law, a person who the *Oregon Health Authority* finds has willfully violated the provisions of ORS 475.300 to 475.346, or rules adopted under ORS 475.300 to 475.346, may be precluded from obtaining or using a registry identification card for the medical use of marijuana for a period of up to six months, at the discretion of the *authority*.

475.319 Defenses–Medical marijuana

(1) Except as provided in ORS 475.316 and 475.342, it is an affirmative defense to a criminal charge of possession or production of marijuana, or any other criminal offense in which possession or production of marijuana is an element, that the person charged with the offense is a person who:
 (a) Has been diagnosed with a debilitating medical condition within 12 months prior to arrest and been advised by the person's attending physician that the medical use of marijuana may mitigate the symptoms or effects of that debilitating medical condition;
 (b) Is engaged in the medical use of marijuana; and
 (c) Possesses or produces marijuana only in amounts permitted under ORS 475.320.
(2) It is not necessary for a person asserting an affirmative defense pursuant to this section to have received a registry identification card in order to assert the affirmative defense established in this section.
(3) No person engaged in the medical use of marijuana who claims that marijuana provides medically necessary benefits and who is charged with a crime pertaining to such use of marijuana shall be precluded from presenting a defense of choice of evils, as set forth in ORS 161.200, or from presenting evidence supporting the necessity of marijuana for treatment of a specific disease or medical condition, provided that the amount of marijuana at issue is no greater than permitted under ORS 475.320 and the patient has taken a substantial step to comply with the provisions of ORS 475.300 to 475.346.
(4) Any defendant proposing to use the affirmative defense provided for by this section in a criminal action shall, not less than five days before the trial of the cause, file and serve upon the district attorney a written notice of the intention to offer such a defense that specifically states the reasons why the defendant is entitled to assert and the factual basis for such affirmative defense. If the defendant fails to file and serve such notice, the defendant is not permitted to assert the affirmative defense at the trial of the cause unless the court for good cause orders otherwise.

475.320 Medical marijuana limits *Amended 2009*

(1)(a) A registry identification cardholder or the designated primary caregiver of the cardholder may possess up to six mature marijuana plants and 24 ounces of usable marijuana.
 (b) Notwithstanding paragraph (a) of this subsection, if a registry identification cardholder has been convicted of a Class A or Class B felony under ORS 475.840 to 475.920 for the manufacture or delivery of a controlled substance in Schedule I or Schedule II, the registry identification cardholder or the designated primary caregiver of the cardholder may possess one

ounce of usable marijuana at any given time for a period of five years from the date of the conviction.
(2) A person authorized under ORS 475.304 to produce marijuana at a marijuana grow site:
 (a) May produce marijuana for and provide marijuana to a registry identification cardholder or that person's designated primary caregiver as authorized under this section.
 (b) May possess up to six mature plants and up to 24 ounces of usable marijuana for each cardholder or caregiver for whom marijuana is being produced.
 (c) May produce marijuana for no more than four registry identification cardholders or designated primary caregivers concurrently.
 (d) Must obtain and display a marijuana grow site registration card issued under ORS 475.304 for each registry identification cardholder or designated primary caregiver for whom marijuana is being produced.
 (e) Must provide all marijuana produced for a registry identification cardholder or designated primary caregiver to the cardholder or caregiver at the time the person responsible for a marijuana grow site ceases producing marijuana for the cardholder or caregiver.
 (f) Must return the marijuana grow site registration card to the registry identification cardholder to whom the card was issued when requested to do so by the cardholder or when the person responsible for a marijuana grow site ceases producing marijuana for the cardholder or caregiver.
(3) Except as provided in subsections (1) and (2) of this section, a registry identification cardholder, the designated primary caregiver of the cardholder and the person responsible for a marijuana grow site producing marijuana for the registry identification cardholder may possess a combined total of up to six mature plants and 24 ounces of usable marijuana for that registry identification cardholder.
(4)(a) A registry identification cardholder and the designated primary caregiver of the cardholder may possess a combined total of up to 18 marijuana seedlings or starts as defined by rule of the *Oregon Health Authority*.
 (b) A person responsible for a marijuana grow site may possess up to 18 marijuana seedlings or starts as defined by rule of the *authority* for each registry identification cardholder for whom the person responsible for the marijuana grow site is producing marijuana.

475.323 Medical marijuana–Search and seizure–Protection of property

(1) Possession of a registry identification card or designated primary caregiver identification card pursuant to ORS 475.309 does not alone constitute probable cause to search the person or property of the cardholder or otherwise subject the person or property of the cardholder to inspection by any governmental agency.
(2) Any property interest possessed, owned or used in connection with the medical use of marijuana or acts incidental to the medical use of marijuana

that has been seized by state or local law enforcement officers may not be harmed, neglected, injured or destroyed while in the possession of any law enforcement agency. A law enforcement agency has no responsibility to maintain live marijuana plants lawfully seized. No such property interest may be forfeited under any provision of law providing for the forfeiture of property other than as a sentence imposed after conviction of a criminal offense. Usable marijuana and paraphernalia used to administer marijuana that was seized by any law enforcement office shall be returned immediately upon a determination by the district attorney in whose county the property was seized, or the district attorney's designee, that the person from whom the marijuana or paraphernalia used to administer marijuana was seized is entitled to the protections contained in ORS 475.300 to 475.346. The determination may be evidenced, for example, by a decision not to prosecute, the dismissal of charges or acquittal.

475.525 Drug paraphernalia

(1) It is unlawful for any person to sell or deliver, possess with intent to sell or deliver or manufacture with intent to sell or deliver drug paraphernalia, knowing that it will be used to unlawfully plant, propagate, cultivate, grow, harvest, manufacture, compound, convert, produce, process, prepare, test, analyze, pack, repack, store, contain, conceal, inject, ingest, inhale or otherwise introduce into the human body a controlled substance as defined by ORS 475.005.

(2) For the purposes of this section, "drug paraphernalia" means all equipment, products and materials of any kind which are marketed for use or designed for use in planting, propagating, cultivating, growing, harvesting, manufacturing, compounding, converting, producing, processing, preparing, testing, analyzing, packaging, repackaging, storing, containing, concealing, injecting, ingesting, inhaling or otherwise introducing into the human body a controlled substance in violation of ORS 475.840 to 475.980. Drug paraphernalia includes, but is not limited to:

(a) Kits marketed for use or designed for use in unlawfully planting, propagating, cultivating, growing or harvesting of any species of plant which is a controlled substance or from which a controlled substance can be derived;

(b) Kits marketed for use or designed for use in manufacturing, compounding, converting, producing, processing or preparing controlled substances;

(c) Isomerization devices marketed for use or designed for use in increasing the potency of any species of plant which is a controlled substance;

(d) Testing equipment marketed for use or designed for use in identifying or in analyzing the strength, effectiveness or purity of controlled substances;

(e) Scales and balances marketed for use or designed for use in weighing or measuring controlled substances;

(f) Diluents and adulterants, such as quinine hydrochloride, mannitol, mannite, dextrose and lactose, marketed for use or designed for use in cutting controlled substances;

(g) Separation gins and sifters marketed for use or designed for use in removing twigs and seeds from, or in otherwise cleaning or refining marijuana;

(h) Containers and other objects marketed for use or designed for use in storing or concealing controlled substances; and

(i) Objects marketed for use or designed specifically for use in ingesting, inhaling or otherwise introducing marijuana, cocaine, hashish or hashish oil into the human body, such as:

  (A) Metal, wooden, acrylic, glass, stone, plastic or ceramic pipes with or without screens, permanent screens or hashish heads;

  (B) Water pipes;

  (C) Carburetion tubes and devices;

  (D) Smoking and carburetion masks;

  (E) Roach clips, meaning objects used to hold burning material that has become too small or too short to be held in the hand, such as a marijuana cigarette;

  (F) Miniature cocaine spoons and cocaine vials;

  (G) Chamber pipes;

  (H) Carburetor pipes;

  (I) Electric pipes;

  (J) Air-driven pipes;

  (K) Chillums;

  (L) Bongs;

  (M) Ice pipes or chillers; and

  (N) Lighting equipment specifically designed for the growing of controlled substances.

(3) Drug paraphernalia does not include hypodermic syringes or needles.

(4) In determining whether an object is drug paraphernalia, a trier of fact should consider, in addition to all other relevant factors, the following:

(a) Instructions, oral or written, provided with the object concerning its use;

(b) Descriptive materials accompanying the object which explain or depict its use;

(c) National and local advertising concerning its use;

(d) The manner in which the object is displayed for sale;

(e) The existence and scope of legitimate uses for the object in the community; and

(f) Any expert testimony which may be introduced concerning its use.

(5) The provisions of ORS 475.525 to 475.565 do not apply to persons registered under the provisions of ORS 475.125 or to persons specified as exempt from registration under the provisions of that statute.

475.840 Controlled substance offenses
Amended 2009

(1) Except as authorized by ORS 475.005 to 475.285 and 475.840 to 475.980, it is unlawful for any person to manufacture or deliver

Amended 2009

a controlled substance. Any person who violates this subsection with respect to:
(a) A controlled substance in Schedule I, is guilty of a Class A felony, except as otherwise provided in ORS 475.860.
(b) A controlled substance in Schedule II, is guilty of a Class B felony, except as otherwise provided in ORS 475.878, 475.880, 475.882, 475.888, 475.890, 475.892, 475.904 and 475.906.
(c) A controlled substance in Schedule III, is guilty of a Class C felony, except as otherwise provided in ORS 475.904 and 475.906.
(d) A controlled substance in Schedule IV, is guilty of a Class B misdemeanor.
(e) A controlled substance in Schedule V, is guilty of a Class C misdemeanor.
(2) Except as authorized in ORS 475.005 to 475.285 and 475.840 to 475.980, it is unlawful for any person to create or deliver a counterfeit substance. Any person who violates this subsection with respect to:
(a) A counterfeit substance in Schedule I, is guilty of a Class A felony.
(b) A counterfeit substance in Schedule II, is guilty of a Class B felony.
(c) A counterfeit substance in Schedule III, is guilty of a Class C felony.
(d) A counterfeit substance in Schedule IV, is guilty of a Class B misdemeanor.
(e) A counterfeit substance in Schedule V, is guilty of a Class C misdemeanor.
(3) It is unlawful for any person knowingly or intentionally to possess a controlled substance unless the substance was obtained directly from, or pursuant to, a valid prescription or order of a practitioner while acting in the course of professional practice, or except as otherwise authorized by ORS 475.005 to 475.285 and 475.840 to 475.980. Any person who violates this subsection with respect to:
(a) A controlled substance in Schedule I, is guilty of a Class B felony, except as otherwise provided in ORS 475.864.
(b) A controlled substance in Schedule II, is guilty of a Class C felony.
(c) A controlled substance in Schedule III, is guilty of a Class A misdemeanor.
(d) A controlled substance in Schedule IV, is guilty of a Class C misdemeanor.
(e) A controlled substance in Schedule V, is guilty of a violation.
(4) In any prosecution under this section for manufacture, possession or delivery of that plant of the genus Lophophora commonly known as peyote, it is an affirmative defense that the peyote is being used or is intended for use:
(a) In connection with the good faith practice of a religious belief;
(b) As directly associated with a religious practice; and
(c) In a manner that is not dangerous to the health of the user or others who are in the proximity of the user.
(5) The affirmative defense created in subsection (4) of this section is not available to any person who has possessed or delivered the peyote while incarcerated in a correctional facility in this state.
(6)(a) Notwithstanding subsection (1) of this section, a person who manufactures or delivers a controlled substance in Schedule IV and who thereby causes death to any person is guilty of a Class C felony.

(b) For purposes of this subsection, causation is established when the controlled substance plays a substantial role in the death of any person.

475.846 Unlawful manufacture of heroin
(1) It is unlawful for any person to manufacture heroin.
(2) Unlawful manufacture of heroin is a Class A felony.

475.848 Unlawful manufacture of heroin within 1000' of a school
(1) It is unlawful for any person to manufacture heroin within 1,000 feet of the real property comprising a public or private elementary, secondary or career school attended primarily by minors.
(2) Unlawful manufacture of heroin within 1,000 feet of a school is a Class A felony.

475.850 Unlawful delivery of heroin
(1) It is unlawful for any person to deliver heroin.
(2) Unlawful delivery of heroin is a Class A felony.

475.852 Unlawful delivery of heroin within 1000' of a school
(1) It is unlawful for any person to deliver heroin within 1,000 feet of the real property comprising a public or private elementary, secondary or career school attended primarily by minors.
(2) Unlawful delivery of heroin within 1,000 feet of a school is a Class A felony.

475.854 Unlawful possession of heroin
(1) It is unlawful for any person knowingly or intentionally to possess heroin.
(2) Unlawful possession of heroin is a Class B felony.

475.856 Unlawful manufacture of marijuana
(1) It is unlawful for any person to manufacture marijuana.
(2) Unlawful manufacture of marijuana is a Class A felony.

475.858 Unlawful manufacture of marijuana within 1000' of a school
(1) It is unlawful for any person to manufacture marijuana within 1,000 feet of the real property comprising a public or private elementary, secondary or career school attended primarily by minors.
(2) Unlawful manufacture of marijuana within 1,000 feet of a school is a Class A felony.

475.860 Unlawful delivery of marijuana
Amended 2009

(1) It is unlawful for any person to deliver marijuana.
(2) Unlawful delivery of marijuana is a:
   (a) Class B felony if the delivery is for consideration.
   (b) Class C felony if the delivery is for no consideration.
(3) Notwithstanding subsection (2) of this section, unlawful delivery of marijuana is a:
   (a) Class A misdemeanor, if the delivery is for no consideration and consists of less than one avoirdupois ounce of the dried leaves, stems and flowers of the plant Cannabis family Moraceae; or
   (b) Violation, if the delivery is for no consideration and consists of less than five grams of the dried leaves, stems and flowers of the plant Cannabis family Moraceae. A violation under this paragraph is punishable by a fine of not less than $500 and not more than $1,000. Fines collected under this paragraph shall be forwarded to the Department of Revenue for deposit in the Criminal Fine and Assessment Account established in ORS 137.300.
(4) Notwithstanding subsections (2) and (3) of this section, unlawful delivery of marijuana is a:
   (a) Class A felony, if the delivery is to a person under 18 years of age and the defendant is at least 18 years of age and is at least three years older than the person to whom the marijuana is delivered; or
   (b) Class C misdemeanor, if the delivery:
      (A) Is for no consideration;
      (B) Consists of less than five grams of the dried leaves, stems and flowers of the plant Cannabis family Moraceae;
      (C) Takes place in a public place, as defined in ORS 161.015, that is within 1,000 feet of the real property comprising a public or private elementary, secondary or career school attended primarily by minors; and
      (D) Is to a person who is 18 years of age or older.

475.862 Unlawful delivery of marijuana within 1000' of a school

(1) It is unlawful for any person to deliver marijuana within 1,000 feet of the real property comprising a public or private elementary, secondary or career school attended primarily by minors.
(2) Unlawful delivery of marijuana within 1,000 feet of a school is a Class A felony.

475.864 Unlawful possession of marijuana

(1) It is unlawful for any person knowingly or intentionally to possess marijuana.
(2) Unlawful possession of marijuana is a Class B felony.
(3) Notwithstanding subsection (2) of this section, unlawful possession of marijuana is a violation if the amount possessed is

less than one avoirdupois ounce of the dried leaves, stems and flowers of the plant Cannabis family Moraceae. A violation under this subsection is punishable by a fine of not less than $500 and not more than $1,000. Fines collected under this subsection shall be forwarded to the Department of Revenue for deposit in the Criminal Fine and Assessment Account established under ORS 137.300.

(4) Notwithstanding subsections (2) and (3) of this section, unlawful possession of marijuana is a Class C misdemeanor if the amount possessed is less than one avoirdupois ounce of the dried leaves, stems and flowers of the plant Cannabis family Moraceae and the possession takes place in a public place, as defined in ORS 161.015, that is within 1,000 feet of the real property comprising a public or private elementary, secondary or career school attended primarily by minors.

475.866 Unlawful manufacture of MDMA

(1) It is unlawful for any person to manufacture 3,4-methylenedioxymethamphetamine.
(2) Unlawful manufacture of 3,4-methylenedioxymethamphetamine is a Class A felony.

475.868 Unlawful manufacture of MDMA within 1000' of a school

(1) It is unlawful for any person to manufacture 3,4-methylenedioxymethamphetamine within 1,000 feet of the real property comprising a public or private elementary, secondary or career school attended primarily by minors.
(2) Unlawful manufacture of 3,4-methylenedioxymethamphetamine within 1,000 feet of a school is a Class A felony.

475.870 Unlawful delivery of MDMA

(1) It is unlawful for any person to deliver 3,4-methylenedioxymethamphetamine.
(2) Unlawful delivery of 3,4-methylenedioxymethamphetamine is a Class A felony.

475.872 Unlawful delivery of MDMA within 1000' of a school

(1) It is unlawful for any person to deliver 3,4-methylenedioxymethamphetamine within 1,000 feet of the real property comprising a public or private elementary, secondary or career school attended primarily by minors.
(2) Unlawful delivery of 3,4-methylenedioxymethamphetamine within 1,000 feet of a school is a Class A felony.

475.874 Unlawful possession of MDMA
(1) It is unlawful for any person knowingly or intentionally to possess 3,4-methylenedioxy methamphetamine.
(2) Unlawful possession of 3,4-methylenedioxymethamphetamine is a Class B felony.

475.876 Unlawful manufacture of cocaine
(1) Except as authorized by ORS 475.005 to 475.285 and 475.840 to 475.980, it is unlawful for any person to manufacture cocaine.
(2) Unlawful manufacture of cocaine is a Class B felony.

475.878 Unlawful manufacture of cocaine within 1000' of a school
(1) Except as authorized by ORS 475.005 to 475.285 and 475.840 to 475.980, it is unlawful for any person to manufacture cocaine within 1,000 feet of the real property comprising a public or private elementary, secondary or career school attended primarily by minors.
(2) Unlawful manufacture of cocaine within 1,000 feet of a school is a Class A felony.

475.880 Unlawful delivery of cocaine
(1) Except as authorized by ORS 475.005 to 475.285 and 475.840 to 475.980, it is unlawful for any person to deliver cocaine.
(2) Unlawful delivery of cocaine is a Class B felony.
(3) Notwithstanding subsection (2) of this section, unlawful delivery of cocaine is a Class A felony if the delivery is to a person under 18 years of age.

475.882 Unlawful delivery of cocaine within 1000' of a school
(1) Except as authorized by ORS 475.005 to 475.285 and 475.840 to 475.980, it is unlawful for any person to deliver cocaine within 1,000 feet of the real property comprising a public or private elementary, secondary or career school attended primarily by minors.
(2) Unlawful delivery of cocaine within 1,000 feet of a school is a Class A felony.

475.884 Unlawful possession of cocaine
(1) It is unlawful for any person knowingly or intentionally to possess cocaine unless the substance was obtained directly from, or pursuant to, a valid prescription or order of a practitioner while acting in the course of professional practice, or except as otherwise authorized by ORS 475.005 to 475.285 and 475.840 to 475.980.
(2) Unlawful possession of cocaine is a Class C felony.

475.886 Unlawful manufacture of methamphetamine

(1) Except as authorized by ORS 475.005 to 475.285 and 475.840 to 475.980, it is unlawful for any person to manufacture methamphetamine.

(2) Unlawful manufacture of methamphetamine is a Class B felony.

475.888 Unlawful manufacture of methamphetamine within 1000' of a school

(1) Except as authorized by ORS 475.005 to 475.285 and 475.840 to 475.980, it is unlawful for any person to manufacture methamphetamine within 1,000 feet of the real property comprising a public or private elementary, secondary or career school attended primarily by minors.

(2) Unlawful manufacture of methamphetamine within 1,000 feet of a school is a Class A felony.

475.890 Unlawful delivery of methamphetamine

(1) Except as authorized by ORS 475.005 to 475.285 and 475.840 to 475.980, it is unlawful for any person to deliver methamphetamine.

(2) Unlawful delivery of methamphetamine is a Class B felony.

(3) Notwithstanding subsection (2) of this section, unlawful delivery of methamphetamine is a Class A felony if the delivery is to a person under 18 years of age.

475.892 Unlawful delivery of methamphetamine within 1000' of a school

(1) Except as authorized by ORS 475.005 to 475.285 and 475.840 to 475.980, it is unlawful for any person to deliver methamphetamine within 1,000 feet of the real property comprising a public or private elementary, secondary or career school attended primarily by minors.

(2) Unlawful delivery of methamphetamine within 1,000 feet of a school is a Class A felony.

475.894 Unlawful possession of methamphetamine

(1) It is unlawful for any person knowingly or intentionally to possess methamphetamine unless the substance was obtained directly from, or pursuant to, a valid prescription or order of a practitioner while acting in the course of professional practice,

or except as otherwise authorized by ORS 475.005 to 475.285 and 475.840 to 475.980.

(2) Unlawful possession of methamphetamine is a Class C felony.

475.900 Classification of controlled substance offenses

(1) A violation of ORS 475.840, 475.846 to 475.894, 475.904 or 475.906 shall be classified as crime category 8 of the sentencing guidelines grid of the Oregon Criminal Justice Commission if:

(a) The violation constitutes delivery or manufacture of a controlled substance and involves substantial quantities of a controlled substance. For purposes of this paragraph, the following amounts constitute substantial quantities of the following controlled substances:

(A) Five grams or more of a mixture or substance containing a detectable amount of heroin;

(B) Ten grams or more of a mixture or substance containing a detectable amount of cocaine;

(C) Ten grams or more of a mixture or substance containing a detectable amount of methamphetamine, its salts, isomers or salts of its isomers;

(D) One hundred grams or more of a mixture or substance containing a detectable amount of hashish;

(E) One hundred and fifty grams or more of a mixture or substance containing a detectable amount of marijuana;

(F) Two hundred or more user units of a mixture or substance containing a detectable amount of lysergic acid diethylamide;

(G) Sixty grams or more of a mixture or substance containing a detectable amount of psilocybin or psilocin; or

(H) Five grams or more or 25 or more pills, tablets or capsules of a mixture or substance containing a detectable amount of:

(i) 3,4-methylenedioxyamphetamine;

(ii) 3,4-methylenedioxymethamphetamine; or

(iii) 3,4-methylenedioxy-N-ethylamphetamine.

(b) The violation constitutes possession, delivery or manufacture of a controlled substance and the possession, delivery or manufacture is a commercial drug offense. A possession, delivery or manufacture is a commercial drug offense for purposes of this subsection if it is accompanied by at least three of the following factors:

(A) The delivery was of heroin, cocaine, hashish, marijuana, methamphetamine, lysergic acid diethylamide, psilocybin or psilocin and was for consideration;

(B) The offender was in possession of $300 or more in cash;

(C) The offender was unlawfully in possession of a firearm or other weapon as described in ORS 166.270 (2), or the offender used, attempted to use or threatened to use a deadly or dangerous weapon as defined in ORS 161.015, or the offender was in possession of a firearm or other deadly or dangerous weapon as defined in ORS 161.015 for the purpose of using it in connection with a controlled substance offense;

(D) The offender was in possession of materials being used for the packaging of controlled substances such as scales, wrapping or foil, other than the material being used to contain the substance that is the subject of the offense;

(E) The offender was in possession of drug transaction records or customer lists;

(F) The offender was in possession of stolen property;

(G) Modification of structures by painting, wiring, plumbing or lighting to facilitate a controlled substance offense;

(H) The offender was in possession of manufacturing paraphernalia, including recipes, precursor chemicals, laboratory equipment, lighting, ventilating or power generating equipment;

(I) The offender was using public lands for the manufacture of controlled substances;

(J) The offender had constructed fortifications or had taken security measures with the potential of injuring persons; or

(K) The offender was in possession of controlled substances in an amount greater than:

(i) Three grams or more of a mixture or substance containing a detectable amount of heroin;

(ii) Eight grams or more of a mixture or substance containing a detectable amount of cocaine;

(iii) Eight grams or more of a mixture or substance containing a detectable amount of methamphetamine;

(iv) Eight grams or more of a mixture or substance containing a detectable amount of hashish;

(v) One hundred ten grams or more of a mixture or substance containing a detectable amount of marijuana;

(vi) Twenty or more user units of a mixture or substance containing a detectable amount of lysergic acid diethylamide;

(vii) Ten grams or more of a mixture or substance containing a detectable amount of psilocybin or psilocin; or

(viii) Four grams or more or 20 or more pills, tablets or capsules of a mixture or substance containing a detectable amount of:

(I) 3,4-methylenedioxyamphetamine;

(II) 3,4-methylenedioxymethamphetamine; or

(III) 3,4-methylenedioxy-N-ethylamphetamine.

(c) The violation constitutes a violation of ORS 475.848, 475.852, 475.858, 475.862, 475.868, 475.872, 475.878, 475.882, 475.888, 475.892 or 475.904.

(d) The violation constitutes manufacturing methamphetamine and the manufacturing consists of:

(A) A chemical reaction involving one or more precursor substances for the purpose of manufacturing methamphetamine; or

(B) Grinding, soaking or otherwise breaking down a precursor substance for the purpose of manufacturing methamphetamine.
    (e) The violation constitutes a violation of ORS 475.860 (4)(a) or 475.906 (1) or (2).
 (2) A violation of ORS 475.840 or 475.846 to 475.894 shall be classified as crime category 6 of the sentencing guidelines grid of the Oregon Criminal Justice Commission if:
    (a) The violation constitutes delivery of heroin, cocaine, methamphetamine or 3,4-methylenedioxyamphetamine, 3,4-methylenedioxymethamphetamine or 3,4-methylenedioxy-N-ethylamphetamine and is for consideration.
    (b) The violation constitutes possession of:
        (A) Five grams or more of a mixture or substance containing a detectable amount of heroin;
        (B) Ten grams or more of a mixture or substance containing a detectable amount of cocaine;
        (C) Ten grams or more of a mixture or substance containing a detectable amount of methamphetamine;
        (D) One hundred grams or more of a mixture or substance containing a detectable amount of hashish;
        (E) One hundred fifty grams or more of a mixture or substance containing a detectable amount of marijuana;
        (F) Two hundred or more user units of a mixture or substance containing a detectable amount of lysergic acid diethylamide;
        (G) Sixty grams or more of a mixture or substance containing a detectable amount of psilocybin or psilocin; or
        (H) Five grams or more or 25 or more pills, tablets or capsules of a mixture or substance containing a detectable amount of:
            (i) 3,4-methylenedioxyamphetamine;
            (ii) 3,4-methylenedioxymethamphetamine; or
            (iii) 3,4-methylenedioxy-N-ethylamphetamine.
(3) Any felony violation of ORS 475.840 or 475.846 to 475.894 not contained in subsection (1) or (2) of this section shall be classified as:
    (a) Crime category 4 of the sentencing guidelines grid of the Oregon Criminal Justice Commission if the violation involves delivery or manufacture of a controlled substance; or
    (b) Crime category 1 of the sentencing guidelines grid of the Oregon Criminal Justice Commission if the violation involves possession of a controlled substance.
(4) In order to prove a commercial drug offense, the state shall plead in the accusatory instrument sufficient factors of a commercial drug offense under subsections (1) and (2) of this section. The state has the burden of proving each factor beyond a reasonable doubt.
(5) As used in this section, "mixture or substance" means any mixture or substance, whether or not the mixture or substance is in an ingestible or marketable form at the time of the offense.

475.904 Manufacture or delivery of controlled substance within 1,000 feet of school

(1) Except as authorized by ORS 475.005 to 475.285 and 475.840 to 475.980, it is unlawful for any person to manufacture or deliver a schedule I, II or III controlled substance within 1,000 feet of the real property comprising a public or private elementary, secondary or career school attended primarily by minors.

(2) Unlawful manufacture or delivery of a controlled substance within 1,000 feet of a school is a Class A felony, except as otherwise provided in ORS 475.860.

475.906 Distribution of controlled substance to minor

Except as authorized by ORS 475.005 to 475.285 and 475.840 to 475.980, it is unlawful for any person to deliver a controlled substance to a person under 18 years of age. Any person who violates this section with respect to:

(1) A controlled substance in Schedule I or II, is guilty of a Class A felony.
(2) A controlled substance in Schedule III, is guilty of a Class B felony.
(3) A controlled substance in Schedule IV, is guilty of a Class A misdemeanor.
(4) A controlled substance in Schedule V, is guilty of a Class B misdemeanor.

475.908 Causing another person to ingest a controlled substance

(1) A person commits the crime of causing another person to ingest a controlled substance if the person knowingly or intentionally causes the other person to ingest, other than by administering or dispensing, a controlled substance or a controlled substance analog without consent of the other person. A person who violates this subsection is guilty of a Class B felony.

(2) Notwithstanding subsection (1) of this section, causing another person to ingest a controlled substance is a Class A felony if the person, with the intent of committing or facilitating a crime of violence against the other person, knowingly or intentionally causes the other person to ingest a controlled substance or a controlled substance analog without consent of the other person.

(3) For the purposes of this section:
  (a)(A) Except as provided in subparagraph (B) of this paragraph, "controlled substance analog" means a substance that:
    (i) Has a chemical structure that is substantially similar to the chemical structure of a controlled substance in Schedule I or II.
    (ii) Has a stimulant, depressant or hallucinogenic effect on the central nervous system that is substantially similar to or greater than the

stimulant, depressant or hallucinogenic effect on the central nervous system of a controlled substance in Schedule I or II.
  (B) "Controlled substance analog" does not include:
    (i) A controlled substance;
    (ii) Any substance that has an approved drug application;
    (iii) Any substance exempted under 21 U.S.C. 355 if the ingestion is within the scope of investigation authorized under 21 U.S.C. 355; or
    (iv) Distilled spirits, wine or malt beverages.
 (b) "Crime of violence" means:
  (A) Rape in the first degree, as defined in ORS 163.375;
  (B) Sodomy in the first degree, as defined in ORS 163.405;
  (C) Unlawful sexual penetration in the first degree, as defined in ORS 163.411;
  (D) Sexual abuse in the first degree, as defined in ORS 163.427;
  (E) Kidnapping in the first degree, as defined in ORS 163.235;
  (F) Kidnapping in the second degree, as defined in ORS 163.225;
  (G) Assault in the first degree, as defined in ORS 163.185; or
  (H) Assault in the second degree, as defined in ORS 163.175.
 (c) "Ingest" means to consume or otherwise deliver a controlled substance into the body of a person, except that "ingest" does not include inhalation of marijuana smoke.

475.910 Applying controlled substance to minor

(1) Except as authorized by ORS 475.005 to 475.285 or 475.840 to 475.980 it is unlawful for any person to intentionally apply a controlled substance to the body of another person by injection, inhalation, ingestion or any other means if the other person is under 18 years of age. A person who violates this section with respect to:
 (a) A controlled substance in Schedule I or II, is guilty of a Class A felony classified as crime category 9 of the sentencing guidelines grid of the Oregon Criminal Justice Commission.
 (b) A controlled substance in Schedule III, is guilty of a Class B felony classified as crime category 8 of the sentencing guidelines grid of the Oregon Criminal Justice Commission.
 (c) A controlled substance in Schedule IV, is guilty of a Class C felony.
 (d) A controlled substance in Schedule V, is guilty of a Class A misdemeanor.
(2) It is a defense to a charge of violating subsection (1) of this section by applying marijuana that the person applying the marijuana was less than three years older than the victim at the time of the alleged offense.

475.912 Unlawful delivery of an imitation controlled substance

(1) A person commits the crime of unlawful delivery of an imitation controlled substance if the person knowingly:

(a) Delivers, other than by administering or dispensing, a substance that is not a controlled substance upon the express or implied representation that the substance is a controlled substance; or

(b) Delivers a substance that is not a controlled substance upon the express or implied representation that the substance is of such nature or appearance that the recipient of the delivery will be able to distribute the substance as a controlled substance.

(2) As used in this section, "deliver" or "delivery" means the actual or constructive transfer, or offer or agreement to transfer, from one person to another of a substance, whether or not there is an agency relationship.

(3) Unlawful delivery of an imitation controlled substance is a Class A misdemeanor.

475.916 Controlled substance fraud

(1) It is unlawful for any person knowingly or intentionally:

(a) To deliver as a registrant a controlled substance classified in Schedule I or II, except pursuant to an order form as required by ORS 475.175;

(b) To use in the course of manufacture or delivery of a controlled substance a registration number which is fictitious, revoked, suspended or issued to another person;

(c) To acquire or to attempt to acquire or obtain or attempt to obtain possession of a controlled substance by misrepresentation, fraud, forgery, deception or subterfuge;

(d) To furnish false or fraudulent material information in, or omit any material information from, any application, report, record or other document required to be kept or filed under ORS 475.005 to 475.285 and 475.840 to 475.980; or

(e) To make, deliver or possess any punch, die, plate, stone or other thing designed to print, imprint or reproduce the trademark, trade name or other identifying mark, imprint or device of another or any likeness of any of the foregoing upon any drug or container or labeling thereof so as to render the drug a counterfeit substance.

(2) Any person who violates this section is guilty of a Class A misdemeanor.

475.918 Falsifying drug test results

(1) A person commits the crime of falsifying drug test results if the person intentionally uses, or possesses with intent to use, any substance or device designed to falsify the results of a drug test of the person.

(2) Falsifying drug test results is a Class B misdemeanor.

(3) As used in this section and ORS 475.920, "drug test" means a lawfully administered test designed to detect the presence of a controlled substance.

475.920 Providing drug test falsification equipment

(1) A person commits the crime of providing drug test falsification equipment if the person intentionally delivers, possesses with intent to deliver or manufactures with intent to deliver a substance or device designed to enable a person to falsify the results of a drug test.

(2) Providing drug test falsification equipment is a Class A misdemeanor.

475.940 Precursor substances

As used in ORS 475.840 to 475.980:
(1) "Iodine matrix" means iodine at a concentration greater than two percent by weight in a matrix or solution.
(2) "Matrix" means something, as a substance, in which something else originates, develops, or is contained.
(3) "Precursor substance" means:
  (a) Phenyl-2-propanone.
  (b) Methylamine.
  (c) D-lysergic acid.
  (d) Ergotamine.
  (e) Diethyl Malonate.
  (f) Malonic acid.
  (g) Ethyl Malonate.
  (h) Barbituric acid.
  (i) Piperidine.
  (j) N-acetylanthranilic acid.
  (k) Ethylamine.
  (L) Pyrolidine.
  (m) Phenylacetic acid.
  (n) Anthranilic acid.
  (o) Morpholine.
  (p) Ephedrine.
  (q) Pseudoephedrine.
  (r) Norpseudoephedrine.
  (s) Phenylpropanolamine.
  (t) Benzyl cyanide.
  (u) Ergonovine.
  (v) 3,4-Methylenedioxyphenyl-2-propanone.
  (w) Propionic anhydride.
  (x) Insosafrole (Isosafrole).
  (y) Safrole.
  (z) Piperonal.

(aa) N-methylephedrine.
(bb) N-ethylephedrine.
(cc) N-methylpseudoephedrine.
(dd) N-ethylpseudoephedrine.
(ee) Hydriotic acid.
(ff) Gamma butyrolactone (GBL), including butyrolactone, 1,2-butanolide, 2-oxanolone, tetrahydro-2-furanone, dihydro-2(3H)-furanone and tetramethylene glycol, but not including gamma aminobutyric acid (GABA).
(gg) 1,4-butanediol.
(hh) Any salt, isomer or salt of an isomer of the chemicals listed in paragraphs (a) to (gg) of this subsection.
(ii) Iodine in its elemental form.
(jj) Iodine matrix.
(kk) Red phosphorus, white phosphorus, yellow phosphorus or hypophosphorus acid and its salts.
(LL) Anhydrous ammonia.
(mm) Lithium metal.
(nn) Sodium metal.
(oo) Any substance established as a precursor substance by rule under authority granted in ORS 475.945.

475.950 Failure to report precursor substances transaction

(1) A person commits the offense of failure to report a precursor substances transaction if the person does any of the following:
 (a) Sells, transfers or otherwise furnishes any precursor substance described in ORS 475.940 (3)(a) to (hh) and (oo) and does not, at least three days before delivery of the substance, submit to the Department of State Police a report that meets the reporting requirements established by rule under ORS 475.945.
 (b) Receives any precursor substance described in ORS 475.940 (3)(a) to (hh) and (oo) and does not, within 10 days after receipt of the substance, submit to the Department of State Police a report that meets the reporting requirements established by rule under ORS 475.945.
(2) This section does not apply to any of the following:
 (a) Any pharmacist or other authorized person who sells or furnishes a precursor substance upon the prescription of a physician, dentist, podiatric physician and surgeon or veterinarian.
 (b) Any practitioner, as defined in ORS 475.005, who administers or furnishes a precursor substance to patients upon prescription.
 (c) Any person licensed by the State Board of Pharmacy who sells, transfers or otherwise furnishes a precursor substance to a licensed pharmacy,

physician, dentist, podiatric physician and surgeon or veterinarian for distribution to patients upon prescription.

(d) Any person who is authorized by rule under ORS 475.945 to report in an alternate manner if the person complies with the alternate reporting requirements.

(e) Any patient of a practitioner, as defined in ORS 475.005, who obtains a precursor substance from a licensed pharmacist, physician, dentist, podiatric physician and surgeon or veterinarian pursuant to a prescription.

(f) Any person who sells or transfers ephedrine, pseudoephedrine or phenylpropanolamine in compliance with ORS 475.973.

(g) Any practitioner, as defined in ORS 475.005, who dispenses a precursor substance to a person with whom the practitioner has a doctor-patient or doctor-client relationship.

(h) Any person who obtains a precursor substance from a practitioner, as defined in ORS 475.005, with whom the person has a doctor-patient or doctor-client relationship.

(i) Any person who sells or transfers an isomer of a precursor substance, unless it is an optical isomer.

(3) Penalties related to providing false information on a report required under this section are provided under ORS 475.965.

(4) The Department of State Police and any law enforcement agency may inspect and remove copies of the sales records of any retail or wholesale distributor of methyl sulfonyl methane or a precursor substance during the normal business hours of the retail or wholesale distributor or may require the retail or wholesale distributor to provide copies of the records.

(5) Failure to report a precursor substances transaction is a Class A misdemeanor.

475.962 Facilitation of controlled substance manufacture

(1) A person commits the crime of distribution of equipment, a solvent, a reagent or a precursor substance with intent to facilitate the manufacture of a controlled substance if the person sells or otherwise transfers equipment, a solvent, a reagent or a precursor substance with knowledge that the equipment, solvent, reagent or precursor substance is intended to be used in the manufacture of a controlled substance in violation of ORS 475.840.

(2) Distribution of equipment, a solvent, a reagent or a precursor substance with intent to facilitate the manufacture of a controlled substance is a Class B felony.

475.967 Possession of precursor substance

(1) A person commits the crime of possession of a precursor substance with intent to manufacture a controlled substance if the person possesses one or more precursor substances with the

intent to manufacture a controlled substance in violation of ORS 475.840 (1), 475.846, 475.848, 475.866, 475.868, 475.876, 475.878, 475.886 or 475.888.

(2) Possession of a precursor substance with intent to manufacture a controlled substance is a Class B felony.

475.969 Unlawful possession of phosphorus

(1) Except as otherwise provided in subsection (2) of this section, a person commits the crime of unlawful possession of phosphorus if the person knowingly possesses any amount of phosphorus.

(2) Subsection (1) of this section does not apply to:
  (a) A person who is conducting a licensed business that involves phosphorus in the manufacture of:
    (A) The striking surface used for lighting matches;
    (B) Flame retardant polymers; or
    (C) Fireworks if the person possesses a federal license to manufacture explosives;
  (b) A person who possesses phosphorus in conjunction with experiments conducted in a chemistry or chemistry related laboratory maintained by a:
    (A) Regularly established public or private secondary school; or
    (B) Public or private institution of higher education that is accredited by a regional or national accrediting agency recognized by the United States Department of Education;
  (c) A retail distributor, wholesaler, manufacturer, warehouseman or common carrier or an agent of any of these persons, who possesses phosphorus in the regular course of lawful business activities;
  (d) The possession of phosphorus as a component of a commercially produced product including, but not limited to, matchbooks, fireworks and emergency flares; or
  (e) A person who possesses phosphorus in a chemical compound in the regular course of a lawful agricultural activity.

(3) Unlawful possession of phosphorus is a Class A misdemeanor.

475.971 Unlawful possession of anhydrous ammonia

(1) A person commits the crime of unlawful possession of anhydrous ammonia if the person knowingly possesses anhydrous ammonia in a container that is not approved by the United States Department of Transportation to hold anhydrous ammonia nor constructed to meet state and federal health and safety standards to hold anhydrous ammonia.

(2) Unlawful possession of anhydrous ammonia is a Class A misdemeanor.

(3) This section does not apply to a person who possesses anhydrous ammonia as part of a cleanup, as defined in ORS 466.605, of anhydrous ammonia by the Department of Environmental Quality under ORS 466.610.

475.975 Unlawful possession or distribution of iodine

(1) Except as otherwise provided in subsection (2) of this section, a person commits the crime of unlawful possession of iodine in its elemental form if the person knowingly possesses iodine in its elemental form.

(2) Subsection (1) of this section does not apply to:
 (a) A physician, pharmacist, retail distributor, wholesaler, manufacturer, warehouseman or common carrier or an agent of any of these persons who possesses iodine in its elemental form in the regular course of lawful business activities;
 (b) A person who possesses iodine in its elemental form in conjunction with experiments conducted in a chemistry or chemistry related laboratory maintained by a:
  (A) Regularly established public or private secondary school;
  (B) Public or private institution of higher education that is accredited by a regional or national accrediting agency recognized by the United States Department of Education; or
  (C) Manufacturing, government agency or research facility in the course of lawful business activities;
 (c) A licensed veterinarian;
 (d) A person working in a general hospital who possesses iodine in its elemental form in the regular course of employment at the hospital; or
 (e) A person who possesses iodine in its elemental form as a prescription drug pursuant to a prescription issued by a licensed veterinarian or physician.

(3) Except as otherwise provided in subsection (4) of this section, a person who sells or otherwise transfers iodine in its elemental form to another person shall make a record of each sale or transfer. The record must be made on a form provided by the Department of State Police, completed pursuant to instructions provided by the department and retained by the person for at least three years or sent to the department if directed to do so by the department. Failure to make and retain or send a record required under this subsection is a Class A misdemeanor.

(4) A licensed veterinarian is not required to make a record of a sale or transfer of iodine in its elemental form under subsection (3) of this section if the veterinarian makes a record of the sale or transfer under other applicable laws or rules regarding the prescribing and dispensing of regulated or controlled substances by veterinarians.

(5) A person commits the crime of unlawful distribution of iodine in its elemental form if the person knowingly sells or otherwise

transfers iodine in its elemental form to a person not listed in subsection (2) of this section.

(6) Unlawful possession of iodine in its elemental form is a Class A misdemeanor.

(7) Unlawful distribution of iodine in its elemental form in a Class A misdemeanor.

475.977 Possessing or disposing of methamphetamine manufacturing waste

(1) As used in this section:
 (a) "Dispose of" means to discharge, deposit, inject, spill, leak or place methamphetamine manufacturing waste into or onto land or water.
 (b) "Methamphetamine manufacturing waste" means chemical waste or debris, used in or resulting from the manufacture of methamphetamine or the grinding, soaking or otherwise breaking down of a precursor substance for the manufacture of methamphetamine.

(2) A person commits the crime of possessing or disposing of methamphetamine manufacturing waste if the person:
 (a) Knowingly possesses methamphetamine manufacturing waste; or
 (b) Knowingly disposes of methamphetamine manufacturing waste.

(3) Subsection (2) of this section does not apply to the possession or disposal of methamphetamine manufacturing waste if:
 (a) The person was storing, treating or disposing of the waste pursuant to state or federal laws regulating the cleanup or disposal of waste products from unlawful methamphetamine manufacturing;
 (b) The person has notified a law enforcement agency of the existence of the waste; or
 (c) The person possesses or disposes of waste that had previously been disposed of by another person on the person's property in violation of subsection (2) of this section.

(4) Possessing or disposing of methamphetamine manufacturing waste is a Class C felony.

475.979 Unlawful possession of lithium or sodium metal

(1) Except as otherwise provided in subsection (2) of this section, a person commits the crime of unlawful possession of lithium metal or sodium metal if the person knowingly possesses lithium metal or sodium metal.

(2) Subsection (1) of this section does not apply to:
 (a) A person who is conducting a lawful manufacturing operation that involves the use of lithium metal or sodium metal;

(b) A person who possesses lithium metal or sodium metal in conjunction with experiments conducted in a chemistry or chemistry related laboratory maintained by a:
(A) Regularly established public or private secondary school; or
(B) Public or private institution of higher education that is accredited by a regional or national accrediting agency recognized by the United States Department of Education;
(c) A retail distributor, wholesaler, manufacturer, warehouseman or common carrier, or an agent of any of these persons, who possesses lithium metal or sodium metal in the regular course of lawful business activities; or
(d) A person who possesses lithium metal or sodium metal as a component of a commercially produced product including, but not limited to, rechargeable batteries.
(3) Unlawful possession of lithium metal or sodium metal is a Class A misdemeanor.

476.715 Throwing away of lighted matches, cigarettes and other materials

No one shall, at any time, throw away any lighted tobacco, cigars, cigarettes, matches or other lighted material, on any forestland, private road, public highway or railroad right of way within this state. Everyone operating a public conveyance shall post a copy of this section in a conspicuous place within the smoking compartments of such conveyance.

476.990 Penalties-Throwing burning material
•••
(5) Subject to ORS 153.022, violation of ORS 476.710 or 476.715 or of any rule or regulation of the State Parks and Recreation Department promulgated thereunder is punishable, upon conviction, by a fine not exceeding $500 or imprisonment in the county jail not exceeding six months, or both.

480.120 Sale, possession and use of fireworks

(1) No person shall sell, keep or offer for sale, expose for sale, possess, use, explode or have exploded any fireworks within Oregon, except as follows:
(a) Sales by manufacturers and wholesalers to customers residing outside this state in accordance with ORS 480.156;
(b) Sales to persons or organizations having obtained a permit from the State Fire Marshal for supervised public display;
(c) Sales to railroads, boats, motor vehicle or other transportation agencies, to be used for signal, warning or illumination purposes in connection with such business;
(d) Sale or use of blank cartridges for licensed shows or theaters or for signal or ceremonial purposes in athletics or sports;

(e) Experimental purposes by a manufacturer of explosives at such places where such experiments are normally conducted;
(f) Sale of blank cartridges for use by the militia or any organization of war veterans or other organization authorized by law to parade in public a color guard armed with firearms;
(g) Sale of shells, cartridges, gunpowder or explosives for use in legally permitted firearms;
(h) Sales of items described in ORS 480.127 to persons who possess the retail sales permit required by ORS 480.127 by a person who holds a manufacturer or wholesaler license issued pursuant to ORS 480.110 to 480.165; or
(i) Sales of items described in ORS 480.127 to individual members of the general public for personal use by taking direct delivery of those items at the time of sale from the holder of a retail sale permit issued pursuant to ORS 480.127.
(2) Law enforcement officers of the state, county or municipality shall enforce the provisions of ORS 480.110 to 480.165.
Note: Penalty for this section is pursuant to ORS 480.990(5).

480.990 Penalties–Fireworks offenses
•••
(5) Violation of any provision of ORS 480.110 to 480.165 is a Class B misdemeanor. Violations thereof may be prosecuted in state or municipal courts when violations occur within the municipality served thereby. Justice courts shall have concurrent jurisdiction with circuit courts in all proceedings arising within ORS 480.110 to 480.165.

•••

609.095 Dog as a public nuisance
(1) A dog is a public nuisance if it:
(a) Chases persons or vehicles on premises other than premises from which the keeper of the dog may lawfully exclude others;
(b) Damages or destroys property of persons other than the keeper of the dog;
(c) Scatters garbage on premises other than premises from which the keeper of the dog may lawfully exclude others;
(d) Trespasses on private property of persons other than the keeper of the dog;
(e) Disturbs any person by frequent or prolonged noises;
(f) Is a female in heat and running at large; or
(g) Is a potentially dangerous dog, but is not a dangerous dog as defined in ORS 609.098.
(2) The keeper of a dog in a county, precinct or city that is subject to ORS 609.030 and 609.040 to 609.110 maintains a public nuisance if the dog commits an act described under subsection (1) of this section. Maintaining a dog that is a public nuisance is a violation.
(3) A keeper of a dog maintains a public nuisance if the keeper fails to comply with reasonable restrictions imposed under ORS 609.990

or if a keeper fails to provide acceptable proof of compliance to the court on or before the 10th day after issuance of the order imposing the restrictions. If the court finds the proof submitted by the keeper unacceptable, the court shall send notice of that finding to the keeper no later than five days after the proof is received.

(4) Any person who has cause to believe a keeper is maintaining a dog that is a public nuisance may complain, either orally or in writing, to the county, precinct or city. The receipt of any complaint is sufficient cause for the county, precinct or city to investigate the matter and determine whether the keeper of the dog is in violation of subsection (2) or (3) of this section.

609.098 Maintaining a dangerous dog

(1) As used in this section, "dangerous dog" means a dog that:
  (a) Without provocation and in an aggressive manner inflicts serious physical injury, as defined in ORS 161.015, on a person or kills a person;
  (b) Acts as a potentially dangerous dog, as defined in ORS 609.035, after having previously committed an act as a potentially dangerous dog that resulted in the keeper being found to have violated ORS 609.095; or
  (c) Is used as a weapon in the commission of a crime.

(2) A person commits the crime of maintaining a dangerous dog if the person is the keeper of a dog and the person, with criminal negligence, fails to prevent the dog from engaging in an act described in subsection (1) of this section.

(3) Maintaining a dangerous dog is punishable as described in ORS 609.990.

609.990 Penalties–Dog offenses

(1) Violation of ORS 609.060 (2), 609.100 or 609.169 is a Class B violation.

(2) Maintaining a public nuisance in violation of ORS 609.095 (2) or (3) is punishable by a fine of not more than $250.

(3)(a) Except as provided in paragraph (b) of this subsection, violation of ORS 609.098 is a Class A misdemeanor.
  (b) If a dog kills a person, violation of ORS 609.098 is a Class C felony.
  (c) If a keeper violates ORS 609.098, the court shall order the dangerous dog killed in a humane manner.

...

Index

Symbols

165.570	911 system–Improper use *112*

A

167.340	Abandonment of animal *159*
163.535	Abandonment of child *57*
167.320	Abuse of animal I *156*
167.322	Abuse of animal I–Aggravated *156*
167.315	Abuse of animal II *156*
166.087	Abuse of corpse I *119*
166.085	Abuse of corpse II *119*
166.076	Abuse of memorial to the dead *118*
166.075	Abuse of venerated objects *118*
127.995	Advance directive–Altering, forging, concealing or destroying *5*
167.090	Advertising–Public display of nudity for *143*
163.345	Age as a defense to sexual offense *48*
165.805	Age misrepresentation by minor *114*
167.322	Aggravated animal abuse I *156*
163.196	Aggravated driving while suspended or revoked *38*
166.070	Aggravated harassment *117*
165.803	Aggravated identity theft *113*
163.095	Aggravated murder defined *29*
164.057	Aggravated theft I *72*
163.149	Aggravated vehicular homicide *34*
164.887	Agricultural operation interference *95*
164.889	Agricultural research interference *95*
163.117	Aiding commission of suicide not murder *32*
164.885	Aircraft endangering *94*
166.638	Airport–Discharging weapon *136*
163.730	Alarm–Defined *67*
471.410	Alcohol–Furnishing to intoxicated person *170*
471.410	Alcohol–Furnishing to minor *170*
471.430	Alcohol–Minor in possession *172*
166.450	Alter identification number on firearm *133*
475.971	Ammonia possession *198*
475.035	Amphetamine–Schedule II *176*

167.340	Animal abandonment	*159*
167.310	Animal abuse–Definitions	*153*
167.320	Animal abuse I	*156*
167.322	Animal abuse I–Aggravated	*156*
167.315	Animal abuse II	*156*
167.310	Animal–Defined	*153*
167.355	Animal fighting–Involvement in	*160*
167.312	Animal interference	*154*
167.330	Animal neglect I	*157*
167.325	Animal neglect II	*157*
167.333	Animal–Sexual assault of	*157*
166.210	Antique firearm–Defined	*122*
166.460	Antique firearms–Exceptions	*134*
167.840	Application of ORS 167.830	*167*
475.910	Applying controlled substance to minor	*193*
164.005	Appropriate–Defined	*70*
163.208	APSO	*41*
166.350	Armor piercing ammo–Possession	*128*
162.315	Arrest–Resisting	*25*
161.249	Arrest–Use of force by assisting person	*13*
164.305	Arson–Definitions	*84*
164.325	Arson I	*85*
164.315	Arson II	*84*
163.185	Assault I	*37*
163.175	Assault II	*36*
163.165	Assault III	*35*
163.160	Assault IV	*34*
167.339	Assault of law enforcement animal	*158*
163.208	Assault of public safety officer	*41*
167.352	Assistance animal–Interfering with	*159*
162.255	Assist in fire-fighting–Refusing to	*24*
162.245	Assist peace officer–Refusing to	*23*
161.405	Attempt–Defined	*15*
161.425	Attempt–Impossibility not a defense	*16*
161.430	Attempt–Renunciation as a defense	*16*
164.276	Authority of sports official to expel	*84*
164.135	Auto theft	*76*

B

165.002	Bad check–Definitions	*96*
165.065	Bad check–Negotiating	*99*

C

163.476	Being where children regularly congregate *55*
162.055	Benefit–Defined *18*
163.515	Bigamy *57*
167.118	Bingo, lotto or raffles or Monte Carlo *148*
166.642	Body armor–Felon in possession of *137*
166.643	Body armor–Unlawful possession of *137*
164.315	Bomb *84*
166.384	Bomb making *132*
166.385	Bomb–Possession of hoax device *132*
162.015	Bribe giving *18*
162.025	Bribe receiving *18*
162.035	Bribery defenses *18*
164.205	Building–Defined *80*
475.912	Bunk dope *193*
164.205	Burglary–Definitions *80*
164.225	Burglary I *81*
164.215	Burglary II *81*
164.235	Burglary tool–Defined *81*
164.235	Burglary tool–Possession *81*
476.715	Burning material–Throwing on road *201*
164.335	Burning–Reckless *85*
163.537	Buying or selling child *57*

C

164.373	Cable television–Tampering with *87*
133.033	Caretaking–Community *6*
164.272	Car prowling *83*
166.240	Carry concealed weapons *124*
164.135	Car theft *76*
164.272	Car–Unlawful entry into *83*
475.908	Cause ingestion of controlled substance *192*
166.076	Cemetery–Abuse of *118*
167.167	Cheating *151*
163.535	Child abandonment *57*
163.665	Child abuse–Defined *61*
163.537	Child–Buying or selling *57*
163.665	Child–Defined *61*
163.577	Child–Fail to supervise *60*
163.547	Child neglect I *58*
163.545	Child neglect II *58*
163.433	Child-Online sexual corruption I *52*

163.432	Child–Online sexual corruption II	*52*
163.690	Child pornography–Defense	*65*
163.665	Child pornography–Definitions	*61*
163.682	Child pornography–Exceptions	*62*
163.676	Child pornography–Exemption	*62*
163.684	Child pornography I	*63*
163.686	Child pornography II	*63*
163.687	Child pornography III	*64*
163.688	Child pornography–Possession I	*64*
163.689	Child pornography–Possession II	*65*
163.684	Child sexual abuse I	*63*
163.686	Child sexual abuse II	*63*
163.687	Child sexual abuse III	*64*
163.479	Child–Unlawful contact with	*56*
163.670	Child–Use in sexually explicit conduct	*62*
161.200	Choice of evils	*10*
476.715	Cigarette–Throwing on road	*201*
133.076	Citation–Failure to appear	*6*
475.900	Classification of drug offenses	*189*
164.270	Closure of premises to motor vehicles	*83*
163.426	Coach–Sexual abuse in the second degree by	*51*
475.882	Cocaine–DCS within 1000' of school	*187*
475.878	Cocaine–MCS within 1000' of school	*187*
475.035	Cocaine–Schedule II	*176*
475.880	Cocaine–Unlawful delivery	*187*
475.876	Cocaine–Unlawful manufacture	*187*
475.884	Cocaine–Unlawful possession	*187*
167.428	Cockfighting	*165*
167.431	Cockfighting–Participation in	*165*
163.730	Coerce–Defined	*67*
163.275	Coercion	*46*
163.285	Coercion–Defense	*46*
165.070	Communications device–Fraudulent	*100*
165.543	Communications–Interception	*111*
165.540	Communications–Obtaining contents	*109*
133.033	Community caretaking	*6*
167.017	Compelling prostitution	*139*
165.002	Complete written instrument–Defined	*96*
162.335	Compounding	*26*
162.345	Compounding–Defenses	*26*

C

164.377	Computer crime	**87**
166.240	Concealed weapons–Carrying	**124**
163.315	Consent–Incapacity	**47**
161.475	Conspiracy–Defense	**17**
161.450	Conspiracy–Defined	**16**
161.465	Conspiracy–Duration of	**17**
161.460	Conspiracy–Renunciation as defense	**17**
161.455	Conspiratorial relationship	**17**
162.135	Contraband–Defined	**20**
162.185	Contraband–Supplying	**21**
163.435	Contributing to sexual delinquency of minor	**52**
	Controlled substance *See also* DCS, MCS, PCS	
475.005	Controlled substance–Defined	**173**
475.916	Controlled substance fraud	**194**
167.222	Controlled substance–Frequenting	**152**
475.840	Controlled substance–Prohibited acts	**182**
166.087	Corpse abuse I	**119**
166.085	Corpse abuse II	**119**
163.448	Correctional facility–Defined	**53**
475.005	Counterfeit substance–Defined	**173**
163.750	Court's stalking protective order	**69**
167.810	Creating hazard	**167**
165.002	Credit card–Definitions	**96**
165.055	Credit card–Fraudulent use of	**99**
133.076	Criminal citation–Failure to appear	**6**
163.005	Criminal homicide–Defined	**29**
162.365	Criminal impersonation	**27**
162.367	Criminal impersonation of officer	**27**
161.150	Criminal liability–Defined	**9**
161.155	Criminal liability for conduct of another	**9**
163.145	Criminally negligent homicide	**34**
164.367	Criminal mischief–Aggregation	**87**
164.305	Criminal mischief–Definitions	**84**
164.365	Criminal mischief I	**86**
164.354	Criminal mischief II	**85**
164.345	Criminal mischief III	**85**
163.205	Criminal mistreatment I	**39**
163.200	Criminal mistreatment II	**39**
163.555	Criminal nonsupport	**58**

165.022	Criminal possession forged inst. I *98*
165.017	Criminal possession forged inst. II *98*
164.138	Criminal possession of a rented or leased motor vehicle *77*
165.032	Criminal possession of forgery device *98*
164.140	Criminal possession rented property *78*
165.037	Criminal simulation *98*
164.255	Criminal trespass I *82*
164.245	Criminal trespass II *82*
164.278	Criminal trespass at sports event *84*
164.243	Criminal trespass II by a guest *82*
164.265	Criminal trespass w/firearm *83*
161.085	Culpability–Definitions *8*
163.257	Custodial interference I *44*
163.245	Custodial interference II *44*
163.452	Custodial sexual misconduct I *53*
163.454	Custodial sexual misconduct II *54*
162.135	Custody–Defined *20*

D

609.098	Dangerous dog–Maintaining *203*
161.015	Dangerous weapon–Defined *7*
475.840	DCS *182*
475.880	DCS–Cocaine *187*
475.882	DCS–Cocaine within 1000' of school *187*
475.850	DCS–Heroin *184*
475.852	DCS–Heroin within 1000' of school *184*
475.912	DCS–Imitation controlled substances *193*
475.860	DCS–Marijuana *185*
475.862	DCS–Marijuana within 1000' of school *185*
475.870	DCS–MDMA *186*
475.872	DCS–MDMA within 1000' of school *186*
475.890	DCS–Methamphetamine *188*
475.892	DCS–Methamphetamine within 1000' of school *188*
475.906	DCS–To minor *192*
475.904	DCS–Within 1000' of School *192*
161.015	Deadly physical force–Defined *7*
161.239	Deadly physical force in making arrest or in preventing escape *12*

D

161.219	Deadly physical force–Limitations on in defense of person *11*
162.015	Deadly weapon–Defined *7*
164.085	Deception–Theft by *73*
161.229	Defense of property–Use of force *12*
163.285	Defenses–Coercion *46*
162.345	Defenses–Hindering or compounding *26*
161.125	Defenses–Intoxication/drug use *8*
163.690	Defenses–Lack of knowledge of age *65*
164.164	Defenses–Mail theft *80*
475.319	Defenses–Medical marijuana *179*
167.085	Defenses–Obscenity *142*
163.434	Defenses–Online sexual corruption of a child *52*
162.095	Defenses–Perjury & false swearing *19*
167.142	Defenses–Possession of gambling records *150*
167.095	Defenses–Publicly displaying nudity *143*
161.440	Defenses–Renunciation *16*
162.105	Defenses–Retraction *19*
161.475	Defenses–Solicitation and conspiracy *17*
164.035	Defenses–Theft *71*
167.310	Definitions–Animal abuse *153*
164.305	Definitions–Arson *84*
165.002	Definitions–Bad check *96*
166.641	Definitions–Body armor offenses *136*
164.205	Definitions–Burglary *80*
163.665	Definitions–Child pornography *61*
167.426	Definitions–Cockfighting *164*
475.005	Definitions–Controlled substance *173*
167.203	Definitions–Controlled substance offenses *151*
165.002	Definitions–Credit card *96*
161.085	Definitions–Culpability *8*
167.360	Definitions–Dogfighting *160*
163.505	Definitions–Family offenses *56*
166.210	Definitions–Firearm *122*
165.002	Definitions–Forgery *96*
167.117	Definitions–Gambling *144*
164.381	Definitions–Graffiti *89*
167.387	Definitions–Interference with livestock *162*

D

167.108	Definitions–Internet gambling *143*
163.261	Definitions–Involuntary servitude and human trafficking *44*
164.160	Definitions–Mail theft *79*
475.302	Definitions–Medical marijuana *177*
165.116	Definitions–Metal property offenses *105*
167.060	Definitions–Obscenity *140*
165.535	Definitions–Obtaining contents of communications *109*
163.431	Definitions-Online sexual corruption of a child *51*
165.072	Definitions–Payment card offenses *100*
167.002	Definitions–Prostitution *138*
164.105	Definitions–Right of possession *75*
181.594	Definitions–Sex offender registration *168*
163.305	Definitions–Sexual Offenses *46*
164.274	Definitions–Sports event trespass *83*
163.730	Definitions–Stalking *67*
163.211	Definitions–Tear gas, mace *42*
164.205	Definitions–Trespass *80*
166.360	Definitions–Weapon in public building *128*
475.005	Deliver or delivery–Defined *173*
475.840	Delivery of controlled substance *182*
	Delivery of controlled substance ***See also*** DCS
475.912	Delivery of imitation controlled substance *193*
162.175	Departure–Unauthorized *21*
164.775	Deposit trash within 100 yds. of waters *91*
164.005	Deprive–Defined *70*
166.384	Destructive device–Manufacture *132*
166.382	Destructive device–Possession *131*
164.367	Determining value of damage *87*
163.305	Deviate sexual intercourse–Defined *46*
166.370	Discharge firearm at school *129*
166.635	Discharge weapon at train *136*
166.638	Discharge weapon on or across airport *136*
166.630	Discharge weapon on or across highway, public utility or ocean shore *135*
166.023	Disorderly conduct I *115*
166.025	Disorderly conduct II *116*
167.080	Displaying obscene material to minor *142*

211

E

609.095	Dog as public nuisance *202*
609.095	Dog at large *202*
167.365	Dogfighting *161*
167.372	Dogfighting paraphernalia *162*
167.370	Dogfighting–Participation in *161*
163.196	Driving while suspended or revoked–Aggavated *38*
475.910	Drug–Administering to minor *193*
475.908	Drug–Administering without consent *192*
	Drug offenses
	See also Controlled substances, DCS, MCS, PCS
475.900	Drug offenses classification *189*
475.525	Drug paraphernalia *181*
167.212	Drug records-Tampering with *152*
475.035	Drug schedules *176 177*
167.222	Drug–Frequenting place where used *152*
475.918	Drug test falsification *194*
475.920	Drug test falsification equipment *195*
161.465	Duration of conspiracy *17*
161.270	Duress *15*
164.205	Dwelling—Defined *80*

E

167.830	Employing minor in place of entertainment *167*
162.257	EMT–Interfering with *24*
163.684	Encouraging child sexual abuse I *63*
163.686	Encouraging child sexual abuse II *63*
163.687	Encouraging child sexual abuse III *64*
164.885	Endangering aircraft *94*
163.195	Endangering–Reckless *38*
163.575	Endangering welfare of a minor *59*
164.205	Enter or remain unlawfully–Defined *80*
161.275	Entrapment *15*
471.430	Entry of licensed premises by minor *172*
162.135	Escape–Defined *20*
162.165	Escape I *21*
162.155	Escape II *21*
162.145	Escape III *21*
167.238	Evidence–Drug offenses *153*

163.565	Evidence of paternity **59**
162.295	Evidence–Tampering with **25**
166.380	Examination of firearm by officer **131**
166.460	Exceptions–Antique firearms **134**
163.702	Exceptions–Invasion of personal privacy **66**
165.124	Exceptions–Metal property offenses **108**
163.412	Exceptions–Sexual penetration **50**
163.206	Exceptions–Criminal mistreatment **41**
166.270	Ex-con in possession of firearm or other weapon **126**
167.335	Exemptions–Animal offenses **158**
163.755	Exemptions–Stalking protective order **69**
161.165	Exemptions to criminal liability **9**
167.075	Exhibiting obscene performance to minor **141**
164.315	Explosive device **84**
166.382	Explosive device–Possession **131**
166.480	Explosives–Sell/give to children **135**
164.075	Extortion–Theft by **73**
163.135	Extreme emotional disturbance as defense **33**

F

475.962	Facilitate controlled substance manufacture **197**
162.205	Fail to appear I **22**
162.195	Fail to appear II **22**
133.076	Fail to appear on criminal citation **6**
164.278	Fail to leave sports event **84**
165.107	Fail to maintain metal purchase record **102**
181.599	Fail to report as sex offender **169**
475.950	Fail to report precursor transaction **196**
163.577	Fail to supervise child **60**
162.385	False information to police **28**
165.002	Falsely alter–Defined **96**
165.002	Falsely complete–Defined **96**
165.002	Falsely make–Defined **96**
162.369	False police ID–Possession of **28**
162.375	False report–Initiating **28**
162.075	False swearing **19**
475.918	Falsifying drug test results **194**
166.642	Felon in possession of body armor **137**

F

166.270	Felon in possession of firearm or other weapon	*126*
165.813	Fictitious identification–Possession of	*115*
166.450	Firearm–Alter identification number on	*133*
164.265	Firearm–Criminal trespass with	*83*
166.210	Firearm–Defined	*122*
166.380	Firearm–Examination by peace officer	*131*
166.370	Firearm–In public building	*129*
166.190	Firearm–Pointing at another	*122*
166.470	Firearm–Sale/transfer of	*134*
166.210	Firearm silencer–Defined	*122*
166.438	Firearm–Transfer at gun shows	*133*
166.250	Firearm–Unlawful possession	*123*
166.425	Firearm–Unlawful purchase of	*132*
166.220	Firearm–Unlawful use	*124*
166.429	Firearm used in felony	*133*
162.225	Firefighter–Defined	*22*
162.257	Firefighter–Interfering with	*24*
480.120	Fireworks–Sale, possession and use	*201*
475.035	Flunitrazepam–Schedule IV	*177*
161.205	Force–Use of physical	*10*
163.305	Forcible compulsion–Defined	*46*
133.318	Foreign restraining order–Providing false	*7*
165.022	Forged instrument–Criminal possession I	*98*
165.017	Forged instrument–Criminal possession II	*98*
165.002	Forged instrument–Defined	*96*
165.002	Forgery–Definitions	*96*
165.032	Forgery device–Criminal possession of	*98*
165.013	Forgery I	*97*
165.007	Forgery II	*97*
165.070	Fraudulent communications device	*100*
165.042	Fraudulently obtaining signature	*98*
165.055	Fraudulently using credit card	*99*
167.222	Frequenting drug house	*152*
131.605	Frisk–Defined	*5*
131.625	Frisk of stopped persons	*6*
133.076	FTA–Citation	*6*
162.205	FTA I	*22*
162.195	FTA II	*22*
165.055	FUCC	*99*
471.410	Furnishing alcohol to intoxicated person	*170*

471.410	Furnishing alcohol to minor	*170*

G

167.117	Gambling–Definitions	*144*
167.147	Gambling device–Possession	*151*
167.109	Gambling over the Internet	*143*
167.137	Gambling records–Possession I	*150*
167.132	Gambling records–Possession II	*150*
167.127	Gambling–Unlawful I	*150*
167.122	Gambling–Unlawful II	*149*
167.808	Glue sniffing	*166*
162.235	Government–Obstructing	*23*
164.383	Graffiti–Applying	*89*
164.381	Graffiti–Definitions	*89*
164.386	Graffiti implement possession	*90*
166.076	Grave–Abuse of	*118*
475.856	Grow op–Marijuana	*184*
164.243	Guest–Defined	*82*
166.438	Gun show–Transfer of firearms at	*133*

H

164.377	Hacking computer	*87*
166.210	Handgun–Defined	*122*
166.065	Harassment	*116*
166.070	Harassment–Aggravated	*117*
166.090	Harassment–Telephonic	*120*
167.810	Hazard–Creating	*167*
163.197	Hazing	*38*
475.852	Heroin–DCS within 1000' of school	*184*
475.848	Heroin–MCS within 1000' of school	*184*
475.035	Heroin–Schedule I	*176*
475.850	Heroin–Unlawful delivery	*184*
475.846	Heroin–Unlawful manufacture	*184*
475.854	Heroin–Unlawful possession	*184*
162.345	Hindering–Defenses	*26*
162.325	Hindering prosecution	*26*
166.385	Hoax destructive device	*132*
163.145	Homicide–Criminally negligent	*34*
163.005	Homicide–Defined	*29*
163.730	Household member–Defined	*67*
163.005	Human being–Defined	*29*

I

163.266	Human trafficking *45*

I

165.800	Identity theft *112*
165.803	Identity theft–Aggravated *113*
163.325	Ignorance or mistake as a defense *47*
475.912	Imitation controlled substance–Delivery of *193*
163.730	Immediate family–Defined *67*
162.365	Impersonation *27*
162.367	Impersonation of officer *27*
165.570	Improper use of 911 *112*
163.315	Incapacity to consent *47*
163.525	Incest *57*
165.002	Incomplete written instrument–Defined *96*
163.467	Indecency–Private *55*
163.465	Indecency–Public *54*
167.808	Inhalants–Unlawful possession *166*
162.375	Initiating a false report *28*
166.180	Injuring–Negligently *122*
166.275	Inmate–Possession of weapons by *128*
165.540	Interception of communications *109*
165.543	Interception of communications *111*
164.887	Interfering with agricultural operations *95*
164.889	Interfering with agricultural research *95*
167.352	Interfering with assistance animal *159*
162.257	Interfering with firefighter or EMT *24*
167.388	Interfering with livestock production *163*
165.572	Interfering with making report *112*
162.247	Interfering with peace officer *23*
167.337	Interfering with police animal *158*
166.116	Interfering with public transportation *120*
167.109	Internet gambling *143*
167.108	Internet gambling–Definitions *143*
163.433	Internet sexual corruption of a child I *52*
163.432	Internet sexual corruption of a child II *52*
166.165	Intimidation I *121*
166.155	Intimidation II *121*
161.125	Intoxication defense *8*
163.700	Invasion of personal privacy *65*
163.264	Involuntary servitude I *45*

163.263	Involuntary servitude II	*44*
167.355	Involvement in animal fighting	*160*
475.975	Iodine–Unlawful possession or distribution	*199*
131.605	Is about to commit–Defined	*5*

J

161.190	Justification as defense	*9*
161.195	Justification–Defined	*9*

K

163.235	Kidnapping I	*43*
163.225	Kidnapping II	*43*

L

163.709	Laser pointer–Unlawful directing	*67*
167.339	Law enforcement animal–Assaulting	*158*
163.215	Lawful custodian–Defined	*43*
164.138	Leased motor vehicle–Criminal possession	*77*
164.140	Leased property–Criminal possession	*78*
162.355	Legal process–Simulating	*26*
161.155	Liability for conduct of another	*9*
475.979	Lithium metal–Unlawful possession	*200*
164.775	Littering in or near waters	*91*
164.805	Littering–Offensive	*92*
167.385	Livestock animal–Unauthorized use	*162*
167.388	Livestock production–Interference	*163*
164.065	Lost property–Theft of	*72*
475.035	LSD–Schedule I	*176*
167.057	Luring a minor	*139*

M

163.211	Mace–Defined	*42*
163.213	Mace–Unlawful use I	*42*
163.212	Mace–Unlawful use II	*42*
166.210	Machine gun–Defined	*122*
166.272	Machine gun–Possession	*127*
164.162	Mail theft	*79*
164.164	Mail theft–Defense	*80*
164.160	Mail theft–Definitions	*79*
609.098	Maintaining dangerous dog	*203*

M

165.572	Making a report–Interference with *112*
163.118	Manslaughter I *32*
163.125	Manslaughter II *33*
475.005	Manufacture–Defined *173*
475.840	Manufacture of controlled substance *182*
	Manufacture of controlled substance **See also** MCS
475.860	Marijuana–DCS *185*
475.862	Marijuana–DCS within 1000' of school *185*
475.005	Marijuana–Defined *173*
475.856	Marijuana–MCS *184*
475.858	Marijuana–MCS within 1000' of school *184*
475.864	Marijuana–PCS *185*
475.035	Marijuana–Schedule I *176*
475.840	MCS *182*
475.876	MCS–Cocaine *187*
475.878	MCS–Cocaine within 1000' of school *187*
475.962	MCS–Facilitation *197*
475.846	MCS–Heroin *184*
475.848	MCS–Heroin within 1000' of school *184*
475.856	MCS–Marijuana *184*
475.858	MCS–Marijuana within 1000' of school *184*
475.866	MCS–MDMA *186*
475.868	MCS–MDMA within 1000' of school *186*
475.886	MCS–Methamphetamine *188*
475.888	MCS–Methamphetamine within 1000' of school *188*
475.904	MCS within 1000' of school *192*
	MDMA–Chemical name 3,4-methylenedioxymethamphetamine *186*
475.872	MDMA–DCS within 1000' of school *186*
475.868	MDMA–MCS within 1000' of school *186*
475.870	MDMA–Unlawful delivery *186*
475.866	MDMA–Unlawful manufacture *186*
475.874	MDMA–Unlawful possession *187*
475.319	Medical marijuana–Defenses *179*
475.316	Medical marijuana immunity *178*
475.320	Medical marijuana limits *179*
475.323	Medical marijuana–Protection of property *180*
475.323	Medical marijuana–Search & seizure *180*
166.076	Memorial to the dead–Abuse of *118*

M

163.190	Menacing **38**
163.305	Mentally defective–Defined **46**
163.305	Mentally incapacitated–Defined **46**
475.035	Mescaline–Schedule I **176**
165.118	Metal property offenses **107**
164.857	Metal property–Transporting unlawfully **93**
165.107	Metal purchase record–Fail to maintain **102**
475.035	Methadone–Schedule II **176**
475.892	Methamphetamine–DCS within 1000' of school **188**
475.977	Methamphetamine manufacturing waste **200**
475.888	Methamphetamine–MCS within 1000' of school **188**
475.035	Methamphetamine–Schedule II **176**
475.890	Methamphetamine–Unlawful delivery **188**
475.886	Methamphetamine–Unlawful manufacture **188**
475.894	Methamphetamine–Unlawful possession **188**
167.310	Minimum care–Defined **153**
167.080	Minor–Displaying obscene material to **142**
475.906	Minor–Distribute controlled substance to **192**
475.910	Minor–Drugging **193**
163.575	Minor–Endangering welfare **59**
167.075	Minor–Exhibiting obscene performance to **141**
167.057	Minor–Luring **139**
165.805	Minor–Misrepresenting age **114**
471.430	Minor–On licensed premises **172**
471.430	Minor–Possession of alcohol **172**
167.400	Minor–Possession of tobacco **163**
167.401	Minor–Tobacco purchase by **163**
471.430	MIP **172**
164.365	Mischief I–Criminal **86**
164.354	Mischief II–Criminal **85**
164.345	Mischief III–Criminal **85**
162.415	Misconduct I **29**
162.405	Misconduct II **29**
163.445	Misconduct–Sexual **53**
166.470	Misdemeanor involving violence–Defined **134**
164.065	Mislaid property–Theft of **72**
165.805	Misrepresentation of age by a minor **114**

163.325	Mistake as a defense *47*
163.205	Mistreatment I–Criminal *39*
163.200	Mistreatment II–Criminal *39*
164.882	Movie piracy *94*
163.115	Murder *30*
163.095	Murder–Aggravated *29*

N

165.065	NABC *99*
167.330	Neglect of animal I *157*
167.325	Neglect of animal II *157*
163.547	Neglect of child I *58*
163.545	Neglect of child II *58*
166.180	Negligently wounding another *122*
165.065	Negotiating a bad check *99*
163.555	Nonsupport–Criminal *58*

O

162.235	Obstruct governmental or judicial administration *23*
164.005	Obtain–Defined *70*
165.540	Obtaining contents of communications *109*
164.805	Offensive littering *92*
164.785	Offensive substances-Placing *92*
162.415	Official misconduct I *29*
162.405	Official misconduct II *29*
163.433	Online sexual corruption of a child I *52*
163.432	Online sexual corruption of a child II *52*
164.205	Open to the public–Defined *80*
164.098	Organized retail theft *74*
166.651	Overpass–Throwing an object off I *138*
166.649	Overpass–Throwing an object off II *137*
164.005	Owner–Defined *70*

P

167.808	Paint sniffing *166*
475.525	Paraphernalia *181*
163.577	Parental responsibility *60*
161.205	Parental use of force *10*
167.431	Participation in cockfighting *165*
167.370	Participation in dogfighting *161*

P

163.565	Paternity evidence	*59*
165.074	Payment card factoring	*101*
475.840	PCS	*182*
475.884	PCS–Cocaine	*187*
475.854	PCS–Heroin	*184*
475.874	PCS–MDMA	*187*
475.894	PCS–Methamphetamine	*188*
162.247	Peace officer–Interfering with	*23*
609.990	Penalties–Dog offenses	*203*
480.990	Penalties–Fireworks offenses	*202*
475.904	Penalties–MCS/DCS within 1000' of school	*192*
476.990	Penalties–Throwing burning material	*201*
163.211	Pepper mace–Defined	*42*
163.213	Pepper mace–Unlawful use I	*42*
163.212	Pepper mace–Unlawful use II	*42*
162.065	Perjury	*19*
162.095	Perjury–Defenses	*19*
163.702	Personal privacy–Exceptions	*66*
163.700	Personal privacy–Invasion of	*65*
166.260	Persons not affected by ORS 166.250	*125*
131.615	Person stop	*5*
167.332	Pet possession restrictions	*157*
475.035	Peyote–Schedule I	*176*
475.969	Phosphorus possession	*198*
162.225	Physical evidence–Defined	*22*
161.249	Physical force by private person assisting arrest	*13*
161.255	Physical force by private person making citizen's arrest	*13*
161.015	Physical force–Defined	*7*
161.205	Physical force–Generally	*10*
161.209	Physical force in defense of person	*11*
161.225	Physical force in defense of premises	*11*
161.229	Physical force in defense of property	*12*
161.235	Physical force in making arrest or in preventing escape	*12*
161.215	Physical force–Limitations on in defense of person	*11*
161.015	Physical injury–Defined	*7*
163.305	Physically helpless–Defined	*46*

P

167.002	Place of prostitution–Defined *138*
164.785	Placing offensive substances *92*
166.190	Pointing firearm at another *122*
167.337	Police animal–Interfere with *158*
162.369	Police ID–Possession of False *28*
163.208	Police officer–Assaulting *41*
162.365	Police officer–Impersonation *27*
162.245	Police officer–Refusing to assist *23*
127.995	POLST–Altering, forging, concealing or destroying *5*
161.015	Possess–Defined *7*
475.971	Possession of anhydrous ammonia *198*
166.350	Possession of armor piercing ammo *128*
164.235	Possession of burglary tool *81*
163.688	Possession of child pornography I *64*
163.689	Possession of child pornography II *65*
	Possession of controlled substance **See also** PCS
475.840	Possession of controlled substance *182*
166.382	Possession of destructive device *131*
167.372	Possession of dogfighting paraphernalia *162*
162.369	Possession of false police ID *28*
165.813	Possession of fictitious identification *115*
166.370	Possession of firearm in public building *129*
166.272	Possession of firearm silencers *127*
166.250	Possession of firearm unlawfully *124*
165.022	Possession of forged instrument I *98*
165.017	Possession of forged instrument II *98*
165.070	Possession of fraudulent communications device *100*
167.147	Possession of gambling device *151*
167.137	Possession of gambling records I *150*
167.132	Possession of gambling records II *150*
166.385	Possession of hoax destructive device *132*
471.430	Possession of liquor while under 21 *172*
166.272	Possession of machine gun *127*
165.810	Possession of personal identification device *115*
475.969	Possession of phosphorus *198*
475.967	Possession of precursor substance *197*
166.272	Possession of short-barreled firearms *127*

164.235	Possession of theft device	*81*
167.400	Possession of tobacco by minor	*163*
166.275	Possession of weapons by inmates	*128*
163.580	Post sign of sale of smoking devices	*61*
475.967	Precursor possession	*197*
475.940	Precursor substances	*195*
475.950	Precursor transaction–Fail to report	*196*
164.388	Preemption–Graffiti	*90*
164.205	Premises–Defined	*80*
475.005	Prescription–Defined	*173*
475.916	Prescription fraud	*194*
167.238	Prima facie evidence–Drug offenses	*153*
166.275	Prisoner–Possession of weapons by	*128*
163.700	Privacy–Invasion of	*65*
163.467	Private indecency	*55*
475.840	Prohibited acts–Drugs	*182*
167.012	Promoting prostitution	*138*
164.005	Property–Defined	*70*
164.305	Property of another–Defined	*84*
162.325	Prosecution–Hindering	*26*
167.002	Prostitute–Defined	*138*
167.007	Prostitution	*138*
167.017	Prostitution–Compelling	*139*
167.002	Prostitution–Definitions	*138*
167.002	Prostitution enterprise–Defined	*138*
167.012	Prostitution–Promoting	*138*
164.305	Protected property–Defined	*84*
133.318	Providing false foreign restraining order	*7*
471.410	Providing liquor to intoxicated person	*170*
471.410	Providing liquor to person under 21	*170*
475.035	Psilocybin–Schedule I	*176*
166.370	Public building–firearm in	*129*
167.090	Public display of nudity for advertising	*143*
163.465	Public indecency	*54*
161.015	Public place–Defined	*7*
162.305	Public records tampering	*25*
166.116	Public transportation–Interfering	*120*

R

163.375	Rape I	*48*
163.365	Rape II	*48*

S

163.355	Rape III *48*
161.245	Reasonable belief–Defined *13*
131.605	Reasonably suspects–Defined *5*
164.162	Receipt of stolen mail *79*
164.095	Receiving–Theft by *74*
164.335	Reckless burning *85*
163.195	Reckless endangering *38*
165.074	Reencoder–Use to access payment card *101*
162.255	Refusing to assist in fire-fighting *24*
162.245	Refusing to assist peace officer *23*
163.215	Relative–Defined *43*
164.138	Rented motor vehicle-Criminal possession *77*
164.140	Rented property–Criminal possession *78*
161.430	Renunciation as defense to attempt *16*
161.460	Renunciation as defense to conspiracy *17*
161.440	Renunciation as defense to solicitation *16*
163.730	Repeated–Defined *67*
165.572	Report–Interference with *112*
167.312	Research & animal interference *154*
162.315	Resisting arrest *25*
133.318	Restraining order–False foreign *7*
164.098	Retail theft-Organized *74*
162.105	Retraction as defense *19*
164.105	Right of possession–Definitions *75*
166.015	Riot *115*
164.415	Robbery I *91*
164.405	Robbery II *90*
164.395	Robbery III *90*

S

167.062	Sadomasochistic abuse *141*
480.120	Sale of fireworks *201*
166.480	Sale or gift of explosives to children *135*
166.470	Sale or transfer of firearm *134*
166.272	Sawed-off shotgun/rifle *127*
165.074	Scanner–Use to access payment card *101*
475.035	Schedule I Drugs *176* *177*
475.035	Schedule II Drugs *176*
	Schedule IV Controlled substances *177*
163.730	School–Defined *67*
166.370	School–Discharging firearm *129*

165.570	School safety hotline abuse	*112*
165.118	Scrap metal property offenses	*107*
167.352	Search & rescue animal–Interfering with	*159*
161.015	Serious physical injury–Defined	*7*
164.125	Services–Theft of	*75*
163.476	Sex offender(certain)–Being where children regularly congregate	*55*
163.479	Sex offender(certain)–Unlawful contact with child	*56*
181.599	Sex offender–Fail to report as	*169*
163.427	Sexual abuse I	*51*
163.425	Sexual abuse II	*50*
163.415	Sexual abuse III	*50*
163.426	Sexual abuse in the second degree by a coach	*51*
167.333	Sexual assault of animal	*157*
167.002	Sexual conduct–Defined	*138*
167.062	Sexual conduct in live show	*141*
163.305	Sexual contact–Defined	*46*
167.002	Sexual contact–Defined	*138*
163.432	Sexual corruption of a child II–Online	*52*
163.433	Sexual corruption of a child I–Online	*52*
163.435	Sexual delinquency of a minor	*52*
163.305	Sexual intercourse–Defined	*46*
163.665	Sexually explicit conduct–Defined	*61*
163.445	Sexual misconduct	*53*
163.452	Sexual misconduct I–Custodial	*53*
163.454	Sexual misconduct II–Custodial	*54*
163.412	Sexual penetration–Exceptions	*50*
163.411	Sexual penetration I	*49*
163.408	Sexual penetration II	*49*
164.098	Shoplifting-Organized	*74*
166.272	Short-barreled firearms–Possession	*127*
166.210	Short-barreled rifle–Defined	*122*
166.210	Short-barreled shotgun–Defined	*122*
165.042	Signature–Fraudulently obtaining	*98*
166.272	Silencers–Possession	*127*
162.355	Simulating legal process	*26*
165.037	Simulation	*98*
163.580	Smoking devices–Post sign of sale of	*61*
167.808	Sniffing inhalants	*166*

475.979	Sodium metal–Unlawful possession	**200**
163.405	Sodomy I	**49**
163.395	Sodomy II	**49**
163.385	Sodomy III	**49**
161.475	Solicitation–Defense	**17**
161.435	Solicitation–Defined	**16**
161.440	Solicitation–Renunciation as defense	**16**
164.278	Sports event trespass	**84**
164.276	Sports official–Authority of to expel	**84**
163.732	Stalking	**68**
163.735	Stalking citation	**68**
163.730	Stalking–Definitions	**67**
162.055	Statement–Defined	**18**
164.162	Stolen mail–Receipt of	**79**
164.115	Stolen property–Value	**75**
131.605	Stop–Defined	**5**
131.615	Stopping of persons	**5**
163.187	Strangulation	**37**
163.213	Stun gun–Unlawful use I	**42**
163.212	Stun gun–Unlawful use II	**42**
163.264	Subjecting another to involuntary servitude I	**45**
163.263	Subjecting another to involuntary servitude II	**44**
163.577	Supervise child–Fail to	**60**
162.185	Supplying contraband	**21**
162.075	Swearing–False	**19**
162.055	Sworn statement–Defined	**18**

T

164.373	Tampering with cable television equipment	**87**
167.212	Tampering with drug records	**152**
162.295	Tampering with physical evidence	**25**
162.305	Tampering with public records	**25**
162.285	Tampering with witness	**24**
163.211	Tear gas–Defined	**42**
163.213	Tear gas–Unlawful use I	**42**
163.212	Tear gas–Unlawful use II	**42**
166.090	Telephonic harassment	**120**
475.035	Tetrahydrocannabinols-Schedule I	**176**
164.882	Theater–Videotaping in	**94**

164.055	Theft I *71*
164.045	Theft II *71*
164.043	Theft III *71*
164.085	Theft by deception *73*
164.075	Theft by extortion *73*
164.095	Theft by receiving *74*
164.015	Theft–Defined *70*
164.235	Theft device-Possession of *81*
164.057	Theft I-Aggravated *72*
164.135	Theft of automobile *76*
165.800	Theft of identity *112*
164.065	Theft of lost, mislaid property *72*
164.125	Theft of services *75*
167.352	Therapy animal–Interfering with *159*
476.715	Throwing away of burning material *201*
166.635	Throwing object at train *136*
166.651	Throwing object off overpass I *138*
166.649	Throwing object off overpass II *137*
167.400	Tobacco possession by minor *163*
167.401	Tobacco purchase by minor *163*
163.266	Trafficking in persons *45*
163.426	Trainer–Sexual abuse in the second degree by *51*
166.438	Transfer of firearms at gun shows *133*
164.857	Transporting metal property *93*
164.857	Transporting metal property unlawfully *93*
164.775	Trash–Deposit in/near waters *91*
164.278	Trespass at sports event *84*
164.205	Trespass–Definitions *80*
164.255	Trespass I–Criminal *82*
164.243	Trespass II by a guest–Criminal *82*
164.245	Trespass II–Criminal *82*
164.265	Trespass with firearm–Criminal *83*

U

475.920	UA falsification equipment *195*
162.175	Unauthorized departure *21*
162.135	Unauthorized departure–Defined *20*
167.385	Unauthorized use of a livestock animal *162*
164.135	Unauthorized use of vehicle *76*
164.383	Unlawful application of graffiti *89*

U

163.479	Unlawful contact with a child	*56*
475.880	Unlawful delivery of cocaine	*187*
475.882	Unlawful delivery of cocaine within 1000' of school	*187*
475.850	Unlawful delivery of heroin	*184*
475.852	Unlawful delivery of heroin within 1000' of school	*184*
475.912	Unlawful delivery of imitation controlled substance	*193*
475.860	Unlawful delivery of marijuana	*185*
475.862	Unlawful delivery of marijuana within 1000' of school	*185*
475.870	Unlawful delivery of MDMA	*186*
475.872	Unlawful delivery of MDMA within 1000' of school	*186*
475.890	Unlawful delivery of methamphetamine	*188*
475.892	Unlawful delivery of methamphetamine within 1000' of school	*188*
163.709	Unlawful directing of light from a laser	*67*
164.272	Unlawful entry into motor vehicle	*83*
167.127	Unlawful gambling I	*150*
167.122	Unlawful gambling II	*149*
164.857	Unlawfully transporting metal property	*93*
475.876	Unlawful manufacture of cocaine	*187*
475.878	Unlawful manufacture of cocaine within 1000' of school	*187*
166.384	Unlawful manufacture of destructive device	*132*
475.846	Unlawful manufacture of heroin	*184*
475.848	Unlawful manufacture of heroin within 1000' of school	*184*
475.856	Unlawful manufacture of marijuana	*184*
475.858	Unlawful manufacture of marijuana within 1000' of school	*184*
475.866	Unlawful manufacture of MDMA	*186*
475.868	Unlawful manufacture of MDMA within 1000' of school	*186*
475.886	Unlawful manufacture of methamphetamine	*188*
475.888	Unlawful manufacture of methamphetamine within 1000' of a school	*188*

U

164.882	Unlawful operation of audiovisual device **94**
166.350	Unlawful possession of armor piercing ammo **128**
166.643	Unlawful possession of body armor **137**
475.884	Unlawful possession of cocaine **187**
166.260	Unlawful possession of firearm–Exceptions **125**
166.262	Unlawful possession of firearm–Limitation **126**
166.250	Unlawful possession of firearm **124**
166.272	Unlawful possession of firearm silencers **127**
164.386	Unlawful possession of graffiti implement **90**
475.854	Unlawful possession of heroin **184**
167.808	Unlawful possession of inhalants **166**
475.979	Unlawful possession of lithium/sodium **200**
166.272	Unlawful possession of machine guns **127**
475.864	Unlawful possession of marijuana **185**
475.874	Unlawful possession of MDMA **187**
475.894	Unlawful possession of methamphetamine **188**
475.969	Unlawful possession of phosphorus **198**
166.272	Unlawful possession of short-barrel firearm **127**
475.975	Unlawful possession or distribution of iodine **199**
163.476	Unlawful presence in location where children regularly congregate **55**
166.425	Unlawful purchase of firearm **132**
163.411	Unlawful sexual penetration I **49**
163.408	Unlawful sexual penetration II **49**
163.213	Unlawful use of stun gun or mace I **42**
163.212	Unlawful use of stun gun or mace II **42**
166.220	Unlawful use of weapon **123**
162.085	Unsworn falsification **19**
161.267	Use of physical force by corrections officer **14**
161.205	Use of physical force–Generally **10**
161.260	Use of physical force in resisting arrest **14**
161.265	Use of physical force to prevent escape **14**
163.670	Using child sexually explicit conduct **62**
167.262	Using minor in drug offense **153**
165.002	Utter–Defined **96**

164.135	UUMV *76*

V

164.115	Value of stolen property *75*
164.272	Vehicle–Unlawful entry into *83*
163.149	Vehicular homicide-Aggravated *34*
166.075	Venerated objects–Abuse of *118*
164.882	Videotaping in theater *94*
163.750	Violate court's stalking order *69*

W

166.240	Weapon–Carrying concealed *124*
161.015	Weapon (Dangerous)–Defined *7*
166.210	Weapon–Definitions *122*
166.360	Weapon in public building–Defined *128*
166.220	Weapon–Unlawful use *123*
163.215	Without consent–Defined *43*
162.285	Witness tampering *24*
166.180	Wounding–Negligently *122*
165.002	Written instrument–Defined *96*

SPANISH FOR LAW ENFORCEMENT

This section contains common situational dialogs and questions useful to street officers. The word choices are designed to apply to most Spanish speakers across different dialects.

The Spanish language consists of the same letters as the English alphabet and the four additional characters: CH, LL, Ñ, and RR.
  CH: Is pronounced like the "ch" in "church" at all times.
  LL: Like the English consonant "Y".
  Ñ: Like the "ny" in "canyon".
  RR: Very strongly trilled, with the front top portion of the tongue on the roof of the mouth behind the teeth.

In Spanish, the letter "H" is always silent. The letter "J" is pronounced like the English "h" in "house". Spanish vowels maintain the following pronunciations at all times:
  A: Sounds like the "a" in "father".
  E: Sounds like the "e" in "they".
  I: Sounds like the "i" in "police".
  O: Sounds like the "O" in "Ohio".
  U: Sounds like the "u" in "rude".
  QU: Sounds like the "c" in "coal".

HIGH RISK VEHICLE STOP

Stop the car! This is the police!
  ¡Pare el carro! ¡Esta es la policía!
  PAH-reh ehl KAH-rroh. EStah ess lah poh-lee-SEE-ah
You are being stopped on suspicion of a crime!
  ¡Lo estamos parando por sospecha de un delito!
  loh es-TAH-mohs pah-RAHN-doh pohr sos-PEH-cha deh oon deh-LEE-toh
Driver, remove the car keys.
  ¡Conductor, saque las llaves del carro!
  kohn-dook-TOHR SAH-keh lahs YAH-behs del KAH-rroh
Put your hands out the window!
  ¡Ponga las manos afuera de la ventana!
  POHN-gah lahs MAH-nohs ah-fooEH-rah deh lah vehn-TAH-nah

Open the door from the outside and get out!
   Abra la puerta de por afuera y salga.
   AH-brah lah PWEHR-tah deh pohr ah-fooEH-rah ee SAHL-gah
Hands up!
   ¡Manos arriba!
   MAH-nohs ah-RREE-bah
Kick the door shut!
   ¡Cierre la puerta con una patada!
   seeEH-rreh lah PWEHR-tah kohn oo-nah pah-TAH-dah
With your hands up, walk backwards toward me!
   ¡Con las manos arriba, camine para atrás hacia mí!
   kohn lahs MAH-nohs ah-RREE-bah, kah-MEE-neh pah-rah ah-TRAHS AH-seeah MEE
You in the car, we know you are there, sit up now!
   Ustedes en el carro, sabemos que están ahí, siéntense derechos ahora mismo.
Take one step to the right (left).
   Tome un paso a la derecha (izquierda).
   TOH-meh oon PAH-soh ah lah deh-REH-chah (ees-keeEHR-dah)
Another step.
   Otro paso.
   OH-troh PAH-soh
Take one step forward (backward).
   Tome un paso hacia adelante (atrás).
   TOH-meh oon PAH-soh ah-ciah ah-deh-LAHN-teh (ah-TRAHS)
Front passenger
   Pasajero delantero
   pah-sah-HEH-roh deh-lan-TEH-roh
Rear passenger
   Pasajero de atrás
   pah-sah-HEH-roh deh ah-TRAHS

LOW RISK STOP

Stop! Police!
   ¡Pare! ¡Policía!
   PAH-reh, poh-lee-SEE-ah
Put your hands up!
   ¡Manos arriba!
   MAH-nohs ah-RREE-bah

Slowly turn around!
> **¡Despacio, voltéese!**
> dehs-PAH-seeoh, vohl-TEH-eh-seh

Stop, spread your feet!
> **¡Pare, separe los pies!**
> PAH-reh, seh-PAH-reh lohs peeEHS

Put your hands on the back of your head!
> **¡Ponga las manos detrás de la cabeza!**
> POHN-gah lahs MAH-nohs deh-TRAHS deh lah kah-BEH-sah

Interlace your fingers!
> **¡Entrelace los dedos!**
> ehn-treh-LAH-seh lohs DEH-dohs

Don't move!
> **¡No se mueva!**
> no seh mooEH-vah

HIGH RISK PRONE

Stop!
> **¡Pare!**
> PAH-reh

Put your hands up!
> **¡Manos arriba!**
> MAH-nohs ah-RREE-bah

Slowly get down on your knees!
> **¡Despacio, Arrodíllese!**
> dehs-PAH-seeoh, ah-rroh-DEE-yeh-seh

Slowly, with your hands in front of you, lie face down!
> **¡Despacio, con las manos en frente de usted, acuéstese boca abajo.**
> dehs-PAH-seeoh, kohn lahs MAH-nohs ehn FREHN-teh deh oos-TEHD, ah-KWEHS-teh-seh BOH-kah ah-BAH-hoh

Face down on the ground!
> **¡Ponga la cara al suelo!**
> POHN-gah lah KAH-rah ahl SWEH-loh

Put your arms out to your side, palms up!
> **¡Estire los brazos a los lados, con las palmas arriba!**
> ehs-TEE-reh lohs BRAH-sohs ah lohs LAH-dohs, kohn lahs PAHL-mahs ah-REE-bah

Spanish for Law Enforcement

Cross your feet at the ankles.
¡Cruce los pies en los tobillos!
CROO-seh lohs peeEHS ehn lohs toh-BEE-yohs

Turn your head to the left (right)!
¡Voltee la cabeza a la izquierda (derecha)!
vohl-TEH-eh lah kah-BEH-sah ah lah eess-keeEHR-dah (deh-REH-chah)

Give me your hand!
¡Déme la mano!
DEH-meh lah MAH-noh

COMMANDS

come here	venga aquí
come with me	venga conmigo
do it	hágalo
don't talk	no hable
give me your license	deme su licencia
go away	váyase
go over there	vaya allá
quickly/hurry up	rápido
let's go	vámonos
listen to me	escúcheme
repeat please	repita por favor
sign your name here	firme su nombre aquí
sit down	siéntese
speak slower	hable más despacio
stand up	párese
stay there	quédese ahí
stop	pare
tell me the truth	dígame la verdad

VEHICLE

turn off the engine	apague el motor
get out of the car	salga del carro

CUSTODY

raise your hands	levante las manos

put your hands on the back of your head	ponga las manos detrás de la cabeza
you are under arrest	usted está arrestado
don't move	no se mueva

GREETINGS, ETC.

Good morning, Miss. (Good day.)
  Buenos días, señorita. (Buen día.)
Good afternoon, Ma'am.
  Buenas tardes, señora.
Good evening, sir. (Good night.)
  Buenas noches, señor. (Buenas noches.)
How are you?
  ¿Cómo está usted?
Very well, thank you.
  Muy bien, gracias.
Hello.
  Hola.
Good-bye.
  Adiós.
So long.
  Hasta luego.
My name is
  Mi nombre es
Excuse me.
  Discúlpeme.

QUESTIONS

Do you have ____ ?	¿Tiene Usted ____ ?
car insurance	seguro de carro
driver's license	licencia de conductor
drugs	drogas
ID	identificación
knives	cuchillos
needles	agujas
pistol	pistola
scars	circatriz
social security #	el número de seguro social
syringes	jeringas

tattoos	**tatuaje**
weapons	**armas**

Your license please.
  Su licencia por favor.
Do you have identification?
  ¿Tiene identificación?
What is your name?
  ¿Cómo se llama usted?
What is your last name?
  ¿Cuál es su apellido?
What is your first name?
  ¿Cuál es su primer nombre?
What is your complete name?
  ¿Cuál es su nombre completo?
How do you spell your name?
  ¿Cómo se escribe su nombre?
What is your address?
  ¿Cuál es su dirección?
How tall are you?
  ¿Cuánto mide usted?
How much do you weigh?
  ¿Cuánto pesa usted?
When were you born? Where were you born?
  ¿Cuándo nació usted? ¿Dónde nació usted?
What is your phone number? (home) (work)
  ¿Cuál es el número de su teléfono? (de casa) (de trabajo)
Where do you work?
  ¿Dónde trabaja usted?
What is your address at work?
  ¿Cuál es la dirección de su trabajo?
Do you have a nickname? (another name?)
  ¿Tiene usted sobrenombre? (¿otro nombre?)
May I search your car?
  ¿Me da permiso para registrar su coche?

MEDICAL

Are you injured?
¿Está herido?
Does your chest hurt? (the) stomach? (the) head?
¿Le duele el pecho? (el) estómago? (la) cabeza?
Where does it hurt? Show me!
¿Dónde le duele? ¡Muéstreme!
You're injured, please don't move.
Usted está herido, por favor no se mueva.
Are you ill?
¿Está usted enfermo?
Are you a diabetic?
¿Es usted diabético?
Are you an epileptic?
¿Es usted epiléptico?
Do you have heart trouble?
¿Sufre del corazón?
How do you feel?
¿Cómo se siente?
Are you taking medicine?
¿Está usted tomando alguna medicina?
Where is your medicine?
¿Dónde está su medicina?
You need medical care.
Usted necesita cuidado médico.
Do you want a doctor?
¿Quiere usted un médico?
Do you want an ambulance?
¿Quiere usted una ambulancia?
You should see a doctor.
Usted debe ver a un médico.
Do you want to go to the hospital?
¿Quiere usted ir al hospital?
You have to go to the hospital.
Usted tiene que ir al hospital.
Where is your medical card?
¿Dónde está su tarjeta médica?

ANATOMY

(the) body	(el) cuerpo
(the) head	(la) cabeza
(the) forehead	(la) frente
(the) face	(la) cara
(the) eyes	(los) ojos
(the) outer ear	(la) oreja
(the) inner ear	(el) oído
(the) lips	(los) labios
(the) nose	(la) nariz
(the) throat	(la) garganta
(the) mouth	(la) boca
(the) back	(la) espalda
(the) chest	(el) pecho
(the) waist	(la) cintura
(the) stomach	(el) estómago
(the) arm	(el) brazo
(the) elbow	(el) codo
(the) wrist	(la) muñeca
(the) hand	(la) mano
(the) fingers	(los) dedos de la mano
(the) toes	(los) dedos del pie
(the) leg	(la) pierna
(the) knee	(la) rodilla
(the) foot	(el) pie
(the) blood	(la) sangre
(the) bone	(el) hueso

Notes

Felony C; 5 years

Criminal Code of Oregon

A full text edition of the Criminal Code of Oregon, is available from:
Legislative Counsel Committee
S101-State Capitol
Salem, OR 97310
(503) 986 1243

Help us make this book more useful to you!!

We want to provide the best compact criminal law reference book available. If there is a statute that you use frequently that is not in this book, or if you didn't find what you wanted in the index on the first try, jot down the missing element and let us know. We will use that information to improve the next edition.

Call us toll free at 888 237 2110, or email us at

info@pocketpressinc.com.

Thanks;

Pocket Press Editorial Staff